Dr Kirstin Ferguson (above left) is an Australian company director. Beginning her career as a military officer, she went on to become the CEO of a successful global consulting business. With university honours degrees in both history and law, Kirstin also has a PhD in leadership and governance for which she has received a number of academic and industry awards. She has been named one of Australia's 100 Women of Influence, is a Sir Winston Churchill Fellow, and was recognised by Women & Leadership Australia with an award for Excellence in Women's Leadership.

Catherine Fox (above right) is a leading commentator on women and the workforce. An award-winning journalist, an author and presenter, she had a long career with the *Australian Financial Review*, where she wrote the weekly Corporate Woman column. In 2017 she was awarded the Walkley Award for Women's Leadership in Media, and is a member of the Australian Defence Force Gender Equality Advisory Board, the Australian Women Donors Network board and co-founder of the Sydney Women's Giving Circle.

UNLOCKING
THE POWER OF WOMEN
SUPPORTING WOMEN

Women
Kind

DR KIRSTIN FERGUSON
and CATHERINE FOX

MURDOCH BOOKS
SYDNEY · LONDON

Published in 2018 by Murdoch Books, an imprint of Allen & Unwin

Murdoch Books
83 Alexander Street, Crows Nest, NSW 2065, Australia
Phone: +61 (0) 2 8425 0100
murdochbooks.com.au
info@murdochbooks.com.au

Murdoch Books UK
Ormond House, 26–27 Boswell Street, London WC1N 3JZ
Phone: +44 (0) 20 8785 5995
murdochbooks.co.uk
info@murdochbooks.co.uk

A catalogue record for this book is available from the National Library of Australia

A catalogue record for this book is available from the British Library.

ISBN 978 1 76052 384 8 Australia
ISBN 978 1 76063 462 9 UK

Cover design by Sandy Cull, gogoGinko
Text design by Vivien Valk

Printed and bound in Australia by Griffin Press

10 9 8 7 6 5 4 3 2 1

The paper in this book is FSC® certified. FSC® promotes environmentally responsible, socially beneficial and economically viable management of the world's forests.

For our daughters

Emily and Zoe Ferguson
Simone, Evie and Antonia Fox Koob

CONTENTS

PREFACE

The first time we met we were both speakers at a women and leadership seminar in Brisbane, and got talking, as you do. Afterwards, Catherine needed to get to the airport and Kirstin, it turned out, had a car. On the way to the airport we didn't stop talking, and haven't stopped talking since. And it's all the highest quality conversation, too: work, family, politics … with the odd bit of gossip and shopping or travel tip thrown in.

Trading notes on how truly fed up we were with the lack of progress for women, which was in danger of stalling, or even going backwards, one of the final straws was witnessing the widespread and pernicious silencing of women's voices on the social media platforms they loved and were using in droves.

After decades of advocacy and effort, we had both had enough. If we could do anything to speed up progress, we were in.

In 2017, when Kirstin asked Catherine to post a short personal profile for an online campaign she'd created, it was quickly done. #CelebratingWomen was well underway at that point, with thousands of followers around the world addicted to these daily uplifting stories of a vast cross-section of random women — but few could have predicted the far-reaching success of Kirstin's humble campaign.

Catching up in Sydney to ponder what it had all meant, and why exactly the campaign had touched so many, and so deeply, we kept talking, and talking. The topic became so big and pressing we decided to write a book together.

Kirstin's year had been highly productive — as indeed her life has been. A skilled businesswoman with a portfolio of board commitments, she is also a regular speaker at conferences and events around the country. Catherine, with a long career in journalism, mostly at the *Australian Financial Review*, had only just launched her last book, *Stop Fixing Women*, and was on the speaking circuit, too. Kirstin lived in Brisbane, and had little time to spare; Catherine was in Sydney and had a busy freelance career. What could possibly go wrong? Actually, not too much, as it turned out.

We have loved writing this book together, about women working together. It has been a true partnership, generating many ideas and the occasional 'light bulb' moment.

It has made us optimistic about women's lives, and reminded us of the power of women's friendships and support in tackling shared challenges.

That's exactly what we hope you find, too.

Kirstin and Catherine
July 2018

INTRODUCTION

At the beginning of 2017, few could have predicted the year ahead would see the biggest global reboot of the women's rights movement since the 1970s. Even as millions of women from all walks of life, communities and age groups started to knit pink 'pussy hats', and took to the streets in their thousands, the outlook was a little grim.

Backlash from efforts to close the gender gap was regularly reported and social media denigration of women was rampant. In Australia there were still 13 ASX 200 companies with no women on their boards, and just eight women chairs; there were fewer women CEOs than there were male CEOs named John, Peter or David.[1] The gender pay gap languished at about 15%.[2] Women's retirement savings were 45% lower than those of men,[3] and domestic violence claimed on average one woman's life a week.[4] Women's voices were noticeable because of their relatively rare presence as sources of authority in the media and on the floor of Parliament.

In the US there were images of President Donald Trump on his first day in office surrounded by an all-male group signing the Global Gag Rule, a law prohibiting US funding of foreign non-governmental organisations that offer abortions to women, or even information about the procedure. The Oscars and Golden Globes were shaping up as yet more award-night ceremonies overwhelmed with male nominees and winners. And somewhere in the crowd was Harvey Weinstein.

Despite — or perhaps because of — this bleak picture, the months that followed unleashed an astounding collective social movement run by and for women, kicked off by those 'pussy hat' marches, and then erupting with a surge of activity around the #MeToo campaign in October 2017. Those Hollywood award nights were very different events the following year, with Oprah Winfrey's rousing 2018 Golden Globe speech thanking all the women who have felt strong and empowered enough to speak up and share their personal stories.

Accepting the Cecil B. deMille award at the 75th Golden Globes, Oprah delivered a powerful speech to loud cheers. 'Each of us in this room are celebrated because of the stories that we tell. And this year we *became* the story,' she said, pointing out that the tales of harassment impacted women from all sectors and walks of life, and had been revealed in a wave of social change and support between women that was just beginning to make its mark. She added:

> I want all the girls watching here now to know
> that a new day is on the horizon. And when that
> new day finally dawns, it will be because of a lot of
> magnificent women, many of whom are right here
> in this room tonight, and some pretty phenomenal
> men fighting hard to make sure that they become
> the leaders who take us to the time when nobody
> ever has to say, 'Me too', again.[5]

As #TimesUp was launched to denote the start of this new era, there was a strong sense that something unstoppable was happening — and happening fast. It was being driven by women who had never seen themselves as political agitators but were yearning for a better world. They didn't want to be told how to run their lives, but to put themselves and their experience front and centre.

Meanwhile, from small beginnings on the Sunshine Coast of Australia, another building block of momentum was being established. With her first tweet, Dr Kirstin Ferguson called out for women — any women — to answer four simple questions about their lives for a short profile post on Twitter and Facebook. The #CelebratingWomen campaign was born.

And it flourished. Before long, an international community was avidly following Kirstin's profiles. At one point, so many women from all corners of the globe had sent in their answers and photos that there was a three-month queue. #CelebratingWomen went on to attract thousands of followers, receive award nominations and grab the attention of Twitter co-founder Jack Dorsey. Kirstin had tapped into an amazingly diverse community of women who were keen to celebrate and support each other's lives and achievements, however large or small.

But this book is about more than the story of #CelebratingWomen. It is about how women — who have always connected and bonded over the teapot, the desk and at the school gate — are grabbing this chance to help each other not just survive, but thrive. How women are challenging the invisibility of their efforts and lives. And how *anyone* can be part of the groundswell.

As we delved deeper, two core themes emerged. Instead of the pervasive stereotype that women are predisposed to stab each other in the back, our research found the opposite: when one woman shines, so do those around her — and that confidence is infectious.

And contrary to the idea that most women inherently lack chutzpah, all kinds of women we spoke to were proud of their achievements. Fed up with their needs being ignored or trivialised, they were more than ready to speak for themselves.

Interestingly, rather than just the stories of high-flying leaders, most #CelebratingWomen followers were inspired by the experiences of women from vastly different backgrounds to their own. As the Australian television journalist Leigh Sales (profile #129 in the campaign) explains, it appealed because:

> ... in an ocean of constant negativity in the news and on social media, it was something really positive. And it highlighted women who are not famous or prominent, but who do awesome work in the community. And people appreciate seeing that.

We saw that, too. But we don't believe for a second that women are nicer or better at empathy than men (that's, after all, a gender stereotype). And we know 'women's programs' can be ineffective and fail to challenge embedded bias or sexist behaviour.

We were fascinated, however, to examine how women's networks do succeed, and how these strong connections were formed because women historically didn't have access to mainstream support. Necessity, as they say, is the mother of invention.

And given a glimpse of what can be achieved from collective pressure — and many mothers, daughters and sisters — there's an appetite for more. The urgency of the task ahead has never been clearer. Women have had enough, and shown they are tired of their work, lives and battles with daily sexism and harassment being disbelieved or ignored.

In fact, women's support for each other has the power to keep challenging sexism and harassment at a critical time for women's rights. If we can leverage this collective social impact, we can circumvent the diversity dead-ends in organisations to produce a fairer playing field for all.

What we have unearthed is a repository of wisdom and suggestions by women about how leaders and workplaces can address the gender gap and rethink the perceived wisdom about women's lives and aspirations. Simple, swift steps that any woman — and man — can take to help change the seemingly intractable status quo.

This is not about women struggling up a ladder on their own, but about throwing down a fishing net and holding the sides so that *all* women can be lifted up together.

Much has changed since #CelebratingWomen began. In Australia, same-sex marriage legislation has been enacted. Women are playing and watching professional sport in record numbers. The number of companies running gender pay gap audits has increased, while those without any women on their boards have decreased. Few employers can ignore the impact of harassment at work, and many are paying attention like never before.

Yet so much remains to do. Decision-making remains mainly in the hands of men. Domestic labour is not valued. And in many parts of the world, more women die in poverty or from domestic violence than men.

Now is the time to come together to challenge the basics of this unfairness because the world, at last, is starting to listen. There are no rules, no borders, and all are welcome to join in.

Women Kind is a call to grasp this opportunity, to find your voice, and to unashamedly celebrate other women's stories — stories about accomplishments, in all their myriad forms, and stories about lives that have been left out, ignored or belittled. Thanks to the immediacy of social media, and our capacity to connect in ways we could only dream of before, women can celebrate the deep satisfaction of working together for the good of all women, and for society. We can all add our voices to keep that momentum going and growing.

The success so far has been astounding, but we're only just getting started.

It may be #TimesUp for some men — but for women everywhere, it's a time like no other.

1

AN ACCIDENTAL ACTIVIST: KIRSTIN'S STORY

There is a small craft brewery at Moffat Beach on Australia's Sunshine Coast popular for its craft beers and friendly atmosphere, as well as its ideal location just metres from the beach. Its owners and clientele, drinking craft beers on tap with intriguing names like the Deadbeat Boyfriend Cream Ale or the Iggy Hop Double IPA, are probably blissfully unaware that it was also the launching pad for a social media campaign that would see me celebrating 757 women from 37 countries around the world. That brewery was 'ground zero', if you like, for the #CelebratingWomen campaign that preoccupied my life for a year and became an active force for collective female empowerment and fulfilment, both locally and globally.

Ironically, I am not much of a drinker, so it was most unusual for me to find myself sitting in a brewery, let alone on my own. Yet perched at a small table and sipping a refreshing shandy (half beer, half lemonade) after walking along the beach, I realised I was no longer prepared to remain a bystander to the widespread denigration of women I was observing in the often-harsh online world. It was too easy to focus on the many negatives encountered by most women who are active online — the virulent abuse, the pile-on behaviour, the endless put-downs. Instead, I wanted to find a way to harness the real strengths of the digital era — its ability to render borders obsolete, its instantaneousness, and its access to a common conversation for millions of people — to produce positive outcomes for women.

Big ambitions and big ideas. I borrowed a pen from the barman, grabbed a napkin and, before I had even finished my shandy, scribbled down four ideas. They were simply some vague concepts and disparate themes that I thought could become the basis for sparking discussion. I could feel a growing sense of excitement and potential ... but first I needed a guinea pig who was brave enough to jump on board with my crazy idea.

Heading back along the beach, I did what generations of women have done instinctively: I called my mum. My mother, Irene, is not an active user of social media, and so was relatively unfamiliar with the escalating and painful issue of online abuse faced by so many women. But Irene has a firm moral compass and is a great believer in social justice and helping disadvantaged women. Standing on the beach with scrawled notes in hand, I asked her to answer four simple questions and to send me some personal photos.

Sand, sun, beer and a fusion of frustration, anger and inspiration. From that unlikely mix and location emerged the structure of the #CelebratingWomen campaign. Little did I realise that those humble beginnings would transform my life, unexpectedly kick-start a global movement and galvanise thousands of women, and men, to publicly support the lives and stories of women they did not previously know.

There was a lot going on for women in the world when I found myself with time to think on my beach holiday. Hillary Clinton had recently lost the US election to Donald Trump, after enduring a disturbing and unmistakable level of misogyny; at the 2016 Republican National Convention, merchandise brandished slogans such as 'Don't be a pussy. Vote for Trump in 2016', '2016: Finally, someone with balls', 'Hillary sucks but not like Monica', and 'Life's a Bitch: Don't vote for one'.[6] Such blatantly sexist messages were confronting for many, reminding us of the kind of rhetoric that could be levelled against any woman daring to aspire to leadership. Comparisons to the signs held behind Australia's first female Prime Minister Julia Gillard in 2011 — including 'Ditch the witch' and 'Juliar ... Bob Brown's Bitch'— were quickly made. Fast forward to 2018 and it was little wonder that Clinton and Gillard announced they would join forces to challenge negative stereotypes of women aspiring to be political leaders.

Arguably, Clinton's loss in the presidential election was due to a range of reasons, including economic insecurity, a generalised distrust in government, the resurrection of Hillary's emails by the FBI, and the various alleged failures of her campaign.[7] Critics of Julia Gillard's tenure mount similar non-gender-related reasons for why she was replaced as Labor leader, and while Gillard admits her gender may explain some things about her experiences as prime minister, it did not explain everything.

Regardless of the political analysis, Clinton's election loss, in particular, felt like a personal blow for millions of ambitious, self-confident, brilliant women who aspired to reach the heights of their careers. If a career politician like Hillary Clinton could lose to a reality television star who had bragged about sexual assault, among numerous other transgressions, we were a very long way from true gender equality at the highest levels. For those women who quickly mobilised in their millions wearing pink 'pussy hats' and marching in the streets, Hillary's loss represented a reality some of us had always feared existed — that regardless of our skills, experiences and aptitude, we would never reach the pinnacle of our chosen careers in the same numbers as our male counterparts. (Political commentator Karrin Anderson has even gone so far as to suggest there is nothing American women can ever do to increase their chances of being elected President, because simply being a competent female candidate appears to breed contempt among voters.[8])

None of this would surprise those who have been studying gender for the past few decades. Globally, the number of female world leaders is astoundingly low: in 2018, only 7.2% heads of state and 5.7% heads of government were women. In 2010, US researchers analysing the career progress of female politicians found that female candidates were negatively influenced by perceptions of their power-seeking intentions, whereas male candidates were not.[9] Power-seeking was seen as incongruent with traditional female values, which in turn resulted in a lower perceived competence of the female politicians, and feelings of moral outrage that they weren't conforming to cultural stereotypes.[10] Further, at the start of their 2010 research paper — well before Hillary announced she would run for President — the researchers included a prescient 2007 quote from a *Los Angeles Times* journalist, who noted, 'Many voters see Senator Hillary Rodham Clinton as coldly ambitious, a perception that could ultimately doom her presidential campaign.'[11] It was to prove true in 2016, and for many women it was another rebuke to the idea that women can ascend to every level of power in society. As former New Zealand Prime Minister Helen Clark more recently remarked:

> **If the full contribution of women to economies and societies isn't realised, it's not only women who won't reach their full potential — whole *countries* won't reach their full potential.**[12]

As a member of several professional women's organisations, these issues had been percolating in my mind for some time. My eyes were being opened daily to the challenges women faced, and the fact that workplace meritocracy remained elusive. However, as a busy professional working woman and mother of two daughters, with a packed diary and heavy travel schedule, finding time to just stop and think felt like an indulgence, and my observations never went beyond a fleeting frustration with the way things were.

I am quite sure that the #CelebratingWomen campaign would not have happened at all if I hadn't been so relaxed while enjoying some long-overdue downtime on a summer holiday at the beach. Away from the daily grind, I had time to really digest what was happening in the world, and the way in which women were being treated — both online, and in the 'real' world. My mind was open to possibilities, rather than being full of the details of my normal day.

Over this particular Christmas holiday break, I was watching with increasing pride and interest as the Women's March in the United States became the largest single-day protest in American history. Similar marches then followed, led by women around the world. At the same time, I could not help but notice a marked increase in the denigration of women online. I knew cyber abuse had always existed, and sadly remembered the tragic death of Australian television personality Charlotte Dawson, who took her own life in 2014 after struggling with the online vitriol levelled against her. Yet I was noticing that cyber-bullying was now even more prevalent, and targeting a much broader range of women.

I felt empathy for American writer and *Teen Vogue* columnist Lauren Duca who, after rejecting an unsolicited offer to accompany now convicted felon Martin Shkreli to an event, found herself the target of his online abuse. Lauren appealed directly to the co-founder of Twitter, Jack Dorsey, to take online harassment seriously. On 9 January 2017, she tweeted this question to Dorsey: 'Why is harassment an automatic career hazard for a woman receiving any amount of professional attention?' I couldn't agree more. Why should any woman be harassed online simply for expressing an opinion?

Although I was fortunate not to have experienced significant online abuse, some of these issues were also particularly relevant to me professionally. After more than two decades in various executive and leadership roles, by January 2017 I had established a career that was challenging, varied and rewarding, and found myself an independent, non-executive director on company boards — including over the previous decade sitting on large private and publicly listed corporate boards, government boards, charitable foundations, professional sporting organisations and a theatre company. I had also developed a busy professional public speaking career, opening conferences and speaking on panels, often about leadership, culture and diversity. Having also received a number of awards, I was aware of my privilege in having the opportunity to influence at this point in my career — I now had a voice, and a responsibility to use it.

I was increasingly conscious of an unstoppable and ever-increasing urge to make a difference wherever I could — not just for women, but for others who did not have the same voice, privilege or opportunities.

In short, by the time I took that walk on the beach, I was primed and ready to speak out.

Years of being an active user of social media meant I certainly wasn't naive about both the opportunities and risks of being active online. The benefits of using platforms like Twitter, Instagram, Facebook and LinkedIn include being able to learn from, and connect with, people we would never otherwise meet. I love interacting with someone living on the other side of the world and finding new connections and networks. By engaging widely on social media, we can learn about views that are different to our own and become awakened to issues within our communities that may otherwise remain obscured. My interest in social media also made me determined to help women claim it back, and make sure their voices were not excluded.

As I enjoyed my holidays that summer afternoon, it was a particular thread of tweets that spurred me from passive, annoyed observer to accidental activist. Looking back, they were not the most memorable of derogatory tweets, and try as I might I can't remember what they were even about. Sadly, that is the point. There is usually nothing original or memorable about the abusive tweets many women receive. They are generally vicious, and often personal, threatening women or seeking to silence them — and there may be an avalanche of such abuse in any given day.

Research conducted in the United Kingdom analysed 50 million tweets received over a six-month period by 152 high-profile women from a range of backgrounds including politics, broadcasting, sports, entertainment and business. The researchers found that each woman received more than 200 abusive tweets — every single day.[13] Of the abusive online messages received by the British Broadcasting Corporation's political editor, Laura Kuenssberg, 91% featured gender-specific slurs or sexual harassment.[14] The BBC was even forced to organise a bodyguard for Laura due to the extent and severity of online trolling she experienced.

The online abuse I read on this particular sunny afternoon as I lay relaxing in a hammock by the beach was targeting a talented, high-profile Australian radio and television broadcaster, Patricia Karvelas. It was unfortunately nothing new for women in the media: in late 2015, a survey of 1054 Australian journalists found that more than 40% of the women had been harassed, bullied or trolled online, ranging from mild examples through to death threats and stalking.[15]

When I read this batch of tweets I was feeling particularly fed up with the way women were being treated, both online and in the public arena, given the strong anti-Hillary Clinton rhetoric at the time. I also knew that if these remarks had been made in person, and I was physically standing there next to the person receiving the abuse, I would definitely do something. In some instances, I would call the police; I just know I would do *something*.

My sense of powerlessness turned into resolve. Experience had taught me everyone can make a difference, even in a small way, through stepping up and speaking out.

And it was in that moment I found myself thinking, 'Enough is enough. Enough.'

Finding my voice

Between getting dumped in the surf and hosting family and friends during those Christmas holidays, I wrote down some thoughts on why it was time to take a stand.

I wrote an opinion piece called 'Let's make 2017 the year of making noise #CelebratingWomen' and sent the article to *Women's Agenda*,[16] an online publication for career-minded women in Australia, whose editor and owner, Angela Priestley, cares deeply about gender equality and issues facing women. My article was published just a few days later.

In hindsight, what I had written was a clear call for action. I argued that we needed to 'make a different kind of noise' — and that we needed to see more celebration, and less denigration, of women online. I had no clear idea what that could look like; I just knew my goal would be to 'celebrate women, from all walks of life, achieving amazing things'. I suggested that 'once you look there are simply endless examples of women doing great things … Every woman we know is doing something extraordinary.'

Without any real planning or forethought, I used the hashtag #CelebratingWomen for the first time, as it seemed to capture the vision in my mind as I hoped that, one day, my news feed on social media might be filled with stories of women who were doing incredible things every day all around us, drowning out some of the negativity we experience.

And that, I thought, was that. Article published, I went back to the beach and my holiday.

Yet I had that nagging thought that it was all very well to share some bold statements in an opinion piece, but words alone were not going to make a change. I wasn't directing my energy at the source, and making a difference on the social media platform where I felt the biggest challenge for women lay. I wanted to proactively support other women, with actions that spoke for themselves.

Looking back, somewhat incredulously, at my own determination over that period brings to mind some advice I heard from photographer and blogger Brandon Stanton that has really resonated with me. Brandon founded the online phenomenon Humans of New York after photographing random people on the streets of New York City and asking them about their lives, then posting their profiles to Facebook. Speaking at the Sydney Opera House in early 2018, he told the audience not to wait for the perfect idea — the important thing is to just begin. This was precisely the stage I'd found myself in only days after I had said 'Enough', and my article had been published. I knew I needed to do more and just begin.

I had no 'permission' to begin #CelebratingWomen, and nor did I ever seek it. I also had no particular position or special entitlement to allow me to try to change the tone for women on Twitter. Unlike so many other decisions in my life, I did not discuss the idea with anyone first, and nor did I ask mentors or trusted advisers whether they thought I should do it. In fact, had I known what was to follow, I am sure I would have over-analysed the options and potential pitfalls, and would've wanted to map out a strategy — and I'm convinced I would have failed early. Instead, I simply jumped in and never looked back. It shows to me that any of us can make a difference; we do not need to wait for someone to say it is okay. As Brandon reminds us, what matters is to just begin.

Ironically, until launching #CelebratingWomen, I had spent my career hoping no one noticed I was a woman at all. It had only been in the previous few years, and after becoming actively involved in women's networks like Chief Executive Women, that I started to find my voice. From early in my career I tried to avoid discussions about 'women's issues' — even in hushed whispers with other women — in case I was tarnished by being labelled as one of those 'difficult women' at work. Like all women I speak to, I wanted to be recognised and acknowledged for my skills and experiences, not for my gender.

As recently as only two years before that afternoon beach walk, I stood on a podium in front of 1000 people in the Brisbane Convention and Exhibition Centre, giving a speech for International Women's Day, and said:

> My gender is the least interesting aspect about me.
> It is the only thing in my life I have had no control
> over. The only thing I had no part in choosing. And
> while I am incredibly proud to be a woman —
> and don't know any other way to be — far more
> interesting, in my view, are the choices I have made
> along the way, the influence I may have had on
> others, my achievements and my mistakes.

During my career I had never set out to loudly celebrate and advocate for women. I had always worked, and largely succeeded, in male-dominated environments through fitting in and avoiding, as best I could, feeling different to the men around me. I worked hard to be recognised *not* for being a woman, but for being a leader in my own right — for doing well at whatever I tried to achieve. I have only ever wanted to be recognised and rewarded for my achievements on merit alone, and I don't know any woman who would want it any other way.

However, over many years of seeing the paltry numbers of women in senior leadership roles and other positions of authority, it had become clear to me that merit was a highly subjective ideal, measured by those who already deemed themselves to have it, and who were already in power. I knew there was no lack of talent among women, but all my preconceived ideas about how women were being treated had finally evolved over the 20-plus years of my professional career to the point where I found myself reading a thread of derogatory tweets and felt ready to act.

It was time.

Four stages of gender awareness

Holly Kramer, a leading Australian company director, and one of the women I was to feature in the #CelebratingWomen campaign (profile #495), has neatly summarised her own path to finding a voice through what she calls the 'four stages of gender awareness'. Although I wasn't familiar with them back then, the stages Holly describes perfectly articulate where I found myself on that afternoon on the beach, and the breakthrough that led to #CelebratingWomen.

In the first stage, Holly describes how she was initially oblivious to issues of gender — how young women, at the start of their careers, may have no perception that they could even experience gender discrimination. And even when women *do* experience obvious gender discrepancies in the workplace, Holly describes how they either don't see them, or *choose* not to see them at all.

Holly then describes how she moved into a stage of denial, where she was still not convinced that bias existed against women — and if problems did arise, it wasn't to do with systemic gender barriers, but the woman herself. When Holly was on maternity leave and her own job was made redundant, rather than thinking this had anything to do with gender discrimination, Holly simply assumed it must have been because she didn't stay in touch well enough with her employer while on leave with her new baby. Researchers in the Netherlands have suggested that such a denial of gender, and related gender discrimination, is actually a direct response to working in a difficult, male-dominated environment in which gender is seen as a liability.[17] Holly was working in a male-dominated industry at the time, just as I — and so many other women — had been for much of my career.

Moving into what she calls the 'stage of awakening', Holly started to notice real, and undeniable, barriers confronting her and other women. Where women were invited into leadership teams, but not given a full seat at the table. Or a woman's contribution in a meeting was ignored, but a male colleague was recognised for saying the same thing. Holly also noticed that men's networks were strong and effective, and often involved activities on a weekend, to which women were not invited. Holly says that in this stage women like herself learned to start advocating for themselves, but were yet to start publicly advocating for others.

The final stage, according to Holly — and the one I found myself thrust into that day on the beach — is advocacy. This is where women recognise that gender discrimination *does* exist, and then focus on understanding *why* it exists, and how to fix it. It is also a point where women may have reached a level of seniority in the workplace, where they have the ability and a sense of responsibility to make a difference for other women.

In a panel to discuss the #MeToo movement in the wake of sexual harassment allegations in Hollywood and elsewhere, Victoria Woodards, the Mayor of Tacoma, Washington, talked honestly about how #MeToo had caused her to re-evaluate parts of her early career. In her own awakening and move to advocacy, Woodards' words resonated with me, and no doubt with so many women:

> How many of us have been in rooms where people say inappropriate things to us, or we overhear something inappropriate said to someone else, and we laugh it off because we don't want to confront it? It makes me think about the responsibility I now have … to speak up when I hear it and when I see it, and not just to brush it under the rug.[18]

Blowing off the covers

This strategy of ignoring my gender, or trying to, had been my modus operandi for much of my adult life. My own career successes, particularly early on, had reinforced the idea that this approach would lead to opportunities and promotions. I spent much of my executive career in denial that there was gender discrimination. Just as Holly described, I had looked at achieving my career goals and assumed that any challenges being faced by other women were the result of their individual circumstances or choices. I avoided being part of women's networks for fear that it would blow my cover on my gender. And like Holly, this denial came in spite of clear evidence of gender bias from the earliest days of my working life.

As a young child, I was thought of as 'bossy' by others and also by myself, with all the negative connotations that word brings. My assertiveness, determination, ambition and willingness to lead were not always attributes welcome in young women, and I recall trying to minimise these traits as I became more aware of what was expected from me.

At one workplace during my career, I had to complete a personality test. I should not have been surprised at my results. It described me as an achiever who is constantly pushed to do more, an activator of ideas impatient for action, a competitor who is invigorated by the contest, a person who thrives on responsibility, and someone who is fascinated and energised by new ideas. My overwhelming memory of that process, however, was thinking that I had been exposed as having masculine personality traits. I remember feeling disheartened that despite my best efforts, my attempts to keep those 'strengths' disguised had been in vain — which, of course, they had been. But looking back now it reminds me how deeply my own notions of gender were entrenched in my behaviours and core beliefs. And looking again at those particular personality strengths as defined by that test, I realise that #CelebratingWomen — and frankly my life to date — would not have been possible without a combination of them all.

But back to my summer holiday, and my increasing frustration at seeing what other women were having to deal with online. As I wrote my opinion piece for *Women's Agenda* and grappled with ideas on how to tackle online denigration, I knew that trying to ignore the double standards and bias women face in their working lives would not make the problem of sexism go away or give other women a fair chance. Nor would pretending to be one of the men in the workplace, as I had learned to do so well. This was also not a case of suggesting to women there were things they needed to 'fix' about themselves — something my co-author Catherine Fox writes about in her book *Stop Fixing Women*. Catherine reminds us that trying to fit women (and some men) into traditional male norms simply hasn't worked, and we need to stop telling women they need to change.

That afternoon walking on the beach I knew that if I wanted to do something, it would need to be about ensuring women's voices — and their work, and the paths they followed – were legitimised and included. I also knew that if I said nothing, then nothing would change. The online abuse would continue, and women would keep being shouted over, and their stories would remain invisible and undervalued. I wanted just the opposite — and to see if I could make even the slightest difference.

I had jotted down four ideas on that napkin from the beachside brewery. My mind was racing: how could I use Twitter to post a very short profile story about these women? How could this work, who might be prepared to be involved, would it be interesting to read?

That's when I called my mum.

Girls can do anything

My mother Irene is a critical part of this story. Not only was she to become the very first #CelebratingWomen profile, but she also reinforced the view I grew up with — that women can do anything.

My mother, and importantly my father as well, never made me think my gender was something to prevent me from succeeding, and always encouraged me to follow my passions. My parents taught me I was incredibly fortunate to have choices, and that for many women the privileged view that 'Girls can do anything' is much more challenging. My mother has been a social-justice campaigner throughout her entire life, and I am grateful to her for ensuring I have always known life is not equal for all. My father was another important role model for me by demonstrating the importance of men supporting women — and men supporting women who support women — as he has always done.

The influence of my parents, and my own life story and experiences, would become a crucial reason I was able to embark on #CelebratingWomen. All of our decisions and experiences in life, both good and bad, help make us the individual, the leader, the parent, the friend and the community member we are today. My life story, as a child who had been told she could do anything, had that reality radically change once I became a minority in a highly male-dominated military environment at the age of 17. Choices I have made in my career and personal life have all had a profound influence on the woman I am today and laid the foundation that led me to celebrate other women so publicly.

My grandmother, Mary Taylor, was another powerful role model in my life. Known as Millie by those close to her, she had lived much of her life very traditionally as a supportive, stay-at-home mother of four, and the wife of a career Army Officer who rose to the rank of Major General in the Australian Army. Millie's mantra for marital harmony was to agree with everything a spouse says — and then go and quietly do whatever you were going to do anyway! This included her passion for 'collecting old ladies' (as she called it), which involved visiting and assisting elderly women whose names were passed on to her by the family doctor. I remember accompanying Millie to visit one of these 'old ladies' when I was a small child, and seeing how much joy my grandmother's visit brought the frail lady, who would otherwise have been alone.

After my grandfather died, and when Millie was 75 years old, rather than stay at home gardening or reading — both of which she loved — she had something else in mind. Her independent spirit, which had been happily subsumed by her other responsibilities for many decades, was unleashed. In the face of curious scepticism, bearing in mind she had only gained her driver's licence at the age of 40, Millie decided to drive herself around Australia, alone, in her trusty, surburban red Honda Jazz. The Grand Circuit, as Millie called it, was 18,000 kilometres (11,000 miles), and her first trip took her nine weeks. She would later tell me it was one of the most thrilling experiences of her life and she loved being on the open road, on her own, watching the world go by. Her passion for driving long distances was not, in her words, about the destination, but about the drive itself.

Having found a way to release her adventurous spirit via the open road, Millie was not content to bottle it again after a single trip, and aged in her late 70s she began her driving obsession. Having returned to her home on the Mornington Peninsula in Victoria after her initial Grand Circuit, Millie set off again, so she could see Australia from the other direction. Before she died, at the age of 93, Millie would drive around Australia on her own 17 times — a feat which I am sure must be some kind of record. She would update us via email on her adventures and regale us with hilarious tales from outback pubs of locals who could not quite believe what she was doing, yet also came to welcome her frequent returns to their towns and motels on her trips.

Millie's new-found independence as a widow and her determination not to have her final years resting at home remains the source of much inspiration for me. Millie never lost her excitement to head off on a new trip, and would tell us endless stories about her beloved Honda, and how she never failed to fulfil her daily evening routine of eating a single can of baked beans for dinner and enjoying a glass of sherry (although, she would insist, never before 5 pm!). She wrote her memoir, with the wonderful title *Baked Beans in the Outback and Curry in Kashmir*, selling 10,000 copies of her book from her back bedroom. In her book Millie wrote about her driving adventures, but also her formative years with my grandfather when he was a British Officer in the Indian Army during the last years of the Raj in India. Her independent spirit showed itself early when, in her words, she 'left home to marry a man she scarcely knew, and whom her family had never met, to live in a country she knew nothing about'.[19]

Millie lived an incredibly full life, and one that never ceased to surprise me. She was self-deprecating to a fault, and in an interview before she died commented, 'Everyone says mine was an interesting life. But it was just what happened.'[20] By the age of 88 she had given 350 talks, about what she called her adventures as 'an elderly unattached female'. I will never forget picking up a magazine and seeing my grandmother in the celebrity pages being photographed with a Winnebago weather van that the Channel Seven Sunrise team named Millie in her honour, or when she was interviewed by Britain's Sky News, who flew to outback Australia to film her travels when she was 91 years old. Millie always had a CB radio in her car for safety, and she would proudly tell us that the truckies on the outback roads had given her a call sign, the Galloping Granny. Millie was the most extraordinary woman — and if I inherit even some of her spirit, I will consider myself very fortunate.

I am a product of the East Coast of Australia, having moved up and down it all of my life. Born in Melbourne in 1973 but moving when I was young, I completed all of my schooling while living in Sydney. I then lived in Canberra for four years, completing my first university degree at the Australian Defence Force Academy (ADFA), before moving at the age of 21 to Brisbane, where I still live today, although I primarily work in Sydney. My younger brother and I completed much of our early schooling at Bundeena Public School, located deep within the Royal National Park on the outskirts of Sydney. We lived in the nearby township of Maianbar, with no more than 500 residents at the time, and as young children spent our days playing in the bush, swimming and sailing on Port Hacking, or riding our bicycles until dark. At this point in my life, thinking about the roles of men and women was far from my mind. I grew up like most kids of the 1970s and 1980s with women often being the primary carers at home, but with increasing numbers of mothers, like my own, having their own careers.

However, I was not blind to the ways in which women were being represented in popular media; I simply did not understand yet how these stereotypes might play a role in my own life. One of my favourite movies was *Working Girl*, starring Sigourney Weaver and Melanie Griffith, nominated for six Academy Awards. The opening credits, with the Oscar-winning song by Carly Simon, take me back to my days as a teen watching this film in awe of so many female lead characters on the screen. In the movie, Tess McGill is a hard-working and ambitious secretary studying for a business degree at night and aspiring to become an executive one day. Katharine Parker is a tough senior executive in the same investment firm, and while she initially appears to mentor and encourage McGill, Parker ultimately betrays the more junior woman, passing McGill's business ideas off as her own. *Working Girl* ends predictably with a confrontation between the two women. The senior woman is fired by an important client (who tells her to 'get your bony ass out of my sight'), and the up-and-coming secretary replaces Parker as the new senior executive.

Even as a teenager, with no real awareness of gender stereotypes, I was confused. The film was celebrating Tess McGill and rewarding her for getting ahead 'the right way' by working hard from the bottom up. And Katharine Parker was vilified for being the cold, selfish caricature of a female executive who wanted to succeed, whatever the cost. I wanted to be a mix of *both* women — an ethical, hardworking and successful female executive — but in *Working Girl* that character was not an option. As much as I loved the movie, it stayed with me and cemented a view that there was only ever room at the top of the ladder for *one* woman. It also built the conviction, exposed in my personality test decades later, that being competitive or ambitious were not traits admired in women.

But an awareness of what this cold, calculating female persona — often referred to as a 'Queen Bee' — might mean to me personally was still some way off.

Looking through the kaleidoscope

My family had relocated mid-way through my high school years, which helped me in accepting differences and valuing diversity of all kinds. We moved from our idyllic beachside town straight to Sydney's inner city. I am not sure I could have lived in two greater extremes in neighbourhoods, and as a teenager I couldn't have been more excited. My parents had bought a run-down nineteenth-century terrace house located on Riley Street in Surry Hills. It was reputed to have been previously owned at one point by organised-crime boss Abe Saffron as one of his many 'massage parlours', although this was never verified beyond family folklore. There were two very well-known Sydney brothels operating on our block, and I do recall naively not quite understanding why our house may have had 36 mattresses in it when we bought it! I really loved living in the middle of all the action. Life was never dull.

For much of the 1980s I would watch the Gay and Lesbian Mardi Gras each year at the end of our street where it joined Oxford Street, when there were significantly fewer people cheering the now world-famous parade beyond the LGBTIQ community and local neighbourhood. At various stages, the terrace next door was used as a halfway house, and I remember one day coming home to heavily armed police inside our own home while a siege was underway next door. I often found myself getting to know the homeless men and women who found places to shelter nearby, and would step over hypodermic needles to get to school on most days. I observed police arrests while wandering through the local streets, and recall a particular morning walking to school when a sex worker was thrown from a car and reversed over, without ever knowing whether she survived. I spent some time volunteering at the now closed Caritas Centre mental health facility, the hospital having been reopened after a century of use as the infamous Lunatic Reception House in Darlinghurst. This exposure to so many different facets of life was a great education for appreciating diversity and equality, and respecting every individual for who they are.

In stark contrast to the lack of access to opportunity I often saw among those in my community, I was very fortunate to finish my schooling at an all-girls' private school, Sydney Church of England Girls Grammar School (SCEGGS) in

Darlinghurst. Reinforcing the message from my parents, our school told us that women could achieve anything we set out to do. In 1990 during my final year of high school, I wrote in my graduation year book that I hoped to be Australia's first female prime minister. I proudly collected stickers produced by a government department at the time that said, 'Girls Can Do Anything'. I still have one stuck on the front of my high school diary from the time, and I remember giving them out to all my friends.

My parents both had professional careers and encouraged me to pursue my own interests, and I was told that doing well at school, working hard and being responsible were the most important ingredients for success. My gender just did not seem relevant to my dreams and aspirations. *Merit* would determine who was to succeed, and I was ready for the challenge. In my world, girls could do whatever they put their mind to if they worked hard and treated people well, and I had strong female friendships that continue today. I was blind to the obvious fact that other women who I walked past every day, like the street walker thrown from the car and the homeless women living in my own street, had very few opportunities at all, and would certainly not have had the same view as me.

Adopting gender camouflage

I had my first taste of being an outsider when I chose to make a sharp change of direction at the age of 17. Even though I did really well in my final exams, I didn't get straight into law at the University of Sydney, which had been my steadfast goal. I briefly considered a career in journalism, since I had been accepted to study at the University of Technology Sydney, but when considering my options, I loved the idea of being paid to go to university — so I decided to relocate and start my career by studying at the Australian Defence Force Academy (ADFA) in Canberra, while training to be an officer in the Royal Australian Air Force. Coming from many generations of military family members, I had been exposed to the armed forces my whole life, so to me this move made sense. At the time, women made up less than 10% of all ADFA cadets, but I don't recall anyone ever making an issue of this statistic or counselling me that women may encounter anything different to their male colleagues. I also don't remember any advice being given to the new female cadets on how best to handle harassment, abuse or any other difficult situations that young women might encounter in this male-dominated environment.

While I had grown up happily believing that men and women lived, worked and all believed in creating a meritorious, equal playing field, at ADFA I soon realised that gender was going to be something others noticed, especially if I didn't find a way to fit in fast. My response was very simple, and learned quickly, as I did my best to survive, trying to avoid discussing gender at all. Gender wasn't relevant to me, I told myself — and I fervently hoped it wouldn't be relevant to anyone else. I became firmly entrenched in Holly Kramer's second stage of denial.

The early 1990s were certainly not a great time to be a woman at ADFA, when bullying, harassment and exclusion of women was commonplace. It was impossible not to notice — but I just thought it was the way things were at ADFA. The biggest priority for me was fitting in so I could succeed. My denial meant I believed that if there were barriers or I didn't feel included, then that had to be due to *my* own shortcomings, and not the attitudes or actions of others.

This blindness seems hard to rationalise now, when recalling such blatant misogyny and sexism. For example, one of the derogatory terms used to describe female cadets when I was at ADFA was 'squids'. In an unpublished compilation of cadet slang produced at the time called *Lego Lingo: The Cadets' Language*, 'squid' was a term used for female cadets because they were considered to be:

> ... flabby, they smelt of fish, were easy to get into and would enfold you with their tentacles and squeeze the moral life out of you. If a female cadet is called a squid in passing, she should not take offence; however, if she is referred to as a 'Dirty fucking squid' then she should get the hint that she's not liked.[21]

When I heard that term used at ADFA I was shockingly ignorant and naive as to how denigrating it was to women. I knew I didn't like hearing it, and it was meant as a dreadful slur — yet at the same time I thought that was just how things were. Finding yourself in such a system, at such a young age, it is much harder to recognise or to know how to address unconscious — let alone such overtly conscious — sexism other than by trying to avoid attention by blending in with the group.

As a woman at ADFA during that period, speaking up about or objecting to the behaviour of some cadets towards women, or the language being used, was so difficult it was nearly impossible. The greatest betrayal, all cadets learned in the very first few days, was to report anything to anyone outside of the Corps of Officer Cadets. To speak with military officers about something that may have been bothering you — and even criminal activity such as rape and sexual assault — would see you ostracised from your classmates very quickly. I recall, with shame, one particular case of a woman who did report a sexual assault. Rather than being supported by those around her for her clear bravery in speaking up, she was instead shunned by all cadets for having 'betrayed' her fellow cadets. The Academy was like *Lord of the Flies* in this regard, and learning how to fit in with its prevailing cultural norms was the only way for both male and female cadets to survive.

It was not just the language or behaviours that made life challenging for a woman at ADFA back then. In my final graduating year, I was interviewed for the most senior cadet position in the hierarchy at the time, Academy Cadet Captain, but missed out and was appointed to the rank below. I was informed ADFA had not yet had a female Academy Cadet Captain, and there was some concern the Academy was not quite ready for a woman in that position.

Despite the difficult climate at the time for women, which the military has acknowledged and has since been working very hard to address, and even with the benefit of hindsight, I don't recall my years at ADFA with any bitterness, and remain incredibly proud to have successfully graduated and served in the Air Force. On graduating I was awarded the Chief of Defence Force Air Force Prize, which made me the most senior Air Force Academy cadet and dux of my Air Force graduating class, both of men and women.

While the first year in particular was extremely testing, I did survive, and I think much of that experience was powerful resilience training for the challenges I have faced since. It also created an enduringly strong bond with my fellow cadets, male and female, as we shared these experiences, and which helped us to survive.

During the first few months, male and female cadets were constantly yelled at by older cadets, punished for failing to make (and remake) beds to an unachievably high standard, or abused while ironing uniforms over and over again as they were crumpled by older cadets. We were screamed at to clean bathrooms, laundries and kitchens, usually accompanied by insults about how useless we were, while under impossible time pressures that ensured failure — with more punishment to follow. We were also humiliated and ridiculed by drill sergeants as we were taught to march around the parade ground. And these are the stories that I can repeat publicly.

It was certainly a world away, both geographically and otherwise, from my all-girls' school in Sydney and it was, as they say, character building. The level of discipline and hard work we were taught has remained with me throughout my career. And the strong relationships I built with my ADFA colleagues led to deep friendships with many women, and men, that continue to this day.

In 2018, on International Women's Day, I was invited back to ADFA to give the keynote speech to 1000 cadets about leadership and gender diversity. It was very moving returning to a place that was so formative in my career, and also heartening to see such significant changes in the two and a half decades since my graduation. The Commandant of the Academy is currently a woman, and women now comprise 25% of all cadets.

Taking questions after my speech, I was asked by one of the male cadets whether I had any regrets from my time at ADFA. After thinking about it for a moment, I said my greatest regret was not having the knowledge, confidence or courage to speak up for other women. It would take a good 25 years to find that voice and to seek to make a difference. Ironically, the reason it took me so long was because I had succeeded at the Academy precisely because I avoided focusing on my gender at all, a tactic I went on to develop for much of my career — adapting to my circumstances, then resolutely avoiding, whenever possible, being identified by my gender.

After my four years at ADFA I graduated with the rank of Flying Officer in the Air Force, and had also completed what would become the first of three university degrees — a Bachelor of Arts, majoring in History. I found myself posted as one of only a few women to an F-111 fighter bomber squadron outside of Brisbane — yet another male-dominated environment. My memories, once again, were of wanting to fit in and excel. But in a lovely twist of fate, and having clearly watched *Top Gun* too many times, as a 21-year-old I met Glen, who was completing his fast-jet training to become an F-111 navigator; he has now been my husband for more than 20 years, and together we have two talented, loving and kind daughters.

In her book *Lean In*, Sheryl Sandberg famously notes that the most important career choice you will make is who you choose as your partner, and Glen has been a wonderful choice for me. Having someone next to me who respects and values my aspirations has been incredibly important in helping me achieve all that I have wanted to, personally and professionally.

A slow awakening

Even while serving in the Air Force as an Administration Officer, I had never lost my original passion to become a lawyer. I had started studying for my law degree as soon as I graduated from ADFA, and took a step closer to my goal when I found an opportunity in 1998 to become a mid-level manager in a corporate law firm — another completely new environment for me, and a long way from the military.

I was in my late twenties, and while I was now working with more women than I had before, most of them were employed in administrative and support roles, with very few at the most senior levels. In the broader legal profession there were the first rumblings of recognition that there may be gender inequality at the partnership level in law firms.

Recalling the Queen Bee idea from the movie *Working Girl*, it was during these years where unhelpful attitudes about working with senior women formed in my mind. I had never worked with any such women before, so when challenges arose I was quick to jump to a flawed explanation. In my role at the law firm I found myself both junior to, and the peer of, a number of highly experienced professional women. A confident and headstrong newcomer, I thought I knew just as much as men and women more senior to me, who may have had one or two decades more experience. Not surprisingly, I had difficult working relationships with a few senior women, which for many years in my mind were explained by the old stereotype of women desperately competing with each other, destined to fight their way to the top of the corporate tree.

Looking back now, with a lot more maturity and insight than I could muster in my twenties, I realise that this was not an issue about women at all. Rather, it was my own unwillingness to listen to others and respect their experience that saw us at loggerheads. On some occasions, it may also have been the other women's unwillingness to be open to new ideas, having learned the need to adapt to their environment and 'stick to the rules'. Our gender was irrelevant to the challenges, rather than being the logical explanation for them. Had I been mature enough to understand this dynamic, I could also have considered the vast numbers of women I *was* working with so constructively, as well as the men I found challenging to work with, and realised that the Queen Bee idea was not real, but simply a reaction to double standards.

In fact, it was as an overwhelmed young mother of a two-year-old and a newborn that I made my first foray into advocating for others. But first, I need to explain how it was actually my very first day on the job in the Air Force that directly led me to start helping women.

Assisting the bereaved

As a brand-new young Flying Officer posted to RAAF Base Amberley, I was assigned what is called a Secondary Duty — a responsibility held in addition to your day job. Within hours of arriving I was given a secondary duty no one seemed to want: Base Burials Officer, which I held for the remaining years of my military service. And on that very first morning I found myself in a car with the Base Chaplain, heading out to comfort the parents of a young airman who had just died.

I was a 21-year-old who had only ever attended one funeral — that of my grandfather, as a child. I had certainly never organised one, yet suddenly I found myself sitting in the living rooms of bereaved families who had lost their sons, daughters, husbands and wives to tragic accidents, illness and suicide. Knowing I could make a difference to people who needed support at the most tragic time in their lives, I threw myself into the role. I discovered that in grief, families desperately need someone to help with key decisions and to organise administrative matters that we otherwise take for granted. I remember having to assist the family of one service member who had taken his own life, and they were having a great deal of difficulty accepting that he had even died, which made organising the funeral challenging. Being sensitive to the trauma these families were experiencing, and then working at a pace that was appropriate in each case while communicating carefully and regularly with them, provided me with skills I have called on as a leader ever since.

My additional task as Burials Officer also became a rewarding part of my Air Force service because it was during such times I found that the military approach is second to none. I felt so proud of the support we could offer, and how the Air Force would do all it could to organise a funeral that helped the families in such pain. By the time I left, I had organised a dozen or more military funerals, and in each one I know we eased the burden those families felt, just a little.

Fast forward to a few years after I began working in the law firm, when tragically two aircrew were killed in an F-111 fighter bomber crash in Malaysia. The pilot and navigator had been Squadron colleagues of mine, and one of their widows in particular had become a close friend. While the military is so supportive of bereaved families in the immediate aftermath of a tragedy, I was concerned to see how simple bureaucratic blunders and perceptions of a lack of transparency during the crash investigation and the months that followed could snowball. Sometimes widows and family members believed their best and only option was expensive litigation, or going to the media to attract attention. With that sense of 'Enough', which I was to call on again almost 20 years later, I applied for, and was awarded, a Sir Winston Churchill Fellowship to investigate support strategies for families of those killed in the Australian Defence Force.

As part of my Churchill Fellowship research I surveyed more than 50 bereaved families of service men and women who were killed on duty, in tragic accidents, or had committed suicide. With my young family in tow, the Fellowship sponsored my travel to the United States to meet with Army personnel at the Pentagon to discuss how they manage military fatalities, and to talk with Australian astronaut Andy Thomas at NASA about the Space Shuttle Columbia disaster, among others. On my return to Australia I met with the then Chief of Defence Force, Sir Peter Cosgrove, and the then Chief of the Air Force, Sir Angus Houston, who received my report and its 37 recommendations for change.

While the report is no doubt now gathering dust somewhere in Canberra, I felt proud for having done what I could to help others. The widow who inspired me to begin this work is convinced that the impact of my recommendations has been absorbed into the cultural change that has happened within the military since that time. Regardless, I continue to feel particularly connected to the people I was able to assist, and in hindsight it probably started me thinking about advocating for other women. But life was busy, I had young children, and I wanted to succeed in my career. I was anxious to 'get somewhere' — even though I had no idea where, or how I would get there, or even why I wanted to get there.

In the decade that followed, the more senior a leader I became, the louder and more pressing my concerns about women's issues grew.

Leaning in to other women

By my early thirties I had spent six years studying law part time. I had raised two young children while listening to lectures on my old cassette player and had qualified as a solicitor. Despite the offer of a role to practise law in the firm, which had been a lifelong goal to that point, I made a decision to switch paths. By this stage I knew the right direction for me was leading others, building businesses and pursuing a wide range of interests beyond practising in a specific area of law. With that in mind, I set off on a new track — one that would see me beginning to understand first-hand the value of empowering and supporting women, to enrich not only my own life, but to benefit the businesses I worked with.

Because I was prepared to move and felt I was able to make brave decisions when needed, I found myself open to left-field opportunities. I am very conscious, now, that I was lucky to have the freedom to make choices, seize opportunities and take risks with my career — for many, many women these kinds of choices are simply unavailable. My eyes were also being opened to the systemic issues other women faced. Many women I knew did not have the same ability to move freely between jobs, due to financial pressures or lack of access to childcare, or did not have the financial or personal support to take on more study, as I had. These practical constraints were becoming increasingly apparent to me. During this 'awakening' stage, as Holly Kramer describes it, I was learning to advocate for myself, but was yet to fully understand how I could advocate for other women.

I left the stability of the corporate law firm and accepted an offer to join a global consulting business chiefly made up of psychologists, offering cognitive-based health and safety training to the mining and resources sector, during the boom years before the Global Financial Crisis. I'd handled the culture shock of moving from a private girls' school to ADFA, then leaving the military to work in a corporate law firm, and now another culture shock lay in store. My learning curve was, yet again, very steep. And I loved it.

In this job I now had many women colleagues, in both support and leadership roles. This brought a diversity of thinking and perspectives which I saw every day and made the business stronger. These were seminal years that forged my understanding about the value of women supporting women, and the benefits this delivers within an organisation. For the first time in my professional career I saw the opportunity that comes from having men and women equally contributing, from the highest levels, to the strategy and direction of the business. And the success of that environment shone through in its culture.

Working so closely with women at all levels of the business was an important counterbalance to our primarily male clients, who ran large mining and resources companies, and I would travel with my colleagues to platinum, diamond and coal mines from the Arctic to the Kalahari. The culture we were able to develop while I was at the helm as CEO resulted in a particularly exciting moment in 2010 when we were named *Business Review Weekly*'s 5th Best Place to Work in Australia, just behind Google, who ranked fourth at the time. It was clear evidence that leading a business based on diversity, authenticity and mutual respect had immense financial, cultural and personal rewards for everyone.

The guilt of a working mum

Travelling around the world was professionally rewarding, but personally very challenging as a mother of two young children. I remember being in high school, imagining what my future might bring, and mapping out that I intended to have my children by the age of 30, while having a professional career as well. During these daydreams I don't recall ever considering how this was all going to happen at the same time. Yet as for so many women juggling a family and career, it did. I met my husband when I was 21, we married when I was 25, had our first daughter when I was 27, and our second when I was 29.

It was now that I came to understand first-hand how challenging it is to balance work outside the home with caring for young children. I was initially very fortunate to be able to create some workplace flexibility in my role, which was relatively uncommon at the time. My husband and I had no family living near us, and just had to get through each week as best we could together, while spending a significant proportion of our income on childcare.

And I remember feeling guilty most of the time.

Guilty that I was a dreadful mother who was away from her children at work. Guilty that when I was at work I was worrying about my children.

Now it is important to note that my memories of this period are vastly different from those of my family. They assure me that I focus on all of the negatives — the times I was away for work, the school occasions I *did* miss, the kids' excursions I wasn't able to attend. But they are quite right in reminding me that for the vast majority of the time I was in fact a present, loving, attentive and proud mother. But the guilt I felt at the time is, I suspect, quite common as we put undue weight on not being what we perceive as the 'perfect' mother — the impossible ideal of 'having it all'. I can look back now with some objectivity that while I may not have been perfect, I was still a great mum who is incredibly proud of the young women my husband and I have raised.

One particular weekend I flew home from a week in Colorado for work, so that I could watch my daughter play soccer, before hopping on a plane the next day for another week working in South Africa. I knew I was taking on much of the guilt and pressure to be all things to all people, yet whether from societal expectations, or my deep-seated views on the role of men and women in parenting, I found the guilt hard to shake, especially as the local primary school knew my girls' carer better than they knew me. On one occasion I was most indignant when the school called my daughter's carer to collect her from school when she was unwell. I happened to be working from home that day, so I collected her from school myself and asked that in future they call me first. So of course, the inevitable happened. The next time one of the girls was ill, the school called me, but I was travelling, and had to regrettably agree that their carer probably was the best person to call first.

There are so many stereotypes in popular culture of the busy working mother who is cold and self-absorbed, leaving her children to be cared for by others, and she is often pitted against the devoted mothers who wait in the playground to collect their children and hear about their days (having baked fresh muffins to boot). Even then I understood that the insecurity I was feeling was not the result of other women doing or saying anything to make me feel guilty. These were my *own* feelings of inadequacy getting in the way. Rationally, I knew my children loved me, and felt loved by me. These were insecurities of my own making, a result of the pressure or stereotypes I imposed on myself — that a 'good mother' stays at home with her children.

Realising this self-imposed guilt was not helping anyone, least of all me or my family, I consciously decided one day to just stop feeling guilty, as hard as that was. It was another occasion when I saw myself say: Enough.

I wish I had understood back then the power I could have drawn from all the remarkable women who were dealing with their own similar challenges. But I was just focused on getting through every day as best I could.

A seat at the table

While CEO, I was invited to join my first corporate board at the age of 35, in the water industry. At the time there was one other woman on the board, but none in the executive team. As a brand-new director, I had a lot to learn, so I quickly completed an Australian Institute of Company Directors course, which dovetailed well with my legal qualifications and hands-on experience leading an international business. It had not been my plan to pursue a full-time career as a company director, but when offered a second board role a few years later, I made the decision to move out of the security of full-time employment to pursue a professional company director career.

The fact I was sitting in a boardroom at all as a woman was unusual in itself, as less than a quarter of all ASX 300 company directors are women. But it was also unusual given my age, as the average age of directors was 57 years for women and 61 years for men. I am fortunate that my board career continued to grow after my initial appointment in 2008.

Among other board roles, I was the first female director of Queensland Rugby Union in its 130-year history. I have also been the only female board director of a multi-billion-dollar construction company, an oil and gas company, and a large timber manufacturing company. In each of these roles I have had to learn to lead through influence, and each situation has required different skills to manage working in a male-dominated environment.

Having now spent a decade as a company director, I am passionate about my profession, with all the fiduciary, fiscal, ethical, cultural and strategic responsibilities that come with it. As a board we are not there to run the business, which is done by skilled and capable executive teams. We are there to set the tone and culture of the business, test assumptions, to ask probing and insightful questions, in order to ensure best-practice corporate governance and the long-term sustainability of the business. It was during the early years of my board career I had also managed to complete a PhD in the field of leadership, corporate culture and governance.

Again, during this time, I was increasingly beginning to understand the widespread challenges women faced. My rationalising had long dismissed any gender barriers I saw as an aberration, or the woman's own fault — a rationalisation I also applied to myself. Now I could look at these issues through the lens of seniority and influence, and actually make a difference to help others drive change. I could ask why there were no women in executive teams. See where women might have been in the organisation's succession plan. And ask for data on gender pay to see if there was a gap or pay discrimination to be addressed.

And I was increasingly gravitating to boards that had other women around the table or in the executive team. From my own experience I know that organisations with boardrooms in which diverse views are welcome — from people with diverse perspectives gained through having a different gender, age, ethnicity, education or experience — are much stronger as a result. With more constructive and mutually respectful dialogue, there tends to be a willingness to hear alternative viewpoints and incorporate different ways of problem solving when addressing critical issues. And the evidence backs up my own observations. Comparing three-year average returns on equity for 428 ASX-listed companies, Bloomberg research found that the strongest correlation with improved performance is a higher share of women on the board, followed by a stronger proportion of women in the company's workforce as a whole.[22] Diversity matters — and particularly having diversity of all kinds, at all levels.

What you see, you cannot unsee

My eyes were also opening, with a growing sense of concern, to behaviour around the board table. Male directors' comments were sometimes acknowledged more seriously than those of their female peers, who may have made the same point just moments earlier. I noticed comments from male board members concluding a woman had only been appointed because of her gender, ignoring her clear qualifications to join the board. During one particularly difficult board meeting, after management updated the board on a stalled negotiation with a client, one male director suggested, with clear sexual innuendo, that the board's only female member be sent in to 'negotiate' the deal.

I noticed all-male executive teams, or teams in which women only held traditional support roles, such as human resources or marketing. I was also noticing more unconscious, structural issues that had arisen in the push to add more women to company boards. Often, head-hunters would be searching to fill 'the diversity spot' for one female director. All this did was set up competition between women for that single seat, or as the analogy keeps reminding us, for the only place at the top of the ladder.

The more senior I became, the more influence I knew I had, and with that came a genuine sense of responsibility to try to help other women succeed. I knew that having other women at the most senior levels of an organisation, and then at every other level of the business, would make it easier for all women to succeed.

The idea of having only one woman at the top of the ladder had to go.

Instead of sticking with my strategy to keep ignoring gender issues, as I had done at the start of my career, I had become drawn to speaking up in support of other women. Seeing campaigns such as #HeforShe, #AllMalePanel, #EverydaySexism and #ShePersisted proliferate on Twitter had helped to change my mind: once you recognise the inequalities facing women, it is impossible to 'unsee' them. And none of us should even try.

Ditching the ladder

My board career propelled me to become part of formal women's networks for the first time — including Chief Executive Women, Women Corporate Directors and the Women's Leadership Institute of Australia. Until that point, I had underestimated the power of joining with other women to make a difference, and had incorrectly believed it could be detrimental to my career. But becoming involved in these organisations very quickly alerted me to the many ways in which gender barriers persist, and the onus to help others. On Twitter, I tentatively retweeted articles on issues facing women and sought out commentary on gender.

My gender awakening had taken almost 25 years to evolve, but was now escalating and waiting to explode into action. I had matured into seniority — Holly Kramer's final stage of advocacy — and wanted to make a difference. 'You have to use your privilege to serve other people,'[23] as Tarana Burke, the founder of #MeToo, says. That was precisely what I wanted to do.

That opportunity came in January 2017 when I finally said 'Enough'. Watching the Women's March with pride, seeing the daily denigration of women online, and all my own experiences meant I could no longer remain silent. It might seem as though my next steps happened overnight, but in reality they were the upshot of decades spent observing the challenges women faced.

I now had the confidence to try to make a difference, and with what turned out to be very fortuitous timing, set out on my most unexpectedly rewarding path of all: creating an online movement that would resonate with women around the world.

Throwing down the fishing net

Back on the beach, having finished my shandy at the brewery, I rang my mum to ask her the four questions I had scribbled on the crumpled napkin.

I wanted to ask questions that could not be answered via Google, but only by an individual woman herself. Questions that would draw out any woman's story, would encourage women from all walks of life to participate online, and would use storytelling to celebrate women — to respond to a frustratingly negative situation in the most positive way I could think of.

The first question I asked Mum was how she describes what she does, without using a position title. (She'd had a very full professional career but was now retired, while also completing a PhD, so I didn't know how she might describe herself.) This simple question turned out to be so important in creating a sense of inclusion in the campaign for so many diverse women — not that I knew this at the time. So I noted down Mum's answer that during her career she had provided health programs in refugee camps in areas of conflict, and post-conflict around the world.

The second question was what Mum had wanted to do when she was at school. Again, I was genuinely curious to understand what her aspirations had been as a young girl. I was quite surprised when she said she'd imagined a career looking after lost dogs at the local pound. But what was revealing — and so common for women of my mother's generation — is that she also answered that her parents had wanted her to be a secretary. Mum initially followed the aspirations of her parents by leaving school at the age of 16 and joining the typing pool of the CSIRO (Commonwealth Scientific and Industrial Research Organisation). Looking back over the campaign, it was fascinating to see the winding paths many women's lives had taken from their original childhood dreams, and how many had found a way back to their original passions. Similarly, their stories reveal how many women were deterred from what they wanted to do because of the expectations of family or others.

The third question asked Mum to describe her life using only three words. This was because, like most women, she had experienced all of life's highs and lows, while also having many incredible adventures. Her response perfectly captured her: Resilience, determination and empathy.

The final question was who Mum hoped to inspire and why. For some women, this turned out to be one of the more challenging questions, but also highly revealing. As the campaign progressed I discovered most women hope to inspire someone who may face similar challenges to themselves, and my mother was no different. She wanted to inspire older women to follow their passions, to never accept age as a barrier, and for women to celebrate their collective wisdom.

That short phone call on the beach set the formula for the hundreds of #CelebratingWomen profiles that would follow.

Starting a celebration

Just two days after my *Women's Agenda* opinion piece appeared online, I posted what would become #CelebratingWomen profile number 1 of Irene, with some photos. I didn't reveal Irene was my mother, but posted it on Twitter in a thread of tweets to see what might happen.

The response was almost immediate. Irene's #CelebratingWomen profile was retweeted and shared dozens of times. People seemed to love her story, and it felt like a tiny glimmer of positivity amidst the endless negative news stories. It was energising to see that maybe, just maybe, celebratory tweets like this could make a small ripple of difference.

Yet it was nerve-racking and unfamiliar territory. I was using social media in a way I hadn't done before, and there were risks involved. I was scared of the reaction I might get, and frankly of the online abuse I might receive myself. I also didn't know whether any positive noise would fizzle out as soon as Mum's profile was posted. Yet encouraged by the response I resolved — in the words of renowned business writer and author of *Good to Great*, Jim Collins — to set myself the biggest, hairiest, most audacious goal I could think of.

Seeing the response to Mum's profile, and buzzing with ideas on the potential ways to build it into an even bigger celebration, I lay in bed that night considering what to do next. With all the courage I could muster I tweeted a very public commitment the following morning that I would celebrate two women — from all walks of life, and from anywhere in the world — every single day in 2017.

I had absolutely no idea where I was going to find so many women willing to share personal photos and answer four personal questions online. Women tend to be reluctant to put themselves forward, to be recognised, and to be willing to say they are proud of what they do — and many don't feel they deserve to be celebrated. And to make things harder, this campaign was asking them to do that in a very public online environment with a reputation as a particularly unsafe place for women. But I was determined to make this work.

I felt it was imperative to finally forget the old saying that when women climb the ladder, they need to send it back down to help other women climb up, too. We need to forget the bloody ladder because it can only ever help one woman at a time. A ladder is designed to be held onto with both hands, so you don't let go. It was time for me to ditch the ladder and throw down a fishing net to bring up many, many women together.

There was an instant response to my public commitment. In the early weeks, before the campaign really established itself, I was sending daily tweets asking women to get involved and help me to achieve my goal, and I was stunned and overwhelmed at the high levels of trust being shown by women — most of whom I had never met — who were sending me their answers to my four questions, along with photos of themselves.

The campaign had tapped into a desire for women to connect with other women, and they were prepared to put themselves forward and be celebrated.

#CelebratingWomen had begun.

'One small rock can move a whole mountain'

The commitment to post two profiles every day for an entire year left me well and truly out of my comfort zone as I found myself loudly and publicly advocating for women every day. Yet despite my initial trepidation, it was a richly energising process, connecting with new women every day and hearing their stories, while seeing first-hand the celebration and response each woman was getting from family, friends and strangers online.

As well as posting their profiles on Twitter, I had created a Facebook page which was attracting hundreds of new followers each week, and it soon became obvious that #CelebratingWomen would grow much more than I had ever anticipated.

The success of #CelebratingWomen led to an incredibly full year. I already had a very busy career, travelling most weeks, so suddenly I found myself posting profiles every morning in the back of taxis, while travelling overseas, on special occasions like birthdays, Easter and Christmas Day, and even when I was unwell. But I never missed a day. And despite many generous offers of assistance, I wrote every woman's profile myself, because I felt strongly that this was a commitment I had made and wanted to see through. Each woman was trusting me to celebrate her and I took that very seriously.

One of my primary goals for #CelebratingWomen was ensuring no woman felt excluded. Anyone who identified as a woman and got in touch before submissions had closed was included. No woman missed out, even when that meant celebrating eight women a day towards the end of the year. The women came from any country, any profession, any educational background, any socioeconomic group or any sexual orientation. Transgender women were also welcomed and celebrated.

Hours were spent each weekend writing the profiles for the week ahead. I laughed one day when someone asked me via Twitter whether I had built an algorithm to write the profiles. And I was often asked to thank the 'team' at #CelebratingWomen for posting the profiles. These lovely comments always made me smile: the 'team' was simply me and my laptop. But more broadly, the wonderful responses I received and the impact I could see it was having on so many women — and men — meant I never felt I was doing this on my own. The network of women I had the privilege of celebrating was beyond my wildest dreams, and the elation each woman felt on the day she was celebrated was shared by many — including me — every day of the year.

That simple idea that began on the beach soon led to media interviews, invitations to speak at events, time in the legendary Twitter 'Blue Room', and to my surprise, my nomination as a finalist in the Walkley Foundation's prestigious Our Watch Awards for best use of social media for #CelebratingWomen.

Parents sent messages to tell me they were showing the women's profiles to their young daughters each day, so young girls could read about diverse role models and career paths. Teachers were using the profiles to show students that it was okay not knowing what lay ahead when leaving school, as other women had been in the same situation and had managed to find their passion. Most importantly, the campaign had created an enormous network of women around the world supporting each other.

The international impact was one of the more exciting aspects of the campaign, but I probably should not have been as surprised by how quickly it spread. As more and more women were celebrated, initially in Australia, women from other nations became involved. By the end of 2017, with a few extra women added to my original goal so that no one missed out, the 757 women came from 37 countries including the United States, United Kingdom and New Zealand, as well as the Faroe Islands, Chile, Japan and South Africa, to name a few. The campaign was written about in Ghana, Indonesia and America, among other locations. Every time a woman from a new country submitted her profile I would be elated. One woman had run as a political candidate for President of Iceland, followed soon after by a teacher from Afghanistan, and a woman who ran a glass-bottomed boat business in Vanuatu.

I was particularly touched by a message from Tina Šipicki, profile #171, who told me how proud she felt to be representing Serbia in the campaign, and that I had shown how 'moving one small rock can move a whole mountain'. Tina is a customs officer and, in her profile, had described herself as providing a safe, secure environment for those using the national airport in Serbia. There seemed no limit to the diversity of women who wanted to get involved and celebrate one another.

Keeping the celebration going

Despite many requests to continue #CelebratingWomen after 2017, I ended the campaign on 31 December, as I had always intended. I always felt that this was a 'point in time' idea — one that generated momentum partly because it was a challenge to see if my original goal could be achieved.

I was also exhausted. Even as someone capable of a huge amount of work, the daily focus on ensuring I celebrated two women every single day, in addition to my busy career, had left little time for much else.

But most importantly, I was also excited to see the next wave of ideas from other women who were also holding the sides of the fishing net to bring other women up.

While the first #CelebratingWomen profile had been of my mother Irene, it felt fitting that the final profile was of my eldest daughter, Emily, after celebrating my younger daughter, Zoe, a week earlier on Christmas Day. Both my daughters had followed the campaign from the very start. They supported me at every stage and I knew they were incredibly proud. The personal is political, as Gloria Steinem famously said, and amid the celebration, my hope was to role-model to these two strong, brilliant young women the different ways we can value women, and offer inspiration for how they may choose to contribute to the world.

I loved that this campaign began so simply, with just one person who had a vision for what might be possible. To think that it made such a difference to so many women, including my daughters, is far more than I ever imagined.

Thanks to the support of other women, and my own support of them, that small ripple of change led to tangible differences for all the women involved. Including me. At a

#CelebratingWomen event in Melbourne while the campaign was still underway, many of the women who had been profiled attended, and to see so many of them come off my screen and into my life was overwhelming. But what really moved me was listening to them all connecting with one another, offering support and truly wanting to lift one another up.

I listened to one woman, who ran a missing persons network after her own brother had disappeared, as she talked to another participant, a news reporter. The two women then collaborated on a news story to highlight the bureaucratic challenges families face when a loved one goes missing. Some women have been offered work, speaking engagements and collaboration opportunities from having been profiled online, while others have formed friendships and professional connections.

Celebrations are truly contagious. Carol Hay (profile #484) self-published a book in Singapore using the four questions to acknowledge many of the women in her personal and professional network. Melanie Brock (profile #600) and Sam Mostyn (profile #756), in collaboration with the Australian Embassy in Japan, launched #CelebratingWomeninJapan on International Women's Day in 2018; and #CelebratingWomen campaigns also appeared in the United States and Papua New Guinea. Businesswoman Natalie Chapman (profile #689) says she used #CelebratingWomen as the inspiration for #AUSinnovates to flag the commercialisation successes of Australian research and innovation companies.

The reaction to the final day of the campaign is something I will never forget. Hundreds of men and women from around the world contacted me on social media, as well as privately, to tell me how much the campaign had meant to them and how much they would miss it. I knew the campaign had been meaningful to many of the women involved, but I hadn't fully appreciated how many other people had enjoyed reading and celebrating from the sidelines. Also unexpected was the strong sense of community which had grown for those hoping I would foster and develop #CelebratingWomen into the future.

There were many suggestions as to other related campaigns people would like to see me involved with, as well as ways to keep the momentum going and turn the campaign into something much more, by selling merchandise and marketing #CelebratingWomen events. The words of Tarana Burke, the founder of #MeToo, really resonated with me, when she described how she felt squeamish about her '15 minutes' when people encouraged her to 'monetise' it through selling merchandise such as #MeToo T-shirts.[24] My motivation for starting #CelebratingWomen had never been about trying to make money or to boost my profile; in fact, I am quite sure that if it had been, the campaign would have failed through a lack of authenticity. I have certainly been rewarded, though, in very different ways. I regularly speak at events around the world about #CelebratingWomen, and more broadly about leadership and diversity, which I love. I was honoured to be awarded the 2018 Queensland Award for Excellence in Women's Leadership, in large part for my work in the campaign, but also for a long career in leading and advocating for others.

Once #CelebratingWomen had finished, people began asking my 'permission' to use the hashtag to create spin-off campaigns, and each time it felt I was being asked for permission that I had no right to give. But what #CelebratingWomen taught me was that being a woman prepared to lift others up, and not succeed at the expense of others, will bring far more in return than you could ever expect — not necessarily more money or a new job, although indirectly they may end up following too. Most importantly, as a result of the campaign I have met countless inspiring women, and have felt enriched, uplifted and rewarded by sharing so many stories, laughs, tears and inspirations with them. And while it was the last thing I ever expected or sought, I too have felt celebrated.

As well as finding myself belonging to a whole vast community of women, #CelebratingWomen also reconnected me with other women after a number of years — including award-winning journalist Catherine Fox.

Catherine and I first met at an event in Brisbane that we had both spoken at several years previously. She needed a lift to the airport; I had a car and our friendship began.

As a perfect example of women supporting women, it seemed entirely appropriate that Catherine and I decided to write this book together.

When women support women, you just never know where it may lead.

2

THE POWER OF
SHARING STORIES

Looking back, it seems fitting that #CelebratingWomen unfolded during 2017 — a watershed year for women around the world. Soon after the campaign launched, there was a surge in social media campaigns focusing on women's issues globally, including #WomensMarch, #MeToo and #TimesUp. 'Feminism' was named 2017 Word of the Year by American dictionary Merriam-Webster; 'The Silence Breakers' who spoke out about sexual harassment were named *Time* People of the Year; and suddenly this was the year for women to not only find their voices, but to have those voices taken seriously. It was also the year that Kirstin found her own.

Kirstin knew #CelebratingWomen might not radically change the tide of abuse women were experiencing online, but the movement nevertheless did help form part of a small but ever-widening current of change.

Standing up, shouting out

There is something awe inspiring when collective power unfolds without formal sanctions, rules, or even appointed leaders.

The global social media movements of 2017 became a sign of the most overt display of collective women's clout since the suffragettes marched in the United Kingdom in the early twentieth century and women took to the streets waving placards in the 1970s. The events were cumulative, and played out against remarkable political activism internationally.

The motivation for many women was the same — to stand up, speak out and be counted, in an outbreak of old-fashioned solidarity. Many were feeling the same sense of frustration that their lives and contributions had been ignored, and a burning desire to help ensure women's lives were recognised and valued. When basic rights, such as reproductive laws, come under threat, it's another stark reminder of the need for eternal vigilance and sustained pressure. This is how social progress has always been made.

By the end of 2017, #CelebratingWomen felt remarkably timely, elevating women's stories when thousands more were supporting and encouraging each other to do the same. Women had found their voices, and they were using social media to make sure they were being heard. While #CelebratingWomen was much smaller in scale, issues and global impact than campaigns such as #MeToo and #TimesUp, they shared a common thread. Watching this unfolding of women's strength and affirmation reinforced the importance of keeping the momentum going.

The power and legitimacy that followed from women feeling safe, included and supported — and the environment on social media this created — could clearly produce incredible change.

Early on, it was apparent that most of the women profiled had never received or sought public recognition. While there were some well-known names among them, and some were acclaimed leaders in their fields, the vast majority had never won awards. They hadn't been in the spotlight before, and were not seeking it. They were mostly women we spend our days with — our families and friends, women we work with or live next door to, who are rarely singled out.

With no qualifying criteria for inclusion, women from all walks of life felt able to be involved. And asking them to explain their various roles by describing their impact, rather than a position title, tended to put their personal values front and centre. This focus and the lack of elitism encouraged even more women to join in the celebration.

This inclusive environment had also resulted from conscious choices during the campaign. Kirstin deliberately published the profiles in the order they were received, to avoid inadvertently 'curating' the campaign, and when writing the profiles was careful to use the women's own words, to minimise any conscious or unconscious bias.

Putting the social back into media

#CelebratingWomen may have begun with the core aim of countering the denigration of women online, but it morphed into something much, much more. By focusing on inclusion as the strategy, diversity became the outcome, spotlighting a rich spectrum of role models who would otherwise have remained invisible. And paradoxically, it could only have happened on social media — the very platform that had become such a fraught arena for many women.

As #MeToo founder Tarana Burke immediately thought when she realised the #MeToo hashtag was gaining worldwide momentum: 'Social media is not a safe space … this is going to be a fucking disaster!'[25] Yet we know that social media can also be used constructively and positively, and the ease with which it allowed women to participate actually increased their willingness to become involved in the campaign.

Suzy Nicoletti (profile #509), Twitter Australia's Managing Director, had a personal and professional interest in #CelebratingWomen. Kirstin's efforts came to her attention in early 2017, as the social media company was redoubling its commitment to user safety by introducing a range of new policies and tools to improve Twitter for everyone.

Kirstin and Suzy had first met at a women's networking event, and reconnected just as #CelebratingWomen started to gain momentum. 'I had to meet (Kirstin) to learn more about what she was doing with #CelebratingWomen and to ensure we could keep amplifying it to promote this story,' Suzy says, adding:

> One of the more defining moments for me
> around the power of the campaign occurred when
> I saw her #CelebratingWomen Melbourne event
> conversation trending above high-rating TV shows
> on Twitter. It really highlighted just how powerful
> this movement had become as women everywhere
> saw the event happening on Twitter and came

together to share their stories about how
the campaign had impacted them.

Extraordinarily, the campaign had attracted no trolling — so the sudden creation of an online haven for women, by an Australian woman with no specific experience in social media, was a revelation, says Suzy:

Here's this woman who decided that there are
incredible women out there who deserve to be
recognised and celebrated. So she took the initiative
to create her own social movement to bring them
together no matter who they were or where they lived.
The uptake on it was incredible! I had her come into
Twitter and we did a Twitter Q&A in our Twitter Blue
Room, and what we loved was how Kirstin utilised
the power of our platform to give a voice to and
connect with women around the world.

Seeing so many women coming together, she says, using the platform in a powerful way on a daily basis, was impressive.

Even for someone on the inside of the social platform, Suzy found #CelebratingWomen a powerful way to amplify her voice, managing to discover and connect with several other women on Twitter, and using the hashtag as a source of meeting interesting and uplifting women.

[#CelebratingWomen] is an example of a thought
leader making an impact in so many ways. Particularly
as a working woman with two young kids I looked to
the campaign everyday as a daily dose of inspiration
from women who were celebrating both work and

family. The movement was holistic and authentic. Women were celebrated for who they were, not just achievements, but the full person and what they valued.

The explosion in social movements online, helped along by powerful female voices, was a sign of entering a new world of digital communication, Suzy adds.

Safety in numbers

Some participants in #CelebratingWomen saw its potential to help reclaim social media. For Sharryn Naylor (profile #531), the campaign set a new benchmark for how social media can be used for good; others said it gave them a public channel to express themselves without being judged. Remarkably, with no evidence of trolling directed at #CelebratingWomen, Kirstin also received none. Neither did any of the women profiled — an unexpected sign of success in meeting the campaign's original aim.

Not surprisingly, many participants were pleased to see the platform being used in a positive way, tired of reading insulting tweets and aggressive views on social media. Others said they had watched the campaign evolve and realised it was a very genuine, non-judgemental and 'safe' forum, which encouraged them to participate, and added to its authenticity. The campaign wasn't being orchestrated by a corporation or brand, to generate views; there was no ulterior motive. Instead, it was all about the profiles and the women. Jo Prigmore (profile #210) said she enjoyed being part of a campaign that was free of bitchiness or hidden agendas.

The unlikely safe haven of a women's online campaign also attracted the attention of Australia's first eSafety Commissioner, Julie Inman-Grant (profile #496), who is leading the only government agency of its kind in the world.[26] A veteran of Silicon Valley tech companies, including a couple of years working for Twitter, she was fascinated to see how #CelebratingWomen built up over the year — unlike many campaigns which are reactive and tend to have a limited life. Its originality and timing also stood out:

> There were a number of different tipping points converging at the same time. It was before #MeToo and #TimesUp, but different movements were pushing towards the same aim: against sexual violence, harassment and for gender equality.
> I happen to think based on what I've seen [#CelebratingWomen's] positive mantra is one that everyone can relate to — even the worst misogynist has a woman in their family who is a role model.

The range of social media activity has been liberating to see, but now the trick is finding ways of continuing to encourage women to raise their voices online, says Julie. After all, the whole idea of social media is to speak truth to power:

> What trolls are trying to do is drive out women's voices and undercut the concept of free speech social media was built on. Kirstin's initiative shows that she wasn't trying to bring anyone down, because there are so many good things to celebrate. It's part of an evolution, rather than a revolution.

In fact, the campaign's positivity helped *repel* trolls, Julie believes, and her office is looking to crowd-source other groups of women to support women online, and build the opposite of a 'dogpile' (when a group of people join in criticising a target online). It's drowning out the trolls with positive stories and killing them with kindness, she adds.

While social media platforms have improved their safety policies, they can't continue to put most of the burden on individual users to protect themselves, she believes. That said, Julie is running a campaign called #WomenWithWITS to give individuals the self-defence skills to read a troll and understand how to respond, and to protect their voices online. So many women have important things to say, and they get nervous — and so do their employers — about going on platforms such as Twitter, because they don't know what sort of reaction they'll get, she adds. Julie's office is taking steps to partner with organisations to deliver this training.

No permission required

It's possible a male leader would have raised the need to tackle online denigration of women at a G7 meeting, but the fact UK Prime Minister Theresa May sent a strong message on this serious problem was particularly notable. She told the 2018 summit that 'women must be able to go online without fear'.[27]

More safety online will no doubt enable many more women to add their voices and propel future activism. In June 2017, mid-way through the campaign, Alison Hallworth (profile #163) wrote in her blog that she had become hooked on social media because 'it gives a voice to individuals and to groups of people that would not necessarily have a platform':

> The power of #CelebratingWomen is it is not
> waiting for Hollywood or 'the establishment' to
> tell us the stories of those everyday women that are
> working hard, chipping away at prejudices, setting
> new standards, mentoring others, inspiring their
> own daughters. We have the power and ability to
> tell those stories now, and we have the power to tell
> them ourselves. And that's worth celebrating.[28]

#CelebratingWomen had allowed women to make some noise in a positive way. No doubt this had a lot to do with the sheer breadth of women involved. It was impossible to categorise them by particular types of occupations. The 757 women were as different as any group of people could be, reminding us once again that gender stereotypes perpetuate the myth that all women think or behave in the same way. They were retirees and women based at home. They were electricians, politicians, house painters, teachers, engineers, customs officers, military officers and social workers. Some were professional sportswomen, Olympians and Paralympians. Each made their own contribution to their local communities, to their country and even to the world.

Importantly, the profiles also included many contributions that are routinely overlooked or ignored — simply because there is little value attached to women's household and caring labour, as author and academic Anne Manne has pointed out[29] in an article about New Zealand academic Marilyn Waring's seminal 1988 book, *Counting For Nothing: What Men Value and What Women are Worth*.[30] Waring's analysis looked at how gross domestic product excluded — and thereby rendered invisible — the huge contribution to society made by women through their life-sustaining unpaid labour.[31] (The Australian Bureau of Statistics has estimated unpaid labour in 2014 was worth $434 billion in Australia alone.[32]) While Waring has considerable influence on governments around the world, much remains to be done to recognise the true value of this unpaid labour, and to credit those doing it, Manne concluded.

Real women, real stories

It was a crucial distinguishing feature of the campaign profiles to include *all* kinds of work and care. Asked what they had wanted to do when they finished school, many spoke about their childhood dreams, and how they had gone on to follow them. But many women ended up finding their path and true passion through a series of unexpected decisions and choices. Sadly, a number of women knew exactly what they had wanted to do or what they were passionate about, but were deterred because of the opinions or lack of encouragement from others. As young girls, many were told they couldn't follow their dreams and got the message, either explicitly or implicitly, that they were not good enough. And this was not a generational issue: even women who had finished school within the past few years had experienced this impasse.

Helene Young (profile #477) epitomised these unusual pathways, describing herself as an airline pilot sailing around Australia while working on her seventh novel. Helene left school with no clear direction, other than knowing she wanted to fly. Her goal waited until she was 24 years old, when she was able to afford flying lessons. By joining the campaign, she hoped to help show other women how dogged determination can help overcome obstacles — but just as importantly, that careers do not define us. To her, the campaign was a welcome reminder that women doing seemingly ordinary roles can be powerful forces for helping other women find their way.

Australian outback station owner Gillian Fennell (profile #595) said the campaign showed her that attitude was more important than education, your ability was more important than your address, and your starting point does not dictate your future. When Gillian left school, she knew she didn't want to go to university, and instead got straight into work and enjoying life. A self-described mum and home tutor, Gillian hoped she could inspire anyone who chooses to stay at home with their kids to know they are doing something great and making a difference to the people around them.

Each woman who participated had provided three words to describe her life. The words women offered from around the world to describe their lives were remarkably consistent. Irrespective of socioeconomic background, educational qualifications or the path through life each woman may have taken, many consistent themes emerged. Plenty described their lives to date as fun, unexpected, fearless, hectic and passionate; others considered their lives had been lucky, purposeful, privileged, while also messy and tragic.

To Kirstin's great surprise, after the campaign ended her father David, and his wife Lori, sent her a printed canvas of a 'word cloud'. They had spent the final month of the campaign manually collating every answer to this question and did a frequency analysis of the results. The word cloud beautifully represented the views of 757 women from around the world — and challenged stereotypes about women being hidebound and risk averse.

The most common word used by women around the world to describe their life to date was 'challenging'. This was followed by 'rewarding', 'fulfilling', 'exciting' and 'adventurous'.

Casting out hope

The answer to the fourth and final question of each #CelebratingWomen profile was equally illuminating. Every woman was asked who they hoped to inspire by sharing their story, and why. Invariably the answers to this question reflected the challenges each woman may have faced and overcome. For single mothers there was often a hope that their story might inspire other women struggling to raise children alone. There were many examples of women wanting to inspire their children — sons and daughters — by their stories, through being able to make their own choices in life to reach their goals. Women who worked in male-dominated fields frequently wished to inspire other women to see that these opportunities were also open to them. And women with physical disabilities often wanted to inspire others facing similar challenges. Universally, the women wanted to make a difference to the lives of others, and more often than not, they hoped to inspire — and support — other women.

Women told us the experience of being celebrated was overwhelmingly positive, with many expressing delight both at seeing their profile online, and receiving well wishes from family, friends and strangers alike. Evelyn Ralph (profile #731) had nervously shared her profile on Instagram; Evelyn's friend saw her tentative Instagram share, found her original profile on Kirstin's Facebook page and then shared it widely, leading to an avalanche of friends and others saying how much Evelyn had inspired them. Again, the simplicity of celebrating a woman for who she was led to a contagious outpouring of support. Evelyn had former students comment on her profile, which meant so much to her, while also helping to inspire a new generation of teachers who may have been feeling a little lost.

Kindness is contagious

The campaign's momentum over the year became a lesson in the power of celebrations. Every woman involved allowed her stories to be shared with the world, in an act of great trust, and the result was positive and joyful — joy for the women themselves, but also for those celebrating them. Celebrations are contagious, and the goodwill and euphoria was transferred from one person to another as kind words, gratitude and well wishes were shared. As stories and accomplishments were re-lived, new ideas, opportunities and inspirations emerged.

The participants themselves best articulated why a more dispersed and collaborative set of role models was such a compelling part of the campaign. And seeing the reaction to their profiles helped them understand they were actually leading by example, which was also revelatory for many. Tweeting in reply to a thread about #CelebratingWomen, Andrea Perry-Petersen (profile #724) made a powerful observation about the breadth of its catchment:

> [#CelebratingWomen] has broadened the
> definition of leadership — by not featuring already
> well-known achievers or those that meet typical
> leadership criteria.

For Fay Calderone (profile #6), the campaign's inclusion of such a disparate array of women was a key reason to be involved. Growing up in Western Sydney as a daughter of refugees from Cyprus and attending public schools, she knew how insurmountable the obstacles can seem — and indeed are, in some cases. Fay wanted to show underprivileged girls who 'think they can't, that they can', knowing the springboard privilege creates in the professions. 'I love that #CelebratingWomen casts the net wide and far,' she says, 'and aims to raise women up indiscriminately.' Dr Mellissa Naidoo (profile #316) told us being part of #CelebratingWomen helped her to acknowledge she was a role model and that she was contributing to changing the culture to one where all women are valued.

UK-based Bijna K. Dasani (profile #81) originally wanted to be a neurologist, but as the eldest child in a single-parent family, left full-time schooling at 16 to undertake full-time employment, and completed her education part-time. Bijna graduated from Oxford University with a Masters level qualification in 2016, and is now a senior executive at the intersection of financial services and technology. She felt her #CelebratingWomen profile presented her in a 'very raw light', and she felt appreciated for simply being her true self — especially in a world where perfection, stereotypes, peer pressure and messages about needing to be 'the best versions of ourselves' are prevalent. The campaign celebrated a truly diverse group of women, and within it is a real-life set of diverse role models, Bijna added.

The sheer scarcity of options, whether in getting an education or following a career, has seen many women take side-tracks and unusual paths rather than following conventional advice, offering up some illuminating narratives throughout the campaign. As medical researcher Dr Caroline Ford (profile #624) told us, seeing the wide-ranging profiles on her Twitter feed each day in 2017 was like a little ray of sunshine. The stories of everyday women were compelling and inspiring, and their influence could be potent and diffuse, even if they were not at the very top of the tree.

Tackling talking taboos

Understandably, many participants had to overcome concerns about 'blowing their own trumpet' before taking the plunge. No one likes a braggard, particularly of the female variety. But on top of those cultural taboos, women historically have also run the gauntlet of being talked over and ignored — or paradoxically, ridiculed for talking too much. Women are routinely told they speak far more than men (a myth several language experts have busted[33]), and the chatty woman is a laughing stock in many societies. But recent campaigns, and the use of social media, have revealed a great unspoken reality for women. While they have always talked among themselves and shared their concerns (just like some men), to do so publicly, or in the workplace, can be fraught with major risks — including of course the vicious trolling Kirstin's campaign was challenging.

The penalties for women using their voices are often about shutting it down. Georgie Somerset (profile #703) has been a leading champion for women in regional Australia, and says she has been 'overlooked in the past' due to her involvement in supporting women, so she 'welcomed an open, embracing movement on social media'. For her, #CelebratingWomen confirmed that the majority of women want to be supportive of other women, but don't always have a mechanism to do that — until now. 'Not everyone wants to join "an organisation" to show their support for other women,' Georgie points out, 'but this has often been one of the few ways to do this.' Finding their own voice through social media and a like-minded supportive audience has helped many women like Georgie bypass the traditional penalties and opened a channel for them to be heard.

During a panel discussion on workplace harassment at Melbourne University, Professor Cordelia Fine said there were two factors that stopped women from speaking out: fear, and lack of efficacy. Both these factors continue to stymie women's ability to speak up, despite the momentum of online social campaigns, and underline the need to sustain and reinforce the power of collective voices to ensure workplace sexism is addressed.

Indeed, it is time to call out the puzzlingly and contradictory reactions women face when they do stand up in the workplace: simultaneously chastised or mocked for favouritism when leaping to each others' defence, and being labelled self-interested Queen Bees if they haven't stepped in.

Over the years we have heard men 'jokingly' — but in reality, passive-aggressively — ticking off women for 'sticking together', or conspiring to get their way (or 'hatching something', as Reserve Bank director Kathryn Fagg told us). Enduring mockery is one thing, but sticking your neck out for another woman, or pointing out some sexism at work, can have serious negative consequences. One US study showed women are penalised for 'diversity-enhancing behaviour' or fronting up about gender inequity, or vocally supporting other women[34] — and while white men didn't get any bonus points for talking up diversity either, at least they weren't marked down for it as women and men of colour were. Women who persist in raising such issues are also often labelled 'trouble makers' — clearly not the way to win friends and influence people. And just like getting a reputation as a 'Queen Bee', those labels tend to stick.

Historically, women who have complained of harassment in the workplace have been at risk not only of losing their job, but never getting another. In Australia in 2010, when Mark McInnes, the high-profile CEO of retailer David Jones, resigned after admitting he had behaved inappropriately with a young female staff member, he went on to another CEO role. The woman in question left her job, her family and the country.

When questions are asked about the difference social media campaigns and collective voices have made, it is worth remembering these past incidents, and the dismissive way in which women's complaints and experience were often handled. Blaming and punishing the victim was all too frequently the outcome. Undoubtedly more workplace complaints will continue to come to light, but more employers are grasping the need to review their workplace policies to deal with them.[35]

The 'F' word

The recent wave of shared female power — and using a virtual community such as #CelebratingWomen to encourage and support each other — represents a rare moment to challenge these corrosive penalties. By keeping the stories coming and stepping up together, there's an opportunity to maintain the pressure for change, and help counter negative stereotypes about women taking the lead or speaking out about their rights and the principles of feminism.

In 2017, when economist Dr Leonora Risse helped set up the Women in Economics Network, she told Catherine there was enthusiastic support from many women, but some were reluctant to join, for fear of being ostracised within their male-dominated workplace and labelled as a feminist — and that this would have repercussions for them at a later stage. This kind of reaction, reminiscent of Kirstin's experiences in chapter 1, also suggests men have a vital role to play in supporting, encouraging and even joining women's networks.

When more than the odd brave woman in an organisation or team overtly supports another, however, it becomes much harder to apply these informal penalties. But it has to be about building collective pressure. And wielding influence. Having more women in leadership roles — supported by male allies, as we will examine further in chapter 7 — who can draw attention to the problem, and use their clout to lead by example obviously helps. They can intervene, and take a different approach to elevating women at a more systemic level.

It's important to be strategic about the role, and ultimate goals, of women's networks in this endeavour. In the past these have mostly been support groups, Dr Risse points out, but have now become an advocacy voice, encouraging women to call out the problem and raising awareness about the value of gender equality.

One of the practical effects of #CelebratingWomen was highlighting the power that can be unlocked when the advantages of women's collaboration are recognised, rather than relying on the usual organisational responses to diversity. Networking groups for women can be highly effective — as we will examine — but in the past have had limited capacity to influence mainstream decision-making. #CelebratingWomen revealed a model that worked and could be emulated in all sorts of environments. But the success of the campaign relied on women overcoming reservations about the penalties for highlighting their achievements.

Spotting the imposter

Many of the comments from women throughout the campaign showed the 'Imposter Syndrome' was alive and well.

First coined in 1978 by two clinical psychologists, the phenomenon describes a person having a deeply held assumption or belief that they do not deserve any success they may have achieved, regardless of any clear external evidence of their competence, and the esteem in which they may be held. When it was first identified, the psychologists had been researching a group of women who dismissed any objective proof of their success as luck, and believed they would be unmasked as frauds, despite many repeated examples of their skills and achievements. Imposter syndrome has been widely validated in research since.

While we can relate to the feeling, it's probably a symptom and not a cause of gender inequity, as research over the last few decades has found no real difference in the numbers of men and women experiencing it. Jack Dorsey, co-founder and CEO of Twitter, has been reported as saying he has moments of self-doubt when he feels he may not be the right person to be CEO of a company that has enjoyed huge success.[36] At a TEDx talk in Sydney, co-founder of Australia's most valuable technology company Atlassian, Mike Cannon-Brookes, said 'Most days, I still feel like I don't know what I'm doing.' He went on to ask the audience:

> Have you ever felt out of your depth, like a fraud?
> And just kind of guessed/bullshitted your way through the situation, petrified at any time someone was going to call you on it?[37]

Feeling like an 'imposter' is something many men and women experience, regardless of their success.

Blaming women's 'imposter' feelings and insecurity is an appealingly simple explanation that takes the blame for gender inequity off employers, suggests writer L.V. Anderson.[38] Whether women are more held back by chronic self-doubt than by discrimination and systemic obstacles is open to debate, although there is no doubt those imposter thoughts are reinforced by many workplace norms.

What became obvious to Kirstin during #CelebratingWomen was the number of women who felt they hadn't been successful in their lives. They wondered whether anything they had done was worthy of celebration, whether anyone would want to hear their story, or what they might have to offer other women as inspiration or as role models. Several said they found the idea of telling others what they had done off-putting, for fear of 'grandstanding', as well as fear of success. Yet as Fay Calderone (profile #6) points out, we can't all be imposters.

Kirstin remembered hearing from one high-profile woman, well known and respected, who said she just could not get involved in #CelebratingWomen, as much as she may have liked to. There was no false humility, but rather a sense for this woman that she hadn't achieved anything worth celebrating.

This feeling is not unusual for senior women, but is also familiar to many women in workplaces who face a well-documented trade-off between likability and competence (a phenomenon Sheryl Sandberg writes about in her book *Lean In*), along with repeated questions about their suitability and capacity for responsibility. Regular criticism is incredibly eroding of anyone's confidence, but is particularly destructive for women already facing double standards. As Marianne Cooper has pointed out, 'decades of social science research has repeatedly found that women face distinct social penalties for doing the very things that lead to success'.[39]

Sometimes criticism of women by senior men tips into a form of harassment. In a newspaper article detailing how a former, older male mentor had overstepped professional boundaries, writer and commentator Dr Julia Baird (profile #708) cited documentary filmmaker Sheila Nevins' definition of 'above the neck harassment'. Julia described how after an older male colleague decided to appoint himself her unofficial 'mentor', his repeated invitations for lunch had made her feel uncomfortable, and one day, she refused to go. The man then wrote a long email to Julia claiming that the only explanation for her long list of achievements, which included numerous awards and a PhD, was that she was a bright, younger woman who, he said, was also good-looking. This meant that opportunities had come her way because 'men can't help themselves'. Julia later wrote that she knew of other women who have also been told 'they have reached too far, been given positions because they are a woman [and] not earned them through slog and sweat'. Women have been 'told to step down, to shrink, to stay home'.[40] These experiences are familiar to many women.

And it is certainly not just public figures who are on the receiving end of such comments. Dr Muneera Bano (profile #553) is a woman of Pashtun ethnicity who was educated in Pakistan. After considerable sacrifice, and breaking many of the patriarchal cultural codes of her home country, Muneera's parents supported her education (despite her mother being denied her own) and Muneera went on to complete a PhD in Australia. Having won the highly competitive award for Women in Science, Technology, Engineering and Mathematics, Muneera was also a recipient of a Google Award for Women in Computer Science. Yet despite her many achievements and overcoming such adversity, a comment was all it took to shatter her confidence. She overheard someone say that because she only had to compete with women in IT and engineering to win the award, and as there very few women working in these fields, it wasn't a 'real' competition. As a result, Muneera says, she felt as if only competing against other women means a competition has less value. And if she competed with men and did win, it would be seen by some as a token effort to boost gender equity targets. These kinds of reactions, she says, make it hard for her to celebrate her own achievements,[41] with the campaign providing a welcome exception.

Kicking the imposter to the curb

Kirstin is also no stranger to imposter syndrome, and can remember it first appearing when she was just 12 years old. At the end of primary school, her parents had encouraged her to apply for one of New South Wales' selective schools, Hurlstone Agricultural High School. She remembered sitting the exam and feeling incredibly nervous and assuming she wouldn't be smart enough to be accepted. While she did do well, was accepted and spent her first two years of high school as a boarding student at Hurlstone, it began a pattern of doubting her own abilities. Some 30 years later, with three university degrees completed, having run a global business and received numerous awards, that same 12-year-old girl will still appear, and Kirstin will wonder whether she is good enough for whatever new opportunity may come her way. Like so many other women with bucketloads of drive, determination and ambition, at the same time she is often struck with anxiety and fear of failure.

These days when the imposter syndrome does sneak back in, as Kirstin often recounts when she speaks to groups:

As I have matured and gained more confidence,
I find I can kick it to the curb much more quickly.
I try to tell myself to stop trying to predict what
might be around the corner or what could
go wrong. I try to remind myself that I have no
reason to think I will fail, and so I should seize
every opportunity and go for it 100%. I also tell
myself that while I may not think I am ready or
that I don't have the precise experience needed,
I need to trust that it will come, that I will be
successful and that I will become a better leader
for being willing to learn. I remind myself that
even if I don't see my potential, clearly others do
so I need to trust in them.

As Dr Julia Baird notes, though, when thinking about 'above the neck harassment', all that confidence and sureness can be chipped at when a man suggests you may have been given an opportunity simply because you are a woman. Often the comments are not so overt, but the meaning is clearly implied. In that instant, it doesn't matter how many university degrees or relevant experience you might have, you can be left feeling small and the imposter can win.

Even during the #CelebratingWomen campaign Kirstin had many moments of doubt, wondering what gave her the right to start #CelebratingWomen, and whether anyone actually valued what it aimed to achieve. When people got in touch to congratulate her on the campaign, Kirstin found she would often minimise their words in her mind and think that all she'd done was post some photos online — something anyone could do.

The campaign revealed many women struggle all the time with feeling like imposters, or unworthy of celebration. And they feel this way regardless of education, career path or age. It can be so ingrained and reinforced by the very real penalties women face for speaking up that they actively avoid promoting themselves. The opportunity to feel proud of, and not judged, for their achievements can feel unnatural and uncomfortable for many — and yet participants found that overcoming that feeling delivered a personal boost, and benefited many others.

Women's business

Women are usually enthusiastic members of all kinds of groups because of their shared experiences and the interests that unite and validate them. We have experienced many women's workplace networks up close, and seen that while they can be affirming for women, they also have much to offer through influencing mainstream workplace and practices. But until now, many of these groups — and their recommendations and insights — haven't been seen as relevant to the serious business agenda.

The women members we've spoken to over the years have been frustrated to find that their — usually voluntary and unpaid — work in setting up these networks and making suggestions has been quarantined as 'women's business', and then either ignored, or regarded as a box-ticking exercise. Clearly the women flocking to contribute to and read the profiles on #CelebratingWomen overcame any doubts about the value of their stories once they saw so many women taking part. The ability to quickly access a community online and draw inspiration from other women — particularly those who have learned from difficult experience — sets up a very different dynamic.

In fact, the tangible results of sharing stories with other women has been measured by researchers Shawn Achor and Michelle Geilan, who worked with the organisers of Conference for Women in the United States to explore the effects of these forums.[42] Their results were surprising. After comparing 2600 women who had attended these conferences with women who hadn't, they found that 'in the year after connecting with peers at the Conference for Women, the likelihood of receiving a promotion doubled' — or indeed slightly more than doubled, with 42% of the women attending the conferences receiving a promotion during that time, compared with only 18% who hadn't. Perhaps less surprisingly, 78% of women attending felt more optimistic after the conference, and 71% of them more connected to others.

Sharing information when enough women coalesce around a challenge can make finding a voice about a specific barrier much easier. In fact, being able to compare notes — either informally, or via networking — can literally pay off in spades. In late 2017 Catherine was interviewed on stage by ABC journalist Annabel Crabb at the Women in Mining and Resources WA (WIMWA) Summit. When the topic of the gender pay gap came up, Annabel mentioned how discussing what they were earning with each other could help women detect when a glaring discrepancy between men and women's pay was occurring, and then provide the evidence to call it out.

Interestingly, this very scenario played out publicly in Britain a few months after the summit at the British Broadcasting Corporation.

The gender pay gap at the BBC originally came to light in early 2017, when a report revealed the salaries of some of its leading personalities. It emerged that the majority of highly paid employees were men, despite many well-known and experienced women in the ranks. While many women employees were outraged, they didn't just get mad, but vowed to get even — using their networks, numbers and social media to rally for change.

As one BBC Women member, *Woman's Hour* presenter Jane Garvey, explained to *The Guardian*:

> Some women who have been raising issues around equal pay since the 1980s were delighted to have new recruits and new tools to address the problem. What's been brilliant over the past year or so is that frankly, social media has allowed us to wage a collective battle, which tactically speaking would have been extraordinarily difficult in the past.[43]

As the furore over the pay revelations continued to unfold — with the obligatory scolding of women for their poor negotiating skills — the women in the BBC stuck to their guns, *The Guardian* reported, and also called on their male peers to help them:

> Women within the corporation show little sign of being blown off course. They described formal and informal groups where stories, salaries and tactics were discussed. Female employees are also looking to their male colleagues to improve transparency in the organisation, with female staff looking for a male 'buddy' doing the same job who is willing to speak to HR about pay discrepancy.[44]

While the pay gap had not been resolved by mid-2018, reports suggested that a cap on news presenters' pay was being considered by the broadcaster, and a number of high-profile men who appear on-air agreed to a pay cut.[45]

Comparing notes like the staff at the BBC allows women to get some perspective on their experience and the value of what they do. According to Laurie Dalton White, founder of the Conferences for Women:

> **Something special happens when you see that you are not alone. Making connections and building relationships with other attendees and speakers helps women form an understanding of their worth, and then they learn strategies to ask for promotions, seek fair pay, and even become mentors to others.[46]**

Towards a new dynamic

When more women see the outcomes from collaborative power and the possibilities for their involvement in every part of the workplace and at every level, the more this will challenge the unhelpful but tenacious idea that women are usually less influential and their connections less valuable than those of men. This belief only reinforces the idea that women usually lack the capacity to help when it comes to mentoring or advancing through the ranks.

While this perceived lack of female clout isn't often acknowledged in formal discussions, we have heard it regularly over the years. Sometimes it's even handed down to women as practical advice for getting ahead: make sure you are on the radar of powerful men and don't waste your time seeking out other women. The rise of shared female power suggests a new and very different definition could be emerging of what makes an influential and effective mentor — and leader (considered in chapter 7).

And connections made through women's campaigns and networks often lead to invaluable referrals. Kirstin and Catherine have lost count of the times they have been asked to speak at an event, write an article, or apply for a job or a board role after a recommendation by another woman — and vice versa, having offered so many women similar opportunities. And we both know of many occasions when informal advice and connections have been offered freely by women to their female peers over the years — sometimes when women are stepping into very senior or new roles that may feel overwhelming.

This isn't just gratifying and good for your own career, but it gets paid forward to other women, and broadens your network. One of the first people to contact Catherine when she took a redundancy from her job at publisher Fairfax after 23 years was Marina Go (profile #9), at the time the CEO of Private Media, which was publishing the online title *Women's Agenda* (now owned and edited by Angela Priestley). She was keen to have Catherine write for the publication, which was clearly a business decision, but the invitation and vote of confidence was much appreciated. Marina has consistently supported and connected many women throughout her career as an executive, and later as she became a successful board director, including one of the few women to chair a rugby league club, Wests Tigers. And many women in senior roles do the same and are eager to help, share insights and hear about other's experiences.

When she was president of the membership group Chief Executive Women (2015–17), company director Diane Smith-Gander (profile #16) saw how much it meant to women making their way through the ranks to connect with and learn from others, during a leadership program the group ran for about 50 women each year.

> One of the things that they do in the course is that each woman speaks for about 5 minutes sharing her personal story, and when I saw that [in the agenda] I thought 'that's a lot of time to spend, I wonder if that time could be better spent?' But when I saw the reaction and heard what the women said, I realised there were so many different ways of being successful — and you could see women were doing things they had been told were detrimental to their careers, and yet they had been ridiculously successful. There's still so much 'fix yourself' feedback, and so many women are just doing things differently.

The #CelebratingWomen stories reminded women they can push back on these expectations about their style of getting things done, Diane Smith-Gander believes. Seeing the range of women's activities and interests in the profiles was also compelling, because it showed they hadn't been restricted. 'That was the affirmation, and it amplified women's voices because it focused only on women.'

Taking advantage of connections to an array of people beyond your own organisation, is actually a very sensible practical strategy. Research on star analysts in Wall Street firms by Harvard Business School Professor Boris Groysberg[47] found that one of the reasons high-performing women did better when they switched jobs was because they had more portable skills, and they placed more emphasis on external business relationships than their male peers. While there were a few possible reasons why women were better at this than men, the research suggested that women found it difficult to crack the 'clubby' internal networks of their firms, so they relied more on their outside contacts. When push came to shove, so to speak, they were able to use their own networks and detailed knowledge of their clients to adjust well to a new employer.

The power of networking led Kimberley Cole to started up a group called Risky Women in 2014, from her Hong Kong base. As Head of Sales, Financial and Risk in Asia for multinational big data company Thomson Reuters, Kimberley saw there were a lot of women working in the area, and it seemed like a good idea to get them together, and for women speakers to give their perspective. Risky Women soon spread to London, Zurich and the United States, with 500 people connected on the LinkedIn site. There has been plenty of business impact and information sharing, both among the members, and with industry leaders speaking to the group. (Not all sessions are strictly professional — we love the sound of a 2018 seminar called 'Don't give up the wine list'!) And it's proved so popular that Kimberley has launched a Risky Women podcast. As one example of the network's practical effect, after an event in Japan, one audience member was elevated to a new job leading fintech initiatives, and subsequently was able to organise a range of meetings with the group to help her in her new position. In early 2018, the Japanese banker set off to London for another role, where she will continue to use and be supported by the network.

Busting out of the silo

Receiving back-up from other women is an experience that also resonates with senior executive Suzanne Young (profile #245). With a background in finance, Suzanne, Executive

General Manager, Operational Partnering at insurance company IAG, and also Chair of its diversity and inclusion committee (called DNA — Diversity Network Advisory), has worked in operational and finance leadership roles at the National Rugby League, Leighton Holdings, Commonwealth Bank, Qantas and Unisys — so she has seen up close the dynamics of some very male-dominated environments.

Suzanne has found her own networks invaluable in forging her career — so much so that after being profiled in Kirstin's campaign, Suzanne decided to launch an internal version of #CelebratingWomen at IAG in 2017. She was prompted to act after a senior male colleague told her that women don't support each other, but also by her own desire for the top team to leave a very different legacy at the organisation:

> I wanted it to be quite overt and pushed for it to be called CelebratingWomen@IAG because we have to celebrate — and it has been incredible. It's now created a physical and digital presence, and a series of what we call 'Thrive' events that focus on different themes our people in the global network want to talk about, such as imposter syndrome, flexibility and goal setting.

Kirstin spoke at the IAG Thrive events in Sydney, Melbourne and Auckland in 2017, as Suzanne was keen for female employees to forge new networks and learn from each other:

> A lot of our women hadn't met before, and I wanted them to connect across divisions. Typically, in large companies it's challenging to network across teams, and women with small children tend to focus on getting their work done and getting home. We try

> to spread the activities around the organisation
> and it has worked well.

The scope for the CelebratingWomen@IAG network has developed as it has grown, to include about 350–400 mid-career and junior women from within the group. Suzanne has been particularly delighted to hear younger women on her own team talk about how uplifting and empowering the network broadly, and the Thrive events, have been for them. Some of the younger women have interviewed senior women about their careers, which has been shared online and provides practical role modelling. The senior women were very happy to help, although a few did question why they were being asked to participate. Suzanne told them, 'This is your time to give back as role models now — and if women want to hear from you, then let's do it.'

Interestingly, Suzanne has her own story about a penny-dropping moment on the value of networks, and how she overcame a resistance to the traditional practice of swapping business cards. She credits a McKinsey Women's Leadership forum with helping dispel her concerns, and to understand the value to be gleaned from active networking:

> I was worried about whether the other person
> would ask me for something — but I learned
> it's not immediately reciprocal, but about
> creating connections.

In fact, in her former role as Chief Operating Officer at the National Rugby League, Suzanne worked to set up a committee for women in the sport, despite some senior men confiding it wasn't worth her effort because it 'wasn't seen as important':

I thought bugger that, I will *make* it important ...
I got women inside and outside the game and set
up a 'Women in League' committee, and one of our
initiatives was the creation of a mentoring program
for 17 women inside the game. I asked my corporate
network to be mentors (free of charge), some of
whom had never had exposure to rugby league, but
who were willing to help as mentors. That's the power
of the network — and for those women it was an
amazing experience having a conversation with other
senior women, and having them support them and
say, 'I've had that happen to me.' It meant they were
not feeling isolated. It's affirming.

Nevertheless, Suzanne does recall some reluctance about putting her own profile on #CelebratingWomen and talking about herself so publicly, despite watching the campaign develop with interest. But once she went ahead the reaction was positive, she built a new network herself through the process, and then encouraged others to take the plunge. One of her direct reports posted her profile 'and we could see her grow 3 inches taller' through feeling proud of the celebration that followed.

Passing the baton

Analysing how women of all ages have been finding and elevating their voices is also a topic close to Holly Ransom's heart. She sees a strong platform for change emerging for many women through campaigns like #CelebratingWomen:

There's an opportunity that social networking
has provided us with — to find like-minded people
connecting and instigating events. To have the means
of doing that at your fingertips when you need it is
unlike physical networking: you can do it in the
moment and that's really empowering, and helps with
the isolation and fear you can feel in these matters.

Holly (profile #90) sits with Kirstin on the board of the charitable foundation, Aim for the Stars, established by seven-time women's world champion surfer, Layne Beachley (profile #710). With Kirstin, she also attended a #CelebratingWomen event in Melbourne, where the enthusiasm amazed her, along with the momentum built over the year. Holly remarks:

It brought me, and the women profiled, into a
community … [many of the women] hadn't been
celebrated before and while this was a rarity, which
depressed me, by the same token I felt how wonderful
for them.

Many women have begun the process of valuing themselves and their stories through online campaigns. As Australian philosopher Kate Manne told *Slate* magazine, the #MeToo movement was very smart in drawing out silence breakers, and giving people voice:

Literally the two words of it — it has the component
of saying, 'Look, me, I belong in this narrative.
Something was done to me that was morally wrong
of a misogynistic nature.' It places you in the centre
of the story in ways that are historically quite

forbidden for women to come forward to say,
'Yeah, me.' Many, if not most, of us have at least one
such narrative in our history. But with the 'too' part,
it passes the baton onto other women … who have
narratives as well. It's both able to centre on yourself
for a moment, but then pass the baton on to the
next person to say, 'Yeah, there's an awareness.
This is ubiquitous and prevalent and not this
unique narrative.'[48]

As more women step up, become silence breakers and
encourage others to do the same, they help rewrite the
assumptions that have undervalued their contributions. They
want to tell their stories and challenge the norms without
fear — and many are just getting going. Amazed at the
response, the participants in #CelebratingWomen told us how
stunned and buoyed they were to realise what they did was
worthwhile, and could help others.

#CelebratingWomen showed that the way ahead for
women's rights is about more — *much* more — sharing and
support. It's about applying the principles of shared power to
meetings and workplaces and communities. It's about
recognising and tapping into the collaborative leadership skills
so many women have, and ensuring more women have a say at
the table to keep driving change.

Such is the power of sharing stories.

3

EVERY WOMAN IS A
ROLE MODEL

They were teachers, scientists, nurses, engineers, politicians, lawyers, carers, students and retirees, living in villages, on farms, and in the world's biggest cities. The more diverse the women who sent in their four answers and photos to Kirstin's campaign, the more the net spread and boundaries dissolved, while enthusiasm for the next story increased.

Any doubts about who would want to read about the lives of a shark scientist in New Zealand, a teacher in Africa, a competitive barbecue cook in the United States or a pharmacist in the United Kingdom melted away. Turns out plenty of people did, and avidly followed the stories as #CelebratingWomen shone a spotlight on hundreds of ordinary women doing extraordinary things.

From the very beginning of the campaign, Kirstin's fundamental belief that every woman is a role model to someone else[49] was reinforced — and then replicated 757 times throughout the year.

This appetite to hear about and learn from the everyday was gratifying, but also reflected something compelling. The jolt of delight and surprise many women felt from being profiled, or reading about others, revealed how effectively these stories and achievements had been hidden from view, or diminished by comparisons to traditional success stories.

It was a revelation, and a motivation to do much more sharing. It challenged the idea that 'success' comes from imitating traditional masculine models that focus heavily on individual impact and less on collaboration. Suddenly it felt as though every woman could take part, without waiting for gatekeepers, or letting others speak on her behalf.

Legitimising and affirming a wide array of women became a core part of the campaign's cumulative power, and a trigger for many followers to keep the good work going. The impact when so many stories emerged was intoxicating for each woman, but together it began to challenge the very idea of who gets to be a role model.

Let's talk about Wonder Woman

The campaign's breadth of profiles neatly turned on its head the unhelpful notion that only 'super women' are considered worthy of attention, or as possible leadership icons. Just like the shoulder pads and stiletto heels of the 1980s 'career woman' in *Working Girl*, the idea of putting all too rare women leaders on pedestals is well past its use-by date. It has, by necessity, reflected a tiny group of outstanding and resilient women. Often enough they are unfairly portrayed as steely perfectionists, such as Facebook's Chief Operating Officer Sheryl Sandberg or Yahoo's former CEO Marissa Mayer, or there has been the sexist focus on the marital status of unmarried driven women, who have been unfairly painted as 'compromising' their personal and family life to reach the top — such as Australia's Foreign Affairs Minister Julie Bishop, and former prime minister Julia Gillard.

Of course, it's still important to include high-profile examples of women succeeding. They show us what is possible, and deserve credit for what they have done — often against greater odds than their male peers. Like most of the population, we love a heart-warming success story about a woman who has overcome the odds to triumph. (Watching the movie *The Post*, about *The Washington Post* owner Katharine Graham, had us virtually cheering from the aisles.) And we have both been motivated by working with and learning from high-achieving women. But this is only one part of the picture, and it can feel unrelatable to many women.

Also restricting women role models to those high achievers narrows the catchment. When it comes to high achievement in science or the arts, few women have reached the very highest levels; since its inaugural ceremony in 1901, the Nobel Prize has been awarded to 881 Nobel Laureates, and of those, only 48 have been women.[50] The term 'genius' is rarely applied to women, as has often been pointed out — but thankfully women are being written back into history for their unsung achievements, such as in the *Good Night Stories for Rebel Girls* books, and in the 2016 film *Hidden Figures*, about the brilliant African American female mathematicians who worked at NASA during the Space Race (another film that had us cheering).

If we haven't even seen these women until recently, little wonder so many other valuable women's achievements have been missing from history.

The tiny cohort who do make it to the top are sometimes depicted as desperately striving to 'have it all', an expression that infuriates many women — and as Kirstin explained in chapter 1, can lead women to harbour a deeply held sense of guilt when it all seems so impossible. 'Having it all' is really shorthand for women who combine a paid occupation with a family; the same description doesn't seem to apply to men.

In fact, the many women featured in #CelebratingWomen did 'have it all' — but in a very different sense. Most had combined a satisfying job — although not always in their original field of choice — with a range of interests, community and caring roles, supported by a network of other women. Suddenly an expression designed to make women feel inadequate became a compliment and a refreshing recognition of achievement.

#CelebratingWomen made it clear there's a pressing need to challenge the societal view that only high-achieving or well-known women should be celebrated. There is no doubt these rare leaders deserve praise — but the women we also need to remember and celebrate are those who are around us every single day. Not every woman wants to become a brilliant scientist or run a Fortune 100 company. Many women want to live their lives in a way that makes a difference to the people closest to them and leaves a positive legacy. Every woman has done important things in her life, even if her stories and contribution have flown largely under the radar. Women deserve to feel proud of their efforts, particularly when they've had to tackle restrictive social norms about what they were meant to do with their lives.

There's no question men act as, and need, role models too. The difference for women is that the narrower prescribed paths women have been encouraged to follow have left many options effectively off the table. Often their achievements and the value they add in lower-paid and lower-status jobs have been invisible to others. In Australia, as elsewhere, women are still disproportionately clustered in a few sections of the economy — healthcare, social assistance, and education and training — with men dominating in a wider range of sectors with higher pay rates.[51] A 2017 report from a Senate committee investigating gender segregation in the workplace attributed this uneven distribution to:

> ... individual workers' choices being constrained
> by structural factors and social norms. Carer
> responsibilities, carried largely by women, as well
> as opportunities for part-time work and flexible
> working arrangements, all conspire to funnel
> women into particular industries and sectors.[52]

Even though legal barriers have been broken down, all these factors make it difficult for women to simply 'choose' whatever they want to do. Formal messages, including from government, have nevertheless reinforced the theory that women can now pursue all career options. Kirstin recalls, as a teenager, writing to a government department for a resupply of 'Girls Can Do Anything' stickers (having already handed the others out to all her friends). But despite the reality that many paths remain difficult for women to access, the #CelebratingWomen campaign helped a new wave of women regain that same sense of optimism by offering up such a wide variety of role models and stories imbued with practical advice.

When we think about the 757 women celebrated, it's not necessarily just their professional accomplishments that spring to mind. We loved every profile because each woman had a fascinating story, and we could relate to elements of each woman's life. We also saw qualities that were universal, regardless of country or background. Qualities of women not otherwise seen or admired nearly enough: courage, resilience, perseverance, ingenuity and audaciousness.

Hearing from all women

When #CelebratingWomen launched, Kirstin was very conscious that the initial catchment would be mostly women from her own network. And she also knew that they could look a lot like her — a Western, middle-class, educated white woman, whose life and experience did not reflect that of many other women, both in Australia and globally.

But she was also determined that she wanted the campaign to celebrate all women as role models, 'from all walks of life and from anywhere in the world'. That meant ensuring women from as many backgrounds as possible were involved, and learning how to amplify a wide range of voices to build true inclusivity.

Like many well-intentioned leaders with the same goal, Kirstin wasn't quite sure where to start, and was nervous about inadvertently making a wrong move and alienating the very women she wanted to seek out and celebrate. This concern is something Aboriginal woman Dr Jessa Rogers (profile #224), Project Director for Indigenous Research and Education Strategy at the University of New England, sees constantly from those with a good heart who genuinely want to support

Indigenous empowerment and social change, but then become paralysed about doing something insensitive — so nothing happens. Instead, Kirstin sought out women of colour and Indigenous women from the community and encouraged them to be part of #CelebratingWomen.

Jessa's story was among the most memorable of the campaign. In Jessa's view, had Kirstin not been as passionate about seeking out diverse women for the campaign, #CelebratingWomen would not have been nearly as rich — and she may not have participated.

Dr Jessa Rogers is a Wiradjuri woman who, after becoming pregnant with her son at the age of 16, became the first in her family to finish high school. With a goal of reshaping stereotypes of Indigenous women, Jessa went to university, where she fell in love with the field of education, particularly for Aboriginal girls. Jessa went on to become a school principal, complete a Master of Education and a PhD, all by the age of 31. In 2017, Jessa was awarded a prestigious Fulbright Scholarship to study at Harvard University.

Kirstin spoke with Jessa after the campaign to understand what motivated her to be part of #CelebratingWomen and why it was so important for diverse women's voices to be heard. 'Generally,' Jessa says, 'as an Aboriginal woman, I do tend to steer clear of generic women's feminist stuff because of the fact it is so often very White.'

A similar view was shared by Roxane Gay in her book *Bad Feminist*:

> For years, I decided feminism wasn't for me as
> a black woman, as a woman who has been queer
> identified at varying points in her life, because
> feminism has, historically, been far more invested

in improving the lives of heterosexual white women
to the detriment of all others.[53]

Yet according to Roxane Gay, feminism's failing should not
mean we abandon it entirely: 'Feminism will better succeed
with collective effort, but feminist success can also rise out of
personal conduct.'[54]

Despite her reservations about mainstream campaigns for
women, Jessa made an exception because she felt strongly that
people don't hear enough about the success stories or challenges
of young Aboriginal women today:

We have great examples of older Aboriginal women
who are leaders in politics, sport and human rights …
and I wanted to put my story out there for followers
of #CelebratingWomen to see an example of a
different generation of young Aboriginal women
leaders that may not look or sound or even appear
to be what people imagine when they hear the term
'Indigenous woman'.

The desire to inspire a younger generation of women was a
common theme from participants with an Indigenous
background and women of colour in Western countries. Fiona
Jose (profile #438) hoped to encourage young Indigenous
women to believe in themselves, be proud of their culture,
challenge the status quo and follow their dreams. Meegan Jia-
Good (profile #230) hoped to inspire other Indigenous girls to
step outside their comfort zones and explore the world we live
in. In the United Kingdom, Tokie Laotan Brown (profile #148)
hoped to inspire black women who, she says, have to work
twice as hard, by knowing that whatever they do — good or

bad — reflects on all other black women. Yemi Adenuga, an Irish woman (profile #263), hoped to encourage girls who were told they will never be anything by a culture that discriminates.

Simply being part of a community of supportive women also encouraged Jessa, who has seen the power through shared leadership and women's skill at doing just that:

> If we can get (inclusion) right with women,
> we can make a huge change in our world. I think
> women at this point in time are so aware of the
> shared experiences we have that can bind us
> together — but also, we need to remind ourselves
> of those experiences we don't share, and then
> work on how to move forward.

Taking a bird's eye view

The way to amplify the voices of Indigenous women and women of colour in communities and workplaces may not be obvious to more privileged women who want to help but, as Jessa points out, often don't know what to do. Yet just as women have become much more aware of an all-male panel at a conference or an all-male board, there is a real need to become skilful at identifying and addressing cultural gaps — and cultural gender gaps — in all kinds of work environments. Jessa says:

> I think a lot of women can speak to the experience of
> being in a board room or meeting and realising they
> are the only woman there, or that they are the youngest
> in the room and knowing you are also female.

She believes women, and men, need to look around that room and consider what kind of people are there — not simply counting the number of men and women. Jessa uses the analogy of what a bird flying high above the community would see:

> **Does it see lots of immigrants? Lots of Aboriginal people? Lots of women? Lots of young people? Then look at the situation you are in and ask if you see that represented around you. If you can't see the same sort of demographics as you see in your community outside, something is not right. You need to ask what has happened, that means some people are shut out? What are the barriers?**

While the diversity of women profiled in #CelebratingWomen was one of its strengths, it only really scratched the surface, with roughly 15% of the 757 profiles being of Indigenous women or women of colour. While Kirstin would have loved to have celebrated many, many more, the campaign also reinforced the cultural challenges some women face.

A woman of Sri Lankan heritage, in the audience at a New Zealand event Kirstin spoke at, described the challenges of having a voice in her society, where women were actively discouraged from speaking out publicly. This had made participating in campaigns like #CelebratingWomen much harder, and was a reminder that far more needs to be done by leaders to genuinely facilitate and support hearing all voices.

There is much progress that needs to be made. In April 2018, the Australian Race Discrimination Commissioner, Dr Tim Soutphommasane, released new research on cultural diversity in Australia.[55] The results are confronting reading, particularly when the paltry levels of cultural diversity in Australian boardrooms and among chief executive officers are combined with the added complexity of gender. In Australia, only 4% of ASX 200 chief executives have a non-European background, and very few of them are women. The report details how:

> ... women of culturally diverse backgrounds ... cop a 'double whammy' when it comes to leadership. Within our collection of statistics on senior leaders, we were able to identify a very small number of female leaders who have a non-Anglo-Celtic background.[56]

This mirrors the experience of Ming Long (profile #468). In an interview with the broadcaster SBS Australia in January 2018,[57] Ming said:

> We see so few women [in leadership] in general because I think the stereotype [that] we make assumptions about are the position of women in society ... When you add the intersection of ethnic or cultural diversity into someone's gender, it makes it twice as hard because the expectation is even stronger that she shouldn't have these roles.

Even in 2018 in multicultural Australia, Ming remains one of the few non-Anglo women to have broken the mould, as the first Asian-Australian woman to lead an ASX 200 company, highlighting the need for far more culturally diverse women in senior leadership.

The cultural mix of profiles appearing in #CelebratingWomen also gave Ming the idea of compiling a list of potential women candidates from non-Anglo-Saxon backgrounds to fill out the very low numbers in leadership and management within Australian organisations. She put out a request on LinkedIn for women of colour who were interested in board positions — and had about 200,000 views from around the world.

Many women within this community, she says, are not well connected to Anglo networks and need to understand that their special power comes from being ethnic and a woman. As new role models emerge, Ming is confident that old-school attitudes and leadership styles are on the way out, particularly given the power of collective advocacy.

Women have always had the capacity and will to speak up and own their achievements, but have encountered powerful deterrents throughout history — particularly those women who are further marginalised by race or sexual orientation.

But as more and more women from across all parts of society find the means to add their voices, bypass the mediators and tell their own story, and to show the breadth of what they do, the parameters and traditional assumptions about achievement and leadership will shift significantly. They already are.

Role models here, there, everywhere

Many women who took part in or followed the campaign found the range of profiles inspiring. Interestingly, this was particularly the case for many of the well-known and senior women featured, who told us this broad array lifted the campaign and had a real impact on them. The campaign showed there is no archetypal woman who deserves celebrating, says business adviser Holly Ransom (profile #90), who saw the platform the campaign provided for women of all backgrounds.

#CelebratingWomen proved a circuit breaker for confronting ingrained stereotypes about women's achievements, and the view that only certain types of success were worthy of celebrating, she says. Dispelling these outdated ideas, the campaign became about a much broader story celebrating every field of endeavour — and this is what made it a game changer.

Holly says the sheer breadth of the profiles also drew attention to how many women with skill and expertise were in the community, and not just at the top — even though they were often poorly represented and far from visible. Similarly, tech start-up accelerator SheStarts director Nicola Hazell (profile #150) says the campaign's range of women and the work they did in the community was an exercise in showing how to create real inclusion.

Many dozens of women who described themselves as 'nothing out of the ordinary' commented on the buzz they got from seeing others just like them included and celebrated for their contribution and inspiration.

Denyse Whelan (profile #298) had wanted to be a primary school teacher since the age of 11, and went on to spend more than 40 years in education and teaching. Recently retired, Denyse had been diagnosed with cancer only two weeks before her profile was posted, and was feeling isolated and 'forgotten' when she decided to participate. Becoming involved helped her to come out of what she described as a relatively sad and lonely life at the time, reminding her of what a role model to others she had been herself, and how much she had contributed to the lives of many during her long teaching career.

Brianna Casey (profile #713), a not-for-profit leader working to help Australians seeking food relief, says the wide range of role models being made visible made her recommend the campaign to other women who might be questioning whether they were in the right role at work, the right personal relationship, or even the right community group, since there were so many examples of other women having faced those same challenges.

A staunch advocate for more gender and cultural diversity in the business sector, company director Ming Long loved the plurality of the campaign, and its celebration of so many women. We don't need the superstars, she says, as they will always be there — but the women in the campaign had their own stories and they needed to be told. Ming, former head of the $2.5 billion Investa Office Fund, tweeted the campaign to connections overseas and helped spread the word internationally. The fact that connections were forged by women providing advice from all around the globe was amazing, she adds. The shared experience of women in their lives and their paid work transcends geographic and ethnic divisions and creates clear bonds. Says Ming:

> That strength comes from the fact we have
> been pushed to the side and we keep fighting
> back and saying, 'we must have a seat at the
> table', and it's fighting it on a daily basis.
> It makes you strong.

The focus of the profiles, which makes them so inspiring, has been on strengths, instead of the more usual preaching to women about how they need 'fixing', says Ming, who is sick of being told she needs a coach to remedy her deficiencies. That is why so many of the women's stories resonated and struck a chord.

The window #CelebratingWomen opened into women's lives across so many boundaries and what they were achieving was a revelation, says former underground miner Sabina Shugg, who set up Women in Mining and Resources WA (WIMWA) in 2003. The sharing of all kinds of stories is crucial for women, Sabina adds, and the impact of connections made through these kinds of networks — particularly on young women — shouldn't be underestimated. It was only during the 1980s that women in Australia were allowed to work in underground mines, and in 2006 women made up only about 6% of workers in the mining and resources sector[58] — but by 2017 that number had climbed to about 16.1%.[59] WIMWA has grown from modest beginnings into a significant community, with 3000 members on the mailing list. The 2017 annual conference, which Catherine attended, sold out in a few hours and attracted 800 people from around the world. One big issue the group addresses is isolation — both physical and mental, says Sabina. Sharing the very broad range of stories of success, both inside and outside the industry, has been very powerful.

Kirstin's original premise, so amply reinforced by the campaign, that every woman is a role model, also helps challenge assumptions about women in leadership, who are depicted as aberrations from the norm, complete with super powers. Casting the net so widely makes women's achievements relatable, but no less inspirational. Role models of all kinds are important for everyone, but this is tricky territory for women when their efforts are so often invisible or dismissed, and they face the trade-off between competence and likability.

Age is no barrier

Traditional male leadership models venerate older men, who are often seen as naturally authoritative and wise. The opposite is often true for women, in Western societies at least. Older women are often the butt of jokes, or ignored, as commentator and author Jane Caro (profile #53) documents in her latest book, *The Women Who Changed Everything*, which examines how older women are now flexing their muscles across society. The rich lives, experience and wisdom of the retired women profiled in #CelebratingWomen came as no surprise to Jane, who has traced the impact this cohort has made on feminism and the ability of women to use their voices. She tells us:

> We all operate on the shoulders of women who came before us. But the women who are over 50 now are the first in the world who have earned their own money over their whole lives. That's because of the Pill which kick-started second wave feminism and gave them new opportunities because they could control their fertility. And the technology change for this generation is social media, which allowed them to join together in campaigns. Both those generations benefited from the turbo charge of a technology revolution that gave women control and agency, and once they got this opportunity they ran with it. It was not being less assertive that was the problem, they vote with their feet.

The acceleration of the women's movement is the legacy of the work and leadership of previous generations of women, she adds. Older women are happily participating on social media, and the campaigns are providing forums where they are heard. Their participation in these movements has made them realise the value of difference and the leadership they have shown in their lives. As Jane points out:

> One of the gifts of being a woman today is that every achievement is more than for you, it's for your entire gender. There's a sense of meaning because it's a bigger issue.

Women have always been remarkable leaders and achievers, but were written out of history, she says. As one example, Jane cites the recent revelation that the brilliant drawings in the famous illustrated book *The Birds of Australia* were often attributed to author John Gould, when in fact they were the work of his wife, Elizabeth Gould.

The age range of the participants in the #CelebratingWomen campaign also stood out to Dr David Cooke, Managing Director of Konica Minolta Australia. His efforts include promoting and employing women in non-traditional roles, so for him the spectrum of the profiles was particularly resonant:

> I found the #CelebratingWomen initiative truly inspiring. Of course, there are millions of women with amazing stories … I particularly loved the range of stories from an age perspective, as well as the diversity of careers and fields that different women worked in.

Gender equity is an issue that needs to be addressed for all women and across society, says David, and online campaigns have been very valuable in broadcasting the breadth of women's contributions — no matter their age — and highlighting what is at stake if this continues to be overlooked or undervalued.

We *can* be what we can't see

It's also clear from Kirstin's campaign — and history — that women have not patiently waited to see a critical mass of other women go ahead of them before trying to pursue their goals. Far from it.

The saying 'you can't be what you can't see' is a bugbear of Kate Jenkins (profile #466), Australia's Sex Discrimination Commissioner. As she explains:

> We'll never get anywhere if we stick to the mantra
> 'we can't be what we can't see'. There have been
> lots of women who were trailblazers. That saying
> dismisses the experience of women who were the first
> — and there are so many of them. Many of those
> 'first' women say they knew it was going to be harder
> for them and they had to perform better than men to
> be seen as equally good. They knew they had to pave
> their own way, with resilience and determination.
> Some of them knew at the time they were the role
> models for future women, others only realised that
> on reflection. For all of those women, they couldn't
> see women ahead of them but they still did it.

History, she notes, doesn't make visible women's leadership, and just about every time you hear stories of leadership it's male. This is why the #CelebratingWomen compilation of so many women's lives offers up such richness and value, legitimising their experiences and emphasising that women can be worthy role models even if they don't have traditional masculine qualities we tend to adulate — such as charisma and overt confidence.

The sheer numbers of women achieving so much out of the spotlight, with very different styles and behaviours to archetypal heroes, also punctures another tenacious and frustrating gender stereotype Kate Jenkins hears all the time:

> It is too easy for people in positions of power
> to declare that the main barrier to women's
> advancement is their lack of 'self-belief and
> confidence'. The suggestion is that women need
> to promote themselves better, including seek pay
> rises and promotions more proactively. Evidence
> tells us that even when women do these things, they
> are less likely to be successful, and their promotions
> are more likely to be questioned. For me it is not
> women's lack of self-belief that explains why they are
> not at the top: there are complex systemic barriers in
> place, barriers that I believe undermine productivity
> and quality … It's not about women's confidence,
> it's about the system.

In fact, a 2018 study by economics researcher Dr Leonora Risse from RMIT University in Melbourne[60] found that while this stereotypical kind of confidence helps some men get ahead, it doesn't make much difference to women. Her review of 7500 male and female employees in Australia found having a confident personality increased men's chances of job promotion, but for women there was virtually no benefit. The gap was most obvious for men with high confidence, who had a 6% greater likelihood of promotion, compared to only a 1% greater chance of promotion for highly confident women. These findings suggest there is a risk that placing the onus on women to change their behaviour simply deflects attention from the bigger issue, which is the gender bias that appears to simmer beneath the surface in many organisational environments. Dr Risse explains:

> Rather than pushing for behavioural change among women, workplaces should instead check for gender biases in how they value their workers' attributes to ensure they don't reward charisma over competence.[61]

In 2017, Dr Risse helped launch the Australian Women in Economics Network (WEN), which aims to connect female economists and address the lack of women moving through the ranks of a profession that has traditionally been seen as aggressive and competitive. While a number of senior women have joined the group, the goal is to involve as many younger women and students as possible, to show that the male-dominated field is changing and offers a wide range of potential careers. The network now has about 500 members nationally, sharing information in a safe environment, with a wide variety of role models.

What collective movements such as #CelebratingWomen and WEN do, says Dr Risse, is send the message to women that they are not alone. And instead of focusing on just women in the boardroom, these movements have spilled into the street, taking in everyday women and commanding a bigger role in the public sphere. She adds:

We've been very conscious in planning our events and publications to illustrate role models who are more relatable. While we do have senior women involved, we also have stories of people who are quite junior, and a lot of young women involved in running the network and on panel discussions. We don't just want the people at the top — we want to represent and connect women at all levels.

The power of a tribe

Running a social media campaign for one year is one thing, but we were also interested to know whether the campaign changed how the women felt about themselves — or about other women — once it ended. Women who participated said they felt part of something bigger than themselves — part of a group of women supporting other women — which made them hopeful for the future; it also reassured them to know so many women were working positively and effectively to change their piece of the world. One woman said the campaign had showed her the power of having a tribe of women around her, and wished she had discovered it earlier.

#CelebratingWomen demonstrated not only to the women involved, but also to those cheering from the side, that women were clearly supporting each other — loudly, proudly, and in significant numbers every day. Women loved being part of something that saw them each rise up, stand tall and connect with one another in positive ways. It reminded them of the importance of publicly noticing and acknowledging other women, and helping to build women up wherever possible.

After the campaign, women told us they felt more confident to give something a go, even if they didn't know what the outcome would be, or whether it would work at all. Many had been nervous about putting themselves forward, with one woman bravely deciding 'it was up to me to celebrate me' before submitting her form. The consistent positive feedback women then received reinforced a new resolve when facing an opportunity or challenge.

During the campaign, women who never felt celebrated found — even if only briefly — that strangers around the world, as well as those closest to them, valued them just for being themselves, and for the essential role they play in the lives of those closest to them. Public affirmation is not only important to the women themselves, but for society. The sound of women's voices during 2017 made it clear women everywhere will not be silenced, and are speaking with one another — and with men — about how they want to be recognised and valued.

All of us wonder, at times, what might have been if we had done things differently. #CelebratingWomen reinforced for us, and so many other women, the fact that every experience can be important. Each setback adds a little bit of scar tissue to our levels of resilience. And every time we make a choice that requires some bravery, and challenge the status quo, we are that little bit more courageous.

There is still much to be done to achieve gender parity, to address gender pay gaps, low levels of women in leadership positions, and tackle community crises such as the chronic levels of domestic and family violence. #CelebratingWomen focused on the important and powerful ways a variety of women are providing role models to others, while also highlighting the need to keep up this crucial work to dismantle the barriers by passing on courage.

Georgie Somerset (profile #703) summed up the lasting impact of #CelebratingWomen beautifully:

> It has been a rich and fabulous celebration of the diversity of women, what they are achieving, the impact they are having and the talent available. It has shone a light on many who we would never hear about, yet also provided high-profile women with the chance to distil their aspirations and impact, and to define what they 'do' rather than what people think they do. It has been an affirming project which will have a wonderfully positive ripple effect.

That ripple, as women united to speak up for and about themselves, was about to turn into a surging current that flowed around the world as the year progressed.

As more women add to the collective voice for the good of their gender, we can also, finally, overturn some outdated and inaccurate beliefs — such as the myth of the Queen Bee — which conveniently suggest women in authority are hardwired to undermine rather than support each other.

4

TAKING THE STING OUT OF THE QUEEN BEE

If you didn't know better, a casual scroll through a list of popular television shows could leave you feeling that women are all either bitchy competitors, nagging housewives or waiting on a man to help them out. Stories that focus on women's friendships, their work and their successes are still rare as hen's teeth. This depressing picture has been much the same in movies — so much so that an American cartoonist, Alison Bechdel, devised a simple measure for gender bias in films and fiction. To pass the Bechdel Test, a movie needs to have at least two female characters, who talk to each other about something other than a man. Not too much to ask, you would think, but even today very few titles pass the test.

The stories from #CelebratingWomen showed the exact opposite: they highlight a strong web of connections and support between women rarely seen in popular culture, or actively encouraged in workplaces where traditional gender norms often prevail.

Long-ingrained stereotypes continue to reinforce pressure on women to be 'nicer' and more caring than men. But many workplace studies have found that while women were consistently seen as warmer, they were also regarded as less competent than their male peers, regardless of their abilities. And if they don't conform to this 'niceness' standard, women were often labelled bitchy or nasty — particularly in leadership. This idea reflects the widespread discomfort that still exists about women's suitability for authority, and has been used to justify the lack of women in decision-making roles. As Professor Cordelia Fine, author of *Delusions of Gender*,[62] points out, there is still:

> a residual unease — both conscious and implicit — with women in positions of power. When women display the necessary confidence in their skills and comfort in power, they run the risk of being regarded as 'competent but cold': the bitch, the ice queen, the iron maiden, the ballbuster, the battle axe, the dragon lady ... the sheer number of synonyms is telling.[63]

Held to higher standards

It hasn't helped that until very recently, most boards or senior teams aiming to show they were diverse would appoint just one woman to tick the 'gender' box. This tactic often fanned fierce competition among candidates for the sole 'woman's seat' at the table — and the women who secured these token appointments, or made it into other forms of leadership, ran a very real risk of being viewed as a 'Queen Bee'.

According to popular thinking, these dreaded women not only fail to help, but actually hinder female underlings, while often denying they have ever faced sexism. Psychological research has revealed three ways women may do this: by presenting themselves more like men; by physically and psychologically distancing themselves from other women; and by endorsing and legitimising the current gender hierarchy.[64]

The Queen Bee was an all too familiar stereotype as Kirstin forged her board career and often found herself the only woman in teams or groups. But after mentoring and seeking advice from women herself in recent years, Kirstin came to see that pressure from conventions, double standards and a scarcity of women at the top played a big part in reinforcing this myth, while leaving the gender-equity status quo unchallenged. The stereotypes about women leaders were so widely circulated and accepted that she thought it was just easier to work with and be mentored by men, which only tended to reinforce her feeling that women were less inclined to help each other.

Women who do make it into the top jobs find they often face additional pressure and double standards. One of Australia's oldest companies, insurer and financial manager AMP, was rocked by the evidence given during the 2018 Royal Commission into Misconduct in the Banking, Superannuation and Financial Services Industry, which saw the resignation of the CEO, Craig Mellor, and Chair, Catherine Brenner. Even before her resignation, there was detailed analysis of Catherine Brenner's downfall. But unlike most of her male colleagues, Catherine faced additional finger pointing and speculation about what went wrong under her leadership. Her drive and ambition were analysed, along with intrusive comments about her family life, whereas none of the male leaders of the organisations appearing before the Commission received the same treatment. As prominent Australian company director, Yasmin Allen, pointed out:

> To be criticised for a business judgement or decision
> is absolutely fine. No one has a problem with that.
> But to move into that kind of personal attack? I feel
> like I have stepped back 50 years. People are saying
> 'Wow, if you put your head up and take a high-profile
> position and something goes wrong this is what is
> going to happen to you if you are a woman.'[65]

Some media columnists even demanded an end to efforts to boost the number of women on boards, claiming it was an experiment that hadn't worked. One writer suggested the events at AMP raised the question of whether women making their way onto boards through the usual corporate networks were any 'better' than the men.[66] Businessman Chris Corrigan asserted that it was 'demonstrably the case' that Brenner was elevated to the role because she was a woman, and any criticism that the commentary about her was sexist was 'so ridiculous'.[67]

Few critics called Catherine Brenner a Queen Bee during her fall from grace, but the implication was certainly there. Some commentary, according to Bloomberg journalist David Fickling:

> ... painted [Brenner's] rise to the job ... as an
> *All About Eve* style tale of charm and connections
> trumping experience and intellect.[68]

Fortunately Fickling was also quick to point out how illogical it was to focus purely on the failings of one individual in the event of a corporate scandal such as AMP's:

> **Given that board decision-making is collective and confidential, the idea that outsiders can pronounce women directors solely responsible for any shortcomings — rather than the majority of board members who are men — barely passes the laugh test.[69]**

Even a quick review of the last few decades of corporate failures show that it has been men who have led both the boards and companies during these times. Yet in none of those cases was it argued that all-male boards should be avoided.[70]

At the time of her resignation, Brenner was one of just 11 female Chairs of ASX 200 companies, about the same as the number of female CEOs. Women held 26% of directorships, and made up just 29.7% of key management ranks[71] in the business sector. While women comprised 46% of the Australian workforce and were more likely than men to hold graduate qualifications, they earned on average 15.3% less, and their average superannuation savings were 42% lower. It's a picture that has remained depressingly unchanged for many years in Australia, and elsewhere.

Little wonder pent-up frustration has erupted into demonstrations, the world over, about equity and basic rights. For all the talk of diversity and a 'post-feminist' world, women have been largely absent from the table when the decisions affecting their lives are negotiated. It's a bleak reality that has propelled women to take yet another stand and call for a different future, unappeased by the glacial progress of the past few decades, and fed up with being blamed for their own marginalisation.

Birth of the Queen Bee

The Queen Bee myth is often used as evidence that women are their own worst enemies, but is actually largely based on a mixture of assumptions and gender stereotypes. Recycling the age-old idea that women are not suited to power — too emotional, too erratic, too bitchy — has been a lazy, outdated and inaccurate way to reinforce the status quo of gender inequity. But the moniker certainly wasn't intended to be used in that way.

Although it feels as though the Queen Bee trope has been around forever, the term was coined in 1973 by three psychologists at the University of Michigan, who traced a pattern of women in power treating their women subordinates more poorly than men. It was certainly a catchy term, but two of the original researchers, Drs Carol Tavris and Toby Jayaratne, regret the way it has been used to beat women over the head.[72] People misunderstood the term, and missed the political and sexist climate that created it, says Dr Jayaratne, who is now a research psychologist in the School of Public Health at the University of Michigan. Queen Bees exist, but are rare, they now claim, and Dr Tavris says that for every one that does exist, there are thousands of women mentoring other women.

However, the premise that women in power mostly hate each other, and do their best to impede workplace opportunities for other women, goes back well before the Queen Bee expression was coined. Australian academic Alana Piper says the idea has been around for centuries with stories, for example, about female brothel owners in the 1800s jealously guarding their power and cheating women out of their pay.[73] These long-standing narratives get repeated so often they become accepted as fact, and many of us are particularly drawn to any new examples that confirm this bias; this is known, unsurprisingly, as 'confirmation bias'. Stories about female rivalry in popular culture, such as between two women in *The Hand That Rocks the Cradle*, the clique in *Pretty Little Liars* and crime queens in *Underbelly*, are seen as more titillating than male violence, Dr Piper explains. It's a distraction from the problems women face, and helps validate pervasive 'women as lesser' attitudes, she adds.[74]

Many workplaces are not an even playing field, but more like a series of deep potholes, where women's achievements continue to be judged very differently to men's. In fact many employers perceive smart women as a threat, according to a US study by sociologist Natasha Quadlin,[75] who sent pairs of job applications with similar content and qualifications — but with a man's name on one, and a woman's on the other — to more than 2000 employers. The men with the highest qualifications were 50% more likely to receive a response than similarly credentialled women. Even worse, women applying for non-traditional jobs, such as mathematicians, were three times less likely to get a response. What employers did value in women candidates was likability, as Dr Quadlin discovered when she also surveyed 261 hiring managers. Despite much attention, gender inequality is still rife, she concluded.

No wonder this discrimination has had behavioural side effects. The deck has been so heavily stacked against women in senior roles it's unsurprising some Queen Bees emerge, says company director Diane Smith-Gander (profile #16):

The ones who have risen to the top have been
successful in masculine situations, and they have
been good at running teams entirely made up of men.
So, what do you expect?

The scarcity effect

Women have long encountered these double standards, and
extra critical attention, particularly in leadership ranks. This
can be highly distracting and debilitating. After their almighty
efforts, the scant few who make it to the top have been
scrutinised intensely (such as Catherine Brenner), and their
behaviour usually held to much higher standards than men.
Just think for a moment about the entrenched sexism faced by
female politicians, including Australia's first female Prime
Minister, Julia Gillard, and Hillary Clinton. Similarly, in the top
ranks of business, a perceived lack of the 'right' qualities is swiftly
punished: when Pacific Brands announced in 2009 that it was
closing seven Australian factories producing iconic Bonds and
King Gee clothing, its CEO, Sue Morphet, received such violent
threats that round-the-clock security was posted at her home.

Nevertheless, despite their actual rarity, we've heard many
women firmly assert the prevalence of Queen Bees. During her
daughters' school years Catherine regularly volunteered for
canteen duty, serving the students at morning tea and lunch
for a few hours one day a month with a group of other parents.
Mothers, usually. (A solitary father joined her roster but gave
up after a few shifts because, he said, it was too much hard
work.) Most women on the teams were well-educated
professionals. Some had left their paid work after having

children, including one woman who had been an investment banker. During a coffee break (an obligatory and essential part of the day's agenda, where much information was exchanged), chatting with a well-bonded group, the former banker told Catherine women couldn't help being nasty to each other at work, and as bosses they were particularly toxic. She was adamant the classic tale about women leaders behaving like Queen Bees was completely accurate, and that it didn't just apply to senior roles.

Pressed (ever so politely) for details, it turned out she had suffered under an unpleasant woman boss shortly before leaving her previous job, and it had remained seared in her memory. As she sat at the table, coffee in hand, surrounded by other women she enjoyed socialising and regularly working with, she swore women were their own worst enemies in the workplace and were predisposed to back-stabbing and cattiness. While she seemed oblivious to the contradiction between what she was saying and her happy participation with the all-female canteen crew, her views were certainly not unusual.

The shadow lingers

Because women in leadership are scarce, it's often easy to recall a Queen Bee or two and assume they are the norm, particularly given the stereotype's broad popularity. Female bosses have been portrayed in unflattering terms over the years — the tough and icy character of Miranda Priestly, played by Meryl Streep in *The Devil Wears Prada*, springs to mind; a bit further back in the 1950s, *Queen Bee* starred Joan Crawford as the evil and conniving Eva Phillips, while *All About Eve* revelled in the catty rivalry between Bette Davis and a younger actress. Television shows like *The Bachelor* thrive on depicting an alpha-female character who undermines the other women in competition for the ultimate prize: a man. There's a long legacy of nasty power-drunk hell cats destroying younger women in fairytales — and often enough it's an evil stepmother, as in 'Cinderella' and 'Snow White'.

The Queen Bee image is also enthusiastically circulated by the media, because it attracts attention and fits perfectly with the assumption that women are to blame for the gender gap in organisations. Telling women they need to be 'fixed' (to help them overcome deficits in confidence and negotiating skills, for example), and reminding them it's their own fault if they are left out of leadership because it usually turns them into destructive Queen Bees, is far less confronting than examining inherent discrimination. Or the bias and sexism that is woven through the 'old boys clubs' that dominate senior ranks. This is despite much research and analysis concluding systemic problems are in fact the culprit, rather than faulty female behaviour.

In 2017, before #MeToo took off, a lengthy feature in *The Atlantic*[76] outlined in detail the various forms of bitchy female professionals, with example after example of 'Beeism'. The article eventually acknowledged that workplaces, not women, were to blame for the syndrome; and that given the complexity of the phenomena, it was impossible to work out its prevalence. Context plays a big role, as Harvard academic Robin Ely explains:

> When there appear to be few opportunities for women, research shows, women begin to view their gender as an impediment; they avoid joining forces, and sometimes turn on one another.[77]

Research confirms this behaviour pattern has much to do with marginalisation rather than gender. Studies[78] show that one way members of minority groups cope with discrimination is by using 'self-group distancing' or denial that it has affected them in an effort to fit in with the dominant group, which then reinforces the status quo. That's one reason we struggle with the Madeleine Albright quote, 'There's a special place in hell for women who don't help other women.' Surely women don't deserve special punishment for occasionally failing to meet unfair and unrealistic expectations of their gender? (All people should help other people, we reckon — and the fires of hell seem a little extreme for common human flaws.)

Workplace pressures often compel women in senior ranks or male-dominated cultures such as the military to downplay their gender to fit in with the prevailing norms, as Kirstin's story shows. Some women who've had a tough climb up the ladder think those behind them should also do it tough — but again, analysis suggests this is a result of being part of the 'out of power' group, rather than some innate female nastiness. Our observations also suggest that women who firmly believe in the syndrome find it helps them justify the often-perplexing levels of bias in the uneven playing field they inhabit, despite being told (and wanting to believe) they work in fair 'meritocracies'.

Given all these findings about workplace gender inequality, it's hardly surprising the sinister shadow of the Queen Bee continues to loom. Just like the plot of *Working Girl*, women are often warned to avoid turning into one of these noxious species as they climb the ranks. After all their extra hurdles to reach senior positions, women often face the prospect of being labelled a turncoat and traitor to their sisters.

Setting the story straight

We have all seen plenty of poor behaviour from men and women at work, and we have suffered under the occasional nasty female boss, too — but this pales into insignificance when compared to the enormous support and life-enhancing company we have received from our women friends, colleagues and networks. We also couldn't help noticing that men's failure to support or mentor peers and younger colleagues doesn't get noticed as much, or labelled in the same way; there just doesn't seem to be an equivalent term for it.

Australia's Sex Discrimination Commissioner, Kate Jenkins (profile #466), believes criticising women for not supporting each other can also be used as an excuse for doing nothing about gender barriers.

> It's part of this idea that gender equality is a battle of the sexes, and feeds into gender stereotypes that women have to all get along and if not, then there's something not okay with that. Not all men support other men. Why should all women support other women?

As she points out, women tend to support each other not because they necessarily have more empathy — that's a gender stereotype — but because they can use their shared experience of marginalisation to bond and leverage for change.

Many women who contacted us about Kirstin's #CelebratingWomen campaign enthusiastically mentioned their outstanding female friends and support networks, as well as professional or workplace women's groups. Quite a few also remembered encountering bitchy or actively unhelpful women

— particularly bosses — and this memory stood out because they had expected better.

Their comments reflect an interesting paradox. It seems no matter how much women recognise the valuable support they get from each other as they go about their daily routines, many still believe an unfortunate change occurs when women move into management jobs, and this nastiness then reflects poorly on all women. It's a pernicious and ubiquitous belief. Several women admitted it had made them reluctant to overtly bond with female colleagues, or speak up about gender issues, for fear of being targeted — until they signed up to #CelebratingWomen, that is, and then many said they felt differently. Instead of being judged or undermined by other women, they felt supported.

Feedback from the campaign, our own experiences, and accumulating research shows us the assumptions behind the Queen Bee syndrome are finally being challenged. The sheer number of women energetically supporting #CelebratingWomen and other online campaigns has offered support for a rethink. And some of the tired old arguments trotted out to bolster the theory have been debunked — women's behaviour is not better or worse than men's, but the result of significant structural and attitudinal bias, particularly in workplaces where senior women have been scarce.

Luckily there are simply more women slowly but surely moving up the ranks, finally countering the so-called 'scarcity' effect. In her 2018 Commencement Address to the graduating class of Barnard College, two-time Olympian and FIFA Women's World Cup champion, Abby Wambach, urged:

Women must champion each other. This can be difficult for us. Women have been pitted against

each other since the beginning of time for that one seat at the table. Scarcity has been planted inside of us and among us. This scarcity is not our fault. But it is our problem. And it is within our power to create abundance for women where scarcity used to live.[79]

Even before shared female power on social media emerged as a dramatic force in 2017, evidence undermining the Queen Bee syndrome was mounting. Laurie Rudman, a social psychologist at Rutgers University, says research shows men are more biased against women at work than are women themselves, and one simple reason for this has been the scarcity of women in authority. 'We need to change our society so that it becomes normative for women to see other women succeeding in all kinds of roles,' she adds.[80]

Other large studies have confirmed that having a woman CEO meant women were more likely to be promoted[81] — one sure-fire way to combat the scarcity effect. But there's still an extraordinarily disproportionate amount of relish when conflict between women surfaces, notes Facebook executive and author of *Lean In*, Sheryl Sandberg, who is herself often accused of being a Queen Bee, despite her vocal support for women. Sheryl too has challenged the default 'catty woman at work' idea,[82] pointing to research supporting the notion that women create opportunities for women.

When men compete, or disagree, it's often viewed as healthy rivalry, but there seems to be a particular fascination with women fighting or undermining each other. As this book was being written, the movie *I, Tonya*, about skater Tonya Harding, was released. The famous attack on Harding's rival Nancy Kerrigan is well known, but as commentary on the film, and a look back at what happened to the two competitors, make clear, they were reduced to opposing caricatures of saint and sinner and 'encouraged to publicly cat fight and were punished by the media — because they were women'.[83] In the build-up to the 2018 French Open, tennis stars Serena Williams and Maria Sharapova, who were due to play each other, were repeatedly described as having a lengthy catfight over their entire careers.[84]

As journalist Tarla Lambert points out:

> It's a trope reinforced time and time again and not one unique to sport. Businesswomen, entertainers, doctors, scientists, teachers, engineers — none are exempt. If you're a woman with ambition, or even a woman with an opinion, society tells us you're likely to scratch another woman's eyes out in the process of getting heard or getting what you want.[85]

In a similar way, Sheryl Sandberg and Marissa Mayer, Yahoo's former CEO, were often pitted against each other in media articles, while business decisions they made were subjected to forensic attention and criticism. Their clothes and their home help were ridiculed, both of which wouldn't have rated a mention for two male CEOs or executives. As one article noted:

> The strange idea that women who are successful must represent all women, or somehow be like all women, is both totally absurd and completely prevalent. How could someone in the position of Sandberg or Mayer live exactly like most women in America?[86]

There is a tricky balancing act at play here, too. Female leaders are often expected to carry the banner for all women — but at the same time, even though many workplaces claim to be true meritocracies, often women in these organisations have been penalised for failing to conform to a feminine ideal which they are assured doesn't operate. As UK academic Sharon Mavin points out:

> It is assumed that women align themselves with
> women; in senior management women are
> responsible for the 'women in management mantle',
> and when they do not conform they are pejoratively
> labelled Queen Bees. Queen Bee 'blames' women
> for *not* supporting each other, constructs women as
> out of place in senior management and maintains
> a gendered status quo.[87]

Men in management have rarely been expected to show such gender affiliation. And while men tend to be less likely to form their own workplace networks — probably because as part of the dominant group they can access support or sponsorship from many of their colleagues — there are strong positive social norms around male bonding and mateship. Until recently many sporting and social clubs were overwhelmingly seen as male preserves.

As Sheryl Sandberg's own analysis reflects, more sophisticated research examining how sexism operates in workforces is finding that the fault lines giving rise to the occasional Queen Bee are often workplace norms, and markedly different assessments of how women and men go about their jobs. What seems like good advice for a man can prove hugely detrimental for a woman. Even telling women to stick up for themselves and draw attention to discrimination can backfire. Women who do this are more likely to be penalised in their performance ratings, while men are often rewarded for the same behaviour.[88]

Turns out it's well-nigh impossible to quantify how many Queen Bees are buzzing around workplaces, says academic Sharon Mavin.[89] In fact adversity often breeds solidarity, as plenty of evidence shows. Indeed, a simple observation makes it obvious that many women in the workforce and the community don't automatically hate each other or routinely tear each other down. Quite the reverse.

Networking groups have thrived in businesses, and across sectors and job categories (as we will see in the next chapter). We often joke that for each role or area of the economy there will be a 'Women in XX' group somewhere — and feedback from #CelebratingWomen participants confirms this. We know how widespread these networks are, across all levels of organisations, because we have spoken at and belonged to many of them over the years. Book clubs, investment circles and mothers' groups have all flourished in recent decades, and women not only make up the bulk of the membership, they are often the founders, and have designed them to address the needs of women. Some groups, as we will examine, have grown internationally and gained thousands of dedicated members. It's the kind of success story many a start-up would love to emulate.

Nurturing not undermining

On top of this overwhelming pattern of women self-organising into support groups, there is accumulating evidence that women do back each other at work, too. Contrary to the assumed rivalry and culture of 'catfighting', it turns out women are more likely to mentor each other than mentor men in the workplace. A study of 318 businesswomen from across 19 countries and 30 different industries observed women more frequently mentoring other women (73% of the time) than men (27% of the time). The authors found:

> ... women do not avoid taking on mentorships because of competition. In fact, the number one reason cited for why women mentor is because they want to be supportive of other women — 80% agreed.[90]

Rather than rival other women in their organisation, the study showed women are actually more likely to sponsor each other and to help others rise to the top. 'We can confidently put to rest the myth that women would rather compete than support one another,' the researchers concluded.

More research by the US firm Catalyst published in 2010 found that 65% of women who received career development support then developed new talent, compared to 56% of men. Of these women, 73% were developing other women, compared to 30% of men.[91]

Queen Bee behaviours are not reflective of some 'mean girl' gene lurking in women's DNA, says US sociologist Marianne Cooper.[92] Rather, to the degree they exist, Queen Bee dynamics are triggered by gender discrimination in male-dominated environments in which women are devalued. There is plenty of evidence to show that women do indeed support one another, she adds:

> When women work with a higher percentage of women they experience lower levels of gender discrimination and harassment. When women have female supervisors, they report receiving more family

and organisational support than when they have male supervisors. And a preponderance of studies shows that when more women are in management positions, the gender pay gap is smaller.[93]

These findings have important implications for how workplaces and women themselves can encourage even greater solidarity. Sheryl Sandberg suggests the way to counter negative assumptions about women's infighting is for women to continue to offer support to their female peers — and to amplify each other's accomplishments. When a woman helps another woman, she says, they both benefit. 'And when women celebrate one another's accomplishments, we're all lifted up.'[94]

This was certainly how #CelebratingWomen made many women feel — including Kirstin, who felt uplifted and personally affirmed from running the year-long campaign. That's why Kirstin uses the idea of a fishing net, rather than pulling women one at a time up a ladder, to fire the imagination and remind women that they are already holding that net in different parts of their lives. The amplification effect also rings true for the many social media campaigns that have galvanised women and attracted massive attention around the world.

That momentum has effectively debunked many strands of the Queen Bee myth — and revealed a startling appetite from women to hear from each other and use their shared power. It's particularly striking that instead of framing and measuring themselves against male models of authority, many of those participating in #CelebratingWomen were fascinated by the way other women had forged their paths across different sectors and countries. They wanted to read about these women, and tell their daughters and colleagues about them. They found them affirming, empowering and encouraging.

Women inspiring women

The sheer breadth of experience, jobs and backgrounds of the #CelebratingWomen participants, which many followers commented on, couldn't be more different to the traditional masculine power figures we've often been told are the only role models that matter, and that Queen Bees are seeking to emulate.

The ruthless competition Queen Bees are said to feel with female peers and underlings was nowhere to be seen in the #CelebratingWomen participants or their followers. Of course, this cohort is self-selecting, yet they are also remarkably diverse, and it's worth noting nearly all the 757 women involved mentioned the delight they felt from seeing their female networks react to their profiles.

As several researchers have noted, the lack of gender diversity at many top tables adds to the pressure on senior women to fight others to keep the 'woman's' role. Blaming these senior women for preventing others progressing could be misguided, according to a 2015 US report, which found:

> … strong evidence that women face an implicit
> quota, whereby a firm's leadership makes an effort to
> have a small number of women in top management,
> but makes less effort to have, or even resists having,
> larger numbers of women. In consequence, the
> presence of a woman on a top management team
> reduces the likelihood that another woman occupies
> a position on that team.[95]

Making the breadth of women's work and achievements visible to a wider audience is a great way to battle the scarcity effect, as it proves women do have the credentials for all kinds of decision-making roles. As feedback from the campaign made clear, many women found reading about others and sharing their own profiles legitimised their careers and decisions, and inspired them to do the same for others. Changing the norms about women succeeding, as Laura Rutger points out, helps mitigate the circumstances that dampen women's aspirations and leave women in power facing double standards.[96] Once that starts to happen, women are also less likely to believe in the Queen Bee myth, and feel safer to aim higher and speak up.

When asked if they thought the Queen Bee was real, or dying away, many #CelebratingWomen participants said it was indeed other women's encouragement that had helped them take the plunge. And many have made a point of paying it back in kind.

'I have been given incredible opportunities by women,' says Melissa Pouliot (profile #674), all of whom she still keeps in touch with. These women have believed in her, nurtured and encouraged her, challenged and taken her outside her comfort zone:

> I would not be where I am today without the women in my life. I have made every effort to do the same to other women who cross my path, both from a personal and professional level. This is why #CelebratingWomen connected with me so strongly, why I wanted to be part of it.

Some, like Dr Muneera Bano (profile #553), refute the existence of widespread Queen Beeism:

> I don't believe in the generalisation of women not
> supporting other women. I look back on all my
> achievements and realise that there were occasions
> I was ready to give up, but there were women in my
> life who would not let me fall and were there to get
> me back on my feet. Among them my mother and
> [PhD] supervisor are on top of the list. Two very
> different women from different parts of the world
> — one illiterate and one a professor — and yet
> both knew the importance of supporting another
> young girl.

For some, the campaign was a refreshing antidote to workplace and pop-culture depictions of women as viperous and backstabbing. Catherine Cahill (profile #354) says we have been constantly told that women don't support women, and it is the most common theme provided to us in media. She wants to see news items that report on women in a positive light — currently few and far between.

The head of BHP's Olympic Dam mine, Jacqui McGill (profile #66), also notes the media reinforcement of the syndrome, and squirms when watching reality TV cooking shows setting women up. Her attitude is clear — she doesn't tolerate bad behaviour no matter who it's from — and she has never had another woman put her down.

The Queen Bee is a myth that we allow to tear us apart, agrees Tracey Clark (profile #543):

> I think if we continue to just accept the idea that
> women are not supportive of each other, it will always
> be a self-fulfilling prophecy. I'd rather support people,
> organisations and projects that *are* helping us build

> each other up, and lead by example. Certainly, in my
> own circle of friends, the women in my life are my
> biggest supporters, so in that aspect, I think my goal
> is working.

Taking part in the campaign actively or as a follower put a fresh perspective on some deeply embedded ideas on women's workplace relationships. It acted as a powerful rebuttal to the catty back-stabbing cliché that has been buttressed by poorly substantiated assumptions and sheer inaccuracies. Allowing it to thrive has reinforced the idea that women lack the wherewithal and leadership skills needed to succeed. But many women who participated now realise from their own experience, and from seeing the public success of social media movements, that sisterhood is the rule, not the exception.

The Queen Bee may not be eradicated quite yet, but she is failing fast.

Evidence of a shift in attitudes to female solidarity is also permeating popular culture and movies, with strong woman leads on the increase. Even female superheroes are hitting the screens, and instead of routinely portraying women in power as competitors there are signs of more nuanced portrayal and sisterhood. We loved the tweet from the author of *Bad Feminist*, Roxane Gay, in early 2018 following the release of movies *Wonder Woman* and *Black Panther* (which features a lead woman character Okoye):

> Wonder Woman and Okoye wouldn't fight. They
> would share intel and collaborate and mutually
> respect each other.[97]

Busting the Queen Bee myth and encouraging workplaces and communities to support — rather than penalise — women who help each other can lift us all up.

The stories and impact of #CelebratingWomen provide clear evidence of a diffuse net of connections and pathways between women, rather than a dagger for the back of a rival. It taps into and builds on the support women have long offered each other, stepping up together to affirm success and contribution, and keeping the pressure on for progress.

That's what women have always done to win their rights. And as the campaign shows, now they have the means to accelerate the pace in a way that past generations of strong women would be cheering on.

5

A BRIEF HISTORY
OF WOMEN'S
NETWORKS

Dazed and confused after giving birth to twins, and with a two-year old in tow, Catherine remembers turning up to a morning tea for new parents held by a multiple-birth association in her area. They were mostly mothers, swapping stories and tactics on conundrums such as how to get baby twins out of the car while keeping an eye on a toddler (shove some food or a toy at the toddler to distract them while getting the twins in the pram first — sounds obvious now, but seemed genius at that point).

It wasn't only the advice that helped, but the perspective on how others were coping when the odds were really against them — one of the mothers at the group had just given birth to her second set of twins in three years! A couple of women already had four children when they discovered twins were on the way. Nobody talked much about their jobs, but it turned out several were lawyers and executives, along with teachers, small business owners and homemakers; none of that made any difference when it came to managing a midnight breastfeeding session for two screaming babies. These meetings were uplifting on a number of levels, even if the humour was a little black at times. Catherine came away from the catch-ups armed with lots of practical tips, and a posse of kindred spirits who made her feel she could cope with three children under the age of three (plus a militant attitude to birth control).

Many mothers have stories of the essential networks they shared at various times in their lives, and you don't need to be a parent to rely on women friends and contacts who see you through and provide a hinterland of generous advice and support. And of course, that same support at the coalface in paid work, as we have noted, is often crucial for sustaining your hold on a job (and your sanity).

Years after gratefully finding solace, coffee and twin expertise in a group, Catherine was delighted to act as a mentor for the Women in Media group, set up by a group of journalists including journalist and activist Tracey Spicer (profile #131). Once again, the shared power of the cohort was obvious — as was the enthusiasm of the younger women turning up in droves for the group's events. Catherine realised that long before such a group existed, the women she worked with in the newsroom of a daily newspaper were providing the same strength and psychological props for each other every day, but often under the radar. Of course, men need this kind of support too, and some of Catherine's male colleagues went out of their way to help each other and women as well. But while those efforts were appreciated there was little judgement about or attention given to whether men offered support or not. The needs of those outside the mainstream were often harder to address in a 'one size fits all' approach — yet obvious mentoring between women was both expected, but also often criticised as 'favouritism'.

Harnessing a social network

The more we analysed the Queen Bee idea that women become unhelpful and unsympathetic to each other as they take on responsibility, the more we realised the clearest evidence to the contrary sat right under our noses. Women from all backgrounds — teachers, nurses, shop assistants, home managers, in high-flying careers — have always helped and supported each other. And what's more, they choose to spend a substantial part of their time in and out of paid work doing just that, whether informally, or through one of the burgeoning women's networks.

While writing this book we sat down one Sunday right next to the beach where Kirstin first had her brainwave about launching a campaign. We soon started discussing the growth of networks for women — and reminisced about book groups and various professional connections we had made. As we chatted, Kirstin thought it might be a good idea to post a short request on Facebook to her 6000 or so followers asking about the networks they were part of or had helped set up.

Within minutes the screen lit up with a wave of groups, from those offering health and nutrition advice for cancer patients, to networks of rural women, indigenous women, in the start-up community, for scientists and engineers ... and the list kept growing: Rotary, UN Women, Queensland Rural, Regional and Remote Women's Network, Business and Professional Women Australia, the STEMMinist Book Club, Plus 600 Women, CBA Women in Focus, YWCA, charities such as Save Our Sisters,

Women in Social Enterprise, Australian Women Donors Network and professional organisations such as Women on Boards, Chief Executive Women, the International Women's Forum, Women Lawyers, Women Corporate Directors, the Women's Indigenous Network, Young Asian Professionals ... and the names continued to come through. Within a few hours, 300 different women's groups had been shared.

We knew about some of these groups, but there were many we hadn't come across. The capacity of women to organise themselves into networks seems to have no limits. Many women responding to the request were tagging friends who had started or ran these groups — a classic case of amplifying other women's achievements.

Women's friendship has of course been a powerful force throughout history, even if acknowledged only peripherally. As Ann Friedman points out:

> **Friendship became a powerful way of challenging**
> **women's subservient roles and pushing forward**
> **other progressive political agendas ... By the time**
> **Betty Friedan called out housewives' malaise and the**
> **second-wave feminist movement was percolating, the**
> **bonds between women were openly acknowledged as**
> **an organising force for political change. Sisterhood,**
> **as the slogan goes, is powerful.[98]**

With such a vast web of informal and formal networks, it's clear women do turn to each other for sustenance, and for increasingly sophisticated levels of practical support and referrals, particularly when they are in environments that are male dominated. And from our feedback, these valuable and diffuse webs of connection haven't been swarming with Queen Bees.

These supporting frameworks are hardly new. In 1916 *The New York Times* breathlessly reported that 125 women had met for what the headline called a 'Manless Dinner'.[99] The (male) reporter explained that the 125 women — including female 'physicians, two authors, a singer, a sculptor, an architect, a lawyer, and workers in philanthropic and semi-charitable callings' — had all gathered together, without men, to 'speak of the achievements of their sex'. While the precise reason for the gathering isn't clear, it's a fair bet this was the start of a network to celebrate women's successes. The 'Manless Dinner' is notable not just for its title and the fact a gathering of women was newsworthy in itself, but also for the diversity of women and their achievements at a time when even eating publicly without a male companion was frowned on. And it's no coincidence that such an event occurred at a time when women were agitating for the right to vote, or had won it in many parts of the Western world, and awareness of the pressure for change was rising. The push for women's rights was in full flight.

Taking to the streets

In fact, the women's rights movement started to appear as an organised social movement over 150 years ago as agitation for basic changes to the law increased. In 1866 Millicent Fawcett set up a petition to support the women's vote in the United Kingdom. She was only 19 and couldn't even sign her own petition, but that certainly didn't stop her — in fact she lobbied for the rights of women for the rest of her life, becoming President of the National Union of Women's Suffrage Societies (NUWSS) from 1907 to 1919, with its staggering 50,000 members. This powerful group that formed more than 150 years ago may not have involved celebrity guest speakers at breakfast events, but was nevertheless an early version of today's ubiquitous women's groups.

The London Society for Women's Suffrage was eventually renamed the Fawcett Society in Millicent's honour in 1953, the year she died. The Society's website notes that hers was the largest organisation agitating for female suffrage at the time, and this strong pressure eventually resulted in securing voting rights for British women (over the age of 30) in 1918. Her efforts are still celebrated today, and Millicent became the first woman to be remembered with a statue in Parliament Square in London. The Society now has about 3000 members and a number of high-profile supporters, including model Kate Moss.

When Carrie Gracie, a former BBC China correspondent who resigned after it was revealed she was paid 50% less than her male counterparts, won back-pay from the broadcaster she donated it to the Fawcett Society.[100] The society then announced the money would be used to set up a fund for women needing legal advice on equal-pay claims.[101] It was another uplifting and practical example of how women tangibly support each other for the greater good.

Cells of activity continued to form around the globe. In 1889, on the other side of the world, the remarkable Louisa Lawson (mother of famous Australian poet, Henry Lawson) established the Dawn Club, where women met to lobby for the vote, discuss broad reform and gain experience in public speaking.

While the centenary of the suffragettes' successes has been celebrated and the work of women at the time lauded, it's often viewed as a movement that appeared to address a particular glaring problem and then disappeared. But women's support for each other and the suffrage movement didn't emerge from the ether and then completely die away. To the contrary, it inspired many. In her book *My Life on the Road*,[102] iconic feminist Gloria Steinem describes how Mahatma Gandhi closely observed the suffragette movement in the United Kingdom and later urged Indians to copy the tactics of the suffragettes in their campaign for self-rule.

The momentum has certainly ebbed and flowed in different eras, with less overt activism by women in the period after the suffragettes, and after World War II as women were strongly encouraged to return to traditional roles in the home. But as social norms shifted and access to education gradually increased, demand for change led to the resurgence of women's collectives and political action that became known as 'second wave' feminism in the 1960s.

Often seen as triggered by Betty Friedan's powerful book *The Feminine Mystique*, this era saw a backlash against the post-war years when women were expected to return obediently to home and hearth, raise a brood of children and give up any ideas about education or paid work. Marches were organised and the agenda moved well beyond the original suffragette demands, pursuing reproductive rights (the Pill became available in 1961), equal pay, maternity leave and education rights. Feminist bookshops and businesses flourished, and all-male enclaves were stormed; in 1971 the unofficial anthem of the era, 'I am woman' was released by Australian singer Helen Reddy.

Lobbying for change

The reach of women's groups in workplaces over the years has extended well beyond the middle classes and white-collar realms, with active lobbying among women running small businesses, in unions and the trades.

The modern women's movement was founded on collective action, and used this power to improve working conditions as industrialisation in the nineteenth century drew so many women into factories and workplaces beyond the home or farm. As UK academics Professor Nicole Busby and Dr Rebecca Zahn explain in an article for the Dangerous Women Project,[103] women joined together to agitate for better working conditions from the early 1800s. Female mill workers went on strike in Britain in 1835, and the first strike for equal pay was organised by 1500 female card-setters in Yorkshire in 1832. Despite women joining forces to push for change just like men, their efforts were not regarded in the same way:

> Although trade unionism and the intellectual underpinnings of the labour movement were instigated around and by women … just as much as they were by men, the fact remains that once institutionalised, the labour movement became focused on the needs and concerns of the 'standard male worker'. Women workers became part of the women's movement.[104]

Professor Busby and Dr Zahn point out women have continued to fight collectively for their rights in the workforce, viewing the strike by women workers at a Ford automative factory in Britain in 1968 (depicted in the 2010 film *Made in Dagenham*) as 'a turning point in the battle for sex equality, which eventually led to the passage of the Equal Pay Act 1970'.[105]

All kinds of working women have used networks to share insights and mobilise around important issues and causes.

More recently in Australia Sally McManus, the first woman to be appointed secretary of the Australian Council of Trade Unions, ran a campaign for equal pay, along with many female colleagues, at the Australian Services Union, on behalf of disability and community workers in the non-government sector. This group is made up of 85% women who work for very low pay while caring for some of the most vulnerable people in the community. McManus had been repeatedly told by lawyers the case was unwinnable, but the Union persisted and after six years, in early 2012, won their hard-fought case. As she told the ABC in 2018:

> from the suffragettes to the AFLW to #MeToo, history is written by women like us, whose determination and persistence in the face of what seems like an inevitable 'no' changes it to a 'yes'.[106]

Worth their salt

Women have also banded together to help break down barriers in traditionally male-dominated sectors including the trades and construction. After working in her husband's painting business, Fi Shewring (profile #33), one of *The Australian Financial Review*'s '100 Women of Influence' winners in 2012, went to technical college to get her qualifications, and wondered why women were so rare in trades — particularly as the practical skills for these jobs were no barrier to entry. Fi eventually became a trade teacher herself and launched a program for young women interested in painting and decorating. In 2009, still appalled at the lack of options, she set up Supporting and Linking Tradeswomen (SALT) to encourage women and girls to take up careers as plumbers, electricians, painters, mechanics and carpenters.

Established in Wollongong, south of Sydney, with seven tradeswomen, SALT now has more than 1730 members in its Facebook group.[107] Their website[108] details the long history of Australian women working in the trades, particularly during the two World Wars, in munitions factories, ship building and steelworks — although most women left these roles at the end of the war periods so men could get their jobs back. There remains plenty of scope for improvement: in 2015 women made up only 14.7% of Australia's technicians and trade workers.[109]

SALT makes good use of social media and has a network across Australia, offering talks and workshops in the community and in schools. As Fi explains:

> When we began there were no other support
> organisations for tradeswomen across all trades and it
> has been wonderful to watch the growth of a number
> of other groups who we have also supported.[110]

In the Australian construction sector, women's groups are also active and widespread. Launched in 1995, the national Women in Construction network holds regular events, conducts research and advocates for change within the sector, which in 2016 employed only about 12% women, down from 17% in 2006.[111]

These efforts, founded by women to unite and support each other, didn't all come from overtly political movements or radical agendas. In 1922 a bunch of enterprising and determined women gathered to set up Australia's largest women's organisation, the Country Women's Association (CWA). Today it has thousands of members working to support each other in remote and regional communities. Like many women's groups it has often been trivialised and the butt of jokes, becoming known in popular culture for its scone recipes and cookbooks, rather than its impact and long history of country women 'fighting isolation and a lack of health facilities'. As the CWA website points out, within a year of forming it was:

> ... a unified, resourceful group that was going from strength to strength. The members worked tirelessly to set up baby health care centres, fund bush nurses, build and staff maternity wards, hospitals, schools, rest homes, seaside and mountain holiday cottages — and much more. The women of the CWA have been initiators, fighters and lobbyists. [112]

Much more, indeed, than baking scones.

All this activity and networking by and for women has left a successful legacy that lives on in the 2017/18 Women's Marches and the solidarity of online campaigns — and offers some potent lessons about the need to keep up the pressure once demand is renewed. If Louisa Lawson was around today, we think she would have instantly appreciated the collective, global clout of social media.

Empowerment has also driven the high-profile #MeToo and #TimesUp campaigns — and China's #WoYeShi, France's #BalanceTonPork, Italy's #QuellaVoltaChea and Norway's #StilleForOpptak — which have built on all these decades of women's lobbying groups in the community.

Back to the future

Women tend to be joiners and collaborators because they traditionally worked in the family and community, where resources and childminding were shared. That's a topic close to the heart of former Australian Governor-General Quentin Bryce, a stalwart of the women's movement over many decades. She recalls her community work in Brisbane during the 1970s when women banded together to address their local needs:

> Our children were brought up in a village.
> If you talk to women my vintage you will hear
> the same experiences. We got into things in our
> neighbourhood. We were part of the emerging
> women's rights movement. When we needed
> childcare we'd ask ourselves, 'How do we get it?'
> Everything started with meetings around kitchen
> tables. We allocated the jobs like fund raising.
> That's when I became involved in mental health
> issues, juvenile justice reform and child health.
> It was an era of vibrant social change, legal reform
> and civil liberties. We learned how to bring people
> with us, how to lobby, to go to see politicians and
> how to write a press release. It developed confidence
> and taught me how things worked.

There's a well-known saying that throughout history small groups of people with shared interest do indeed change the world. Australian Sex Discrimination Commissioner, and former law firm partner Kate Jenkins (profile #466), told us there's a long history of women's collective action dating back over 100 years of activism. Support for those affected by family violence, with women helping women in safe houses and fighting for justice and protection, has been around for a long time. More recently, that advocacy has resulted in the appointment of Ministers for Family Violence Prevention in several States and a Royal Commission being conducted in Victoria with similar initiatives in other States. Campaigns such as #MeToo have been a perfect example of women's voices coming together and taking strength from each other to advocate for change as a collective, rather than rely on the individual complaints system offered by the law, Kate says.

The legacy of the suffragettes and other women who led the way on crucial changes has been noted as, a century later, the wave of social media campaigns unfolded. As journalist Eva Wiseman points out:

> In 1918 Fawcett, Emmeline Pankhurst and their
> fellow suffragists and suffragettes won a 50-year
> campaign for (some) women to be given the same
> political rights as men. Today, the battle lines are
> different, but the wars rage on.[113]

Interviewing a group of leading British women activists she dubs 'the new suffragettes', Eva Wiseman describes the long battle for change. This modern band of activists have:

> ... bravery and strength that almost vibrates the
> windows. It's not the jolly strength of Instagram
> aphorisms; it's gritty, it requires hard work and
> banding together.[114]

A century after women got the vote, says Sophie Walker, who set up the Women's Equality Party in the United Kingdom, there's a different kind of disenfranchisement: 'Today women have the vote — the fight is to empower them to use it',[115] an insight that is particularly relevant in the United Kingdom where voting is not compulsory.

Emmeline Pankhurst's leadership a century ago has also been proudly reflected in the work of her great-granddaughter, Dr Helen Pankhurst. She used the motto of the suffragettes 'Deeds not words' as the title of her book on the last hundred years of the women's rights movement, released in early 2018. She has no doubt that the campaigns around the world signal a new era for women's rights:

> 2018 has become symbolic and important in its own right ... We've got enough women speaking up, supported by enough other women and men saying 'It's not good enough, all these norms we've had for a century, for longer, we're just fed up with it and we need a change.'[116]

Helen added that her great-grandmother and supporters were adept at marketing, branding and motivating their followers — and had they been able to use social media, their impact would have been even greater. The similarities between the fight for the vote and #MeToo were striking — women saying 'Enough', coming together and saying, 'We can change things'.

Flicking a switch

It was saying 'enough' to online denigration that also helped set Kirstin on the path to creating her campaign. Sometimes anger and frustration propel action, and when enough of us join together, the encouragement brings a new pace to the exercise.

High rates of education of girls and women, the voices of women through social media campaigns, and the spread of networks and groups for women, make it clear that lack of supply is no longer a valid reason for lack of progress, Australia's Sex Discrimination Commissioner Kate Jenkins (profile #466) points out. There are increasing numbers of educated and empowered women who want to know what they can do to change the status quo, and who are supporting each other, and making a difference — and will not be sidelined, she adds.

Men have always congregated in forums such as business, social and sporting groups to exchange information and contacts, and their bonding and support for each other has traditionally been lauded, particularly in sports arenas and the military. Indeed, in the Australian Defence Force and across Australian society, the notion of the noble ANZAC is a sacred masculine model, built on the historic ideal of an heroic, hardy and self-deprecating soldier who always sticks by his mates. When toxic behaviour in male sports teams or the Australian Defence Force emerges, it is often attributed to 'letting the team down'. Women's bonding, it's fair to say, has rarely been accorded much attention, nor the same kind of respect. As we examined the story of women's support and networking, it became clear that as well as having common experiences and challenges, the unifying factor for many women's groups and their activism has been exclusion from traditional power structures, and dealing with embedded barriers that continue to hamper them and compromise their ability to earn a living.

Shared challenges make strong ties among women that can be very liberating. Female friendships, as writer Ann Friedman points out, have no defined boundaries or gatekeepers, unlike traditional family relationships:

> **Friendships have no ceremonial beginning or end, no biological definition. They are not sanctioned by any church, nor recognised officially by any state. This is perhaps why women, historically diminished by the government and burdened by the family, find such fulfilment and power among friends.**[117]

It's a strong indication of the need for a radical shift in valuing women in society and workplaces that so many women rely on their friends and flock to various networks and groups to get a hearing and advice. As a result, these groups span a broad swathe of social sectors, interests, jobs and occupations, and also use all kinds of media, which gives them extra breadth and clout.

Women have always been enthusiastic members of social, mothers' and other community groups, which have played such an important role in community building and bonding, as former Governor-General Quentin Bryce has pointed out. They have been invaluable for women in a range of communities where isolation and financial hardship make it hard to get crucial daily support, much less access to paid work. But in recent years there has been a boom in women's networks in organisations, across sectors and professions, with many building powerful global connections and impact that has astonished even their founders.

Stemminists

The #CelebratingWomen campaign unearthed and elevated these connections among women, while also showing how effective they could be in all kinds of areas. It even converted some previously hesitant social media users into fans and innovators.

Although initially reluctant, cancer researcher Dr Caroline Ford (profile #624) joined Twitter in 2015 after a dinner with peers who said it was a fantastic way to connect with others in the same field. For Caroline it proved an eye opener:

> [Twitter] is incredible for women and scientists in
> Science, Technology, Engineering, Mathematics
> and Medicine (STEMM), and for collaboration and
> meeting people. The thing I found wonderful about
> Twitter is this kick-arse sisterhood of women who
> are willing to champion and advocate for each other,
> which is incredible. I'm in the medical area, where
> there are lots of women, but if you are the sole
> woman in an area like engineering then Twitter
> is an incredible way to get the support and know
> you are not the only one.

Caroline leads the Gynaecological Cancer Research Group at the University of NSW, which aims to understand why gynaecological cancers develop, how and why they spread throughout the body, and how best to treat them. In a story reminiscent of Kirstin's, she came up with an idea to make more use of social media while on her summer holidays, out having a run. Caroline had just read the book *Inferior* by UK journalist Angela Saini, which outlines how sexism has been woven through scientific analysis of gender, and discovered from social media that a fellow scientist, Professor Renae Ryan, was also reading it.

The plan for a feminist book club for women in STEMM was hatched. But instead of setting up a small group of local women, Caroline decided to use Twitter to spread the word more widely — and there was an immediate response.

Launched in early 2018, the STEMMinist Book Club grew to more than 2000 members globally in a few months. Members were meeting up in Istanbul, Dublin and Berlin, Caroline says in surprise, with people making new connections and important professional links around the world.

Caroline is also part of Franklin Women, another valuable network that hosts events online for women in science and research. And she has joined the Superstars of STEM group, facilitated by Science & Technology Australia, with about 30 other women who were hand-picked as mentees to learn how to effectively use their voice and raise their profile. These connections have become a significant backstop for Caroline and offer invaluable advice. And they do something more:

> These women don't fit the scientist mould. They are
> so diverse in age and ethnicity and are all the things
> you don't think of when you think of a scientist,
> who is usually seen as an old white dude with a wife.
> They are doing amazing things, and they are a very
> important part of my life.

Spreading the net

We spoke to a range of women leading various networks to get a sense of their aims, scope, outcomes, and what they saw making a difference for women in the workforce, whatever kinds of jobs they held. One of the most successful and with a very broad catchment is Business Chicks, developed by Emma Isaacs, an Australian who now lives in the United States. Crowds of women in all sorts of jobs flock into mid-city venues, often early in the morning, to hear a well-known speaker. They do a fair bit of networking, too, if the noise levels at these events are anything to go by. Emma bought the business in 2005 after attending one of these occasions and saw thousands of switched-on, successful women. She explains:

> We only had 250 members, and the business only operated on the east coast of Australia. These days we operate across two continents, 11 cities, and we reach more than 400,000 people a year. We've evolved the business into a membership organisation and media business, including a digital offering at www.businesschicks.com, a print magazine called *Latte* and an offline events program that sees us producing over 100 live events nationally each year, with past speakers such as Sir Richard Branson, Gloria Steinem, Diane von Furstenberg, Arianna Huffington, Julia Gillard, Dr Brené Brown, Nicole Kidman.

The Business Chicks members are an eclectic bunch. They range in age from age 16 to 86, some are running their own businesses, while others are employed across all sectors and at all levels. 'Many have dreams of starting their own business. But the commonality that unites these women is a passion for sharing ideas, knowledge, experience and skills,' Emma explains. The stories from speakers offer inspiration and courage to women to move ahead with their careers or businesses, she adds. But the power of this extensive network moves beyond education to also provide a reading on gender issues, which shouldn't be underestimated — it's a classic example of the shift that can occur as these groups mature and move from a core supporting role to advocacy as well.

> Having a community as big as Business Chicks
> means that we're kept abreast of issues facing
> our membership each day, and there are recurring
> patterns, particularly with gender equality, that
> need to be addressed — for example, policies
> around parental leave and truly flexible working
> arrangements. I've seen so many companies give lip
> service to flexible working arrangements, but their
> written policy paints a very different picture to what
> their management say and truly believe about this.

The women's campaigns of 2017 made it clear that women still need to use their collective clout to pressure for change, says Emma:

> It's somewhat contentious to think a women's
> network is still needed in 2018 and indeed into
> the future, but all our research and the campaigns
> of the last year have confirmed it, and the reality is
> that we still work in a world where unconscious (and
> conscious) bias exists, and still have a long way to go

in order to close the gender pay gap and equal the scales when it comes to representation.

If this past year has taught us anything, it's that women are united. And we're ready to work to catalyse real change, together. The challenge now is that we keep the momentum going, and that's where I think women's groups are going to be the difference — we're going to continue to stand beside each other and continue to encourage each other to demand change.

The success of networks such as Business Chicks has helped pave the way for a range of other business forums in recent years, often not confined to a particular sector, but offering women all across the workforce a chance to catch up and debrief. A group that was designed by Sydney businesswomen Jane Lu and Gen George to be a bit of fun has attracted an extraordinary 50,000 members. You have to admire the nous of the founders calling their group Like Minded Bitches Drinking Wine, and making sure it has few barriers to entry besides a small fee. The wine-drinking members now hail from all around the world.

Stellar frontiers

Age is no barrier to setting up networks. While still in her twenties, Dr Jillian Kenny founded Machinam, which produces educational material designed to make maths engaging for Year 9 and 10 students — and as if that wasn't enough, she also co-founded the non-profit organisation

Power of Engineering, which runs nationwide events designed to inspire female students from across Australia, as well as regional and Indigenous male and female students into the engineering profession. In high school she had few role models and originally wanted to be a lawyer, until work experience with an engineering firm opened her eyes to new possibilities. Wondering why no one had told her about engineering, she decided it was time to do something about it.

Like Dr Caroline Ford, Jillian is also a member of Science & Technology Australia's Superstars of STEM group. Jillian has found a real sense of sisterhood from the connections with women members and the support to have their voices heard. She explains:

> The other part, which has been more powerful for some people, is just belonging to something, and the sense of being able to be yourself with a group of people who understand your experience. When the program started there were 30 of us and we started a Slack messaging group — there's discussion every single day, and people can bring whatever they are dealing with, from bullying to just looking for support and advice.

The advice has ranged from career steps to quite practical ideas, such as how to negotiate fees for speaking at events. And it's about valuing themselves and their time. Given the goal of the group is to lift members' media profiles and accept more speaking requests, this information from more experienced members has been enormously helpful, and includes advice on how to set boundaries and occasionally say no to some invitations. Jillian wouldn't have been doing that, she says, without the backing from the group.

Kylie Walker, CEO of Science & Technology Australia, helped establish the Superstars of STEM group. While there were many programs for women in science, as a former journalist she wanted to help make the work of these women visible in the public arena. Women make up 16% of the most senior scientists in Australia, but just 8% of the most followed scientists on Twitter are women, according to analysis Kylie has done of the top 100 'influencers' on Twitter, as judged by the number of followers. She works with members of the program over 12 months to give them training in communicating their work in a way that is relevant for the public, whether through social media or writing opinion pieces.

It's not a case of fixing the women, Kylie says, but giving them skills they haven't had the opportunity to develop, particularly in academia. This includes speaking on stage for public events and in schools, where they provide girls with clear role models. The members range in age from their twenties up to retirement, and come from a range of ethnic backgrounds, as well as the LGBTI community. There has been great cohesion in the group as members support and encourage each other. Kylie explains:

> The beautiful side-effect of it has been all the
> women on the program have had opportunities made
> available to them from joining — new jobs, founding
> a company, some have new career paths.

One example of how the group has amplified and given members their voice is RMIT academic Dr Tien Huynh, who arrived in Australia from Vietnam and completed her postdoctoral studies in cancer, tissue repair, neuropharmacology and drug discovery technologies. Dr Huynh never thought to talk about her own story or life before the program, but it has given her the confidence to own who she is and tell it proudly. Dr Huynh has become something of a celebrity in Vietnam, invited there to speak at forums, and to the media as well.

Even with the strength of the Superstars of STEM, participating has not been without its challenges and backlash for some women. They have faced criticism from colleagues for getting too big for their boots, but none have dropped out to date — which may also reflect the strong bonds and support they give each other. At the same time, it's apparent that having more women in leadership — who have strong connections and influence throughout their workplace — is ensuring that these networks are most effective.

Behind the scenes, Kylie says, many senior women also offer a largely unrecognised boost to other women through active but informal referrals, so more women can contribute, progress, and be heard.

Starting up

Women's programs that provide context and tools to get around workplace barriers have fanned demand in one of the most dynamic and high-profile areas of the economy: the start-up and entrepreneurial space, where women remain poorly represented. (About 25% of Australian start-ups were founded by women in 2017, according to the StartUp Muster survey.[118]) A burst of activity in recent years has seen some thriving groups set up to support women in the sector, and help access capital and the kinds of informal networks that get a business off the ground.

These groups — including SheStarts, Heads Over Heels and Springboard Enterprises, amongst many others — also actively bust the myth that women aren't interested in technology, or are restricted to businesses that fall under the 'mumpreneurs' tag. As Fiona Boyd, the CEO of networking group Heads Over Heels, explains, women who access their events are setting up in the health, logistics, engineering, financial services and technology sectors. And the programs are working. In late 2017 Heads Over Heels had seen $24 million invested in women's businesses and helped facilitate 2890 offers of introduction for members. The same year it ran a total of 20 events in Sydney and Melbourne, and partnered in the CAASTRO Galaxy Convention for students held at The University of Sydney, focusing on women in STEM, innovation and entrepreneurship.

In a similar way, the SheStarts accelerator program at BlueChilli invests in up to 10 female-led technology businesses a year to help them get off the ground. SheStarts Director Nicola Hazell (profile #150) says having a program focused on women leaders in the start-up space is needed to deliver real change, instead of just tinkering around the edges:

> What we are doing is changing the ratio of female
> leadership in the most dynamic part of the economy.
> We're now seeing more women coming forward,
> getting started and accessing venture capital to grow.

Having allies when setting up a business is enormously helpful, something reinforced for Nicola when she was profiled for #CelebratingWomen and found herself part of a wide new circle of women. She really appreciated the range of women celebrated, and the work they did in the community. It was challenging our ideas of what leadership is meant to look like, she says — there was no hierarchy, and you didn't have to be the person with the most privilege. It was refreshing, and gave people a voice who had never had one before — and on a global scale.

Launched in 2016, SheStarts has already had more than 1000 women registered to apply, although the program only takes up to 10 start-ups each year. But the community that has built around the program is huge, Nicola says, with thousands of women following online, and more than half a million views on the SheStarts documentary series on social media. The accelerator supports women to build their technology, grow their tech businesses and develop skills as a leader and entrepreneur, including how to be confident in a world that is telling you not to be.

SheStarts works in collaboration with other organisations like Heads Over Heels, Scale Ventures and Springboard Enterprises, another accelerator program for tech companies led by women. It's all helping to build crucial networks, explains Nicola:

> **There's a reason for creating opportunities for women and a space for them. It's not about doing a gender split — we just require participating start-ups to be female-led — but trying to drive a different environment.**

On a personal level, Nicola has developed an increased appreciation of the magic of networking:

> **Over the last five years the networking effect has been hugely transformational for me. Before**

that I was really just focused on *doing* my job —
I would connect with incredible people through my
work but never had the time for those cups of coffee.
So I completely flunked networking in my twenties.
I didn't realise how much I was missing women's
networks until I was about to hit 30 and realised
I wanted to have those deeper discussions — where
you try and solve the biggest world problems over
a cup of coffee — and so I started organising regular
gatherings with like-minded women every two
months ... Now I've seen that happen here, too, in
#CelebratingWomen and through the SheStarts
community. It's a powerful force for change.

Everyone loves a 'bestie'

The communities built by women sometimes extend beyond
networks and coalesce around shared interests — or people.
Few Australians could fail to recognise the voices of Leigh
Sales and Annabel Crabb, journalists at the very top of their
game with a string of reporting, writing and television credits to
their name. The pair are firm friends, and a few years ago
launched a podcast called 'Chat 10 Looks 3' to capture their
conversations about what they were reading, watching and
doing in their busy lives. It's been a smash hit and has attracted
tens of thousands of dedicated followers, who also turn up for
special events held from time to time around the country.

Leigh (profile #129) says the pair launched the podcast for
a couple of reasons:

One was that we enjoyed each other's company a lot,
but catching up always seemed to be well down our
list of priorities. We thought if we had an 'enforced'
catch-up as part of work, we would do it more
often. Two, we also wanted a chance to do a project
together, but every idea we had took up too much
time, given our other commitments. A podcast
seemed like something that would take minimal
time, yet allow us to indulge our shared interests.

It's obvious neither Leigh nor Annabel need to find their
voice — they have skills in that area most of us could only
dream of acquiring. But the podcast gave them a chance to
connect with each other in a very different milieu to their
professional circles, and has let them show the value they place
on their strong bond — and why this rich backdrop has
sustained them as women in such high-profile media jobs. And
this connection is highly relatable. They think it has been
successful because it is about friendship, says Leigh:

Initially, we thought it was about books and movies
and politics and cooking. But it became clear that
while people enjoy hearing about those things, what
they mostly love is our interaction with each other.
I think that particularly for female listeners, it gives
them the same buzz that they get from catching up
with their close female friends when they don't have
time to see them as much as they'd like.

The audience is roughly 90% women, about half of whom are
aged 25–55, which is obvious at the live events.

> I think they are attracted to the events because
> it's a chance to catch up with their own girlfriends.
> Plus, I think they view us as their friends, too, and
> they enjoy 'catching up' with us.

By sharing their friendship, Chat 10 Looks 3 has obviously struck a deep chord. For the die-hard fans, it seems to have elevated the value of these connections, which many #CelebratingWomen campaign participants told us they'd once felt self-conscious about.

Keeping things moving

With the most senior women leaders from the Australian corporate, public service, academic and not-for-profit sectors among its members, the Australian Chief Executive Women (CEW) organisation, which was founded in 1985, has supporting women as its core mission. The group describes its main purpose as 'Women leaders enabling women leaders', and its more than 500 members come from most sectors of the economy.

Being invited to join CEW was an important step in helping Kirstin understand more about workplace gender inequality issues, and how collective thinking can help address them. Women asked to join the group are being recognised as role models, says director Kathryn Fagg, who was elected CEW President in late 2016. She has been a member for about 10 years, and having worked in male-dominated sectors such as manufacturing and logistics, found the group invigorating:

> I got pretty involved early on and discovered the joy
> of working with other women at senior levels. There's
> this enormous commitment to creating opportunities
> and trying to make it easier for others and make
> Australia a better society.

Looking back, the year 2008 was a galvanising point for CEW. Census data released by the Workplace Gender Equality Agency showed that the number of women at senior levels, in both boards and executive roles, was going backwards, Kathryn recalls:

> That's when women said, 'This is ridiculous.'
> [Progress] had been glacial, but going backwards
> was unacceptable — and some men also stepped
> up and said, 'Something has to change here.'

To amplify its message, and help women leaders have more impact, CEW runs a range of activities, including the leaders program, which takes 100 women members a year and provides expertise and support. The group also runs the CEO Conversation series, which takes members to talk to top teams in a range of large organisations to share their stories, and helps the firms work out what they need to do differently, particularly for leaders.

There's a very collegiate climate among the members, which is at odds with the idea that senior women are at loggerheads, Kathryn says. Over the years, she has noticed that a group of women chatting together in a workplace would often attract comments such as 'What are you hatching?' — but these days it's less likely to be noted, and women are more overt about the power of their connections.

> I find it really interesting in groups at a big event
> like the Reserve Bank dinner, that the women tend
> to know each other, and are very pleased to see each
> other, too, which I think is really lovely and it's
> showing the strong relationships — and it's good for
> everyone to see that.

Having watched Kirstin's campaign unfold, Kathryn was struck by its perfect timing, as the concern about progress not just stalling but rolling backwards galvanised many women. The concept of #CelebratingWomen:

> ... showed you can make a big difference quite
> quickly. You can keep it simple and step forward and
> you don't need to go to a highly complex model. It
> said, here's the way we are recognising women. And
> just do it. And I love the fact it is positive — the whole
> #MeToo campaign is very important about recognising
> bad behaviour, but it's also important to have the
> positive stories. I always think, 'Why wouldn't you
> support a network?' It's such a straightforward action
> to say 'I'm supporting this', and see others involved.

Kathryn took on the position of CEW President from predecessor and board director Diane Smith-Gander (profile #16). Diane says she has observed some differences and evolution in how women approach networking.

> I would say women have been mostly naive about
> what networks are for. It is a sweeping generalisation
> that women go to mentors, while men look for
> supporters who will get them their next job. When

> you get into women's networks, if you have a major
> bump in the road, you may not see a lot of women
> who can offer the next job, whereas men tend to pop
> up again in a job very quickly. At CEW I tried to point
> out we should be providing the pastoral care, and that
> has to extend to helping [women] get another job.

The power and impact of congregating with kindred spirits crosses many boundaries and arenas. Networks of women have also been very active in the philanthropic arena, supporting causes from large not-for-profits to domestic violence shelters and through giving circles (a kind of book club for raising money for causes). Most giving circles are made up of women; they have tripled in the ten years to 2017, and raised an estimated US$1.29 billion.[119]

Catherine is on the board of the Australian Women Donors Network, which advocates for greater philanthropic investment in women and girls and educates donors on how to apply a gender lens to their social investments. Evidence suggests that even with the best intentions, women can miss out unless the design and delivery of philanthropically funded programs takes into account their specific needs and circumstances. According to CEO Julie Reilly, research reveals that only 12% of donor funds in Australia are directed specifically to programs for women and girls.[120] This shows why it's pivotal for the work of women supporting women to be amplified.

Our analysis of the history of women's solidarity, and how #CelebratingWomen and the many thriving women's networks continue the momentum, proves that among the key benefits — along with the ability to access advice, skills and connections — is a real sense of validity and encouragement, which many women have not found elsewhere.

In particular, women who were running or members of these groups said talking about their experiences gave them a renewed sense that their story was worth telling, and how to do that effectively, whether they were starting out, in the professions or working in the community. Many of the groups have been formed to combat the isolation, scarcity and marginalisation of women.

Social media movements offer participants and followers another avenue to unite at a crucial time, to keep up pressure to help women everywhere. This collaboration, buoyed by these platforms, is once again showing that shared power can legitimise and improve all women's lives and help pave the way for better outcomes in generations to come. Women everywhere are now connecting for all sorts of reasons — but they are united in showing loudly and clearly that this long-awaited opportunity for change cannot, and must not, be lost.

Without these connections women would never have got the vote, access to education, equal pay or childcare — and some still haven't.

Women don't need anyone else to talk for them. They are doing it for themselves.

6

THE AMPLIFICATION EFFECT

'If you want something done, ask a busy woman' is a bit of a cliché, but has a ring of truth nevertheless.

Women, as we have seen, are already doing a lot to support each other — often on top of a heavy family or domestic load — and every time a woman managed to fit in the time to read or submit a profile to #CelebratingWomen, she played a role in supporting other women by using her voice, sharing her story and adding clout to a collective call for social change. This, it became apparent to Kirstin early on, was both the attraction for women, and the result of their participation. It also became a model for the power and encouragement women can leverage, when they openly build on the support they have always offered each other and join their voices together.

In workplaces, the implications of this shift continue to unfurl, and many women are hopeful they can contribute and drive practical change in their jobs. Women have been backing each other up for millennia, but the rewards of active support between women have certainly become more apparent and topical, with a focus on how to keep the momentum going. In the United States, Ann Friedman and Aminatou Sow coined the term 'Shine Theory' in 2013 to describe the simple premise that 'I don't shine if you don't shine', and 'to describe a commitment to collaborating with rather than competing against other people — especially other women.'[121] They explain:

> We practise Shine Theory because true confidence is infectious. Because powerful women make the greatest friends. Because people know you by the company you keep. Because we want the strongest, happiest, smartest women in our corner — and we want to support each other in pursuing success and happiness on our own terms.

This was a refreshing alternative to the pervasive finger-wagging women have faced when they back each other up, and warnings about turning into Queen Bees or coming a cropper from trying to 'have it all'.

The practical application of Shine Theory was illustrated throughout the #CelebratingWomen campaigns, but there are other key ways women have shown they can make a difference. We also felt that two-time Olympic soccer champion, Abby Wambach, perfectly captured the imagination of how we can help other women shine during her 2018 commencement address at Barnard College:

As you go out into the world: amplify each others'
voices. Demand seats for women, people of colour
and all marginalised people at every table where
decisions are made. Call out each other's wins just
like we do on the field: claim the success of one
woman, as a collective success for *all* women.[122]

The 'amplification' effect

As the #CelebratingWomen profiles were posted and the year
wound to an end, some lessons from the shared power of the
campaign emerged for women, men and workplaces. Even
before social media provided such an effective — and
paradoxically safe — means for women to tell their stories,
and support each other, some pointed tactics aimed for
similar outcomes in daily routines in the workplace, where
good old-fashioned human dynamics make it hard for women
to be heard.

One of the upsides of women feeling supported by like-
minded colleagues — and sufficiently exasperated with the
status quo — is that they can come up with strategies among
themselves, especially around the meeting table — and even in
the White House. Despite his very vocal support for women,
and describing himself as a feminist, former US President
Barack Obama had far fewer women in powerful roles than
men in his first administration. Not only outnumbered, the
women in the Obama White House soon also realised they
were getting fewer chances to contribute than their male
colleagues, particularly in meetings and formal discussions. So,
they took matters into their own hands.

In a strategy that was quickly dubbed 'amplification', the women made a deliberate decision to back up each other's suggestions around the table by repeating them and crediting the woman who had contributed the idea. It was a way of countering the well-documented tendency for women to be interrupted, spoken over, or have their input 'appropriated' in groups — and it worked. By Obama's second term, the gender split among the top team was closer to fifty/fifty and the President regularly asked women, including younger women, for input.

The difference was made possible by women using their collective power, as White House senior adviser Valerie Jarrett described in 2016:

> I think having a critical mass makes a difference …
> It's fair to say that there was a lot of testosterone
> flowing in those early days. Now we have a little
> more oestrogen that provides a counterbalance.[123]

Women not only used their numbers, but made a strategic effort to support each other, rather than accepting conventional advice and concentrating all their efforts on the often-thankless task of persuading their male peers to get on board — or hoping their efforts would somehow eventually be recognised. As one article noted, the exercise shows that women have:

> … tremendous strength in numbers, but gathering
> those numbers in the first place takes courage and
> conscious effort. Maybe one day we won't need that
> tool to be treated equally, but that day isn't today.[124]

Former White House Communications Director during the Obama Administration, Jennifer Palmieri, advises that women need to lift other women up, always. She reminds us of why we should reflect on the scarcity idea that women can only ever be at senior levels in limited numbers:

> Don't let the thought enter your head that you are in a competition with other women — that there is only room for one woman on that team, or that there is only room for one woman in that meeting. That contributes to the sense that women still don't quite fit into the workplace; that there is only so much room for women here. It's not true. It's not pie. One woman's gain isn't another woman's loss. It's when we get lots of women in leadership positions that real change happens.[125]

As #CelebratingWomen has shown, along with the myriad social media movements allowing women to shine together, now is a better time than ever to build on the effort and strength that has made women's collegiality such a powerful force for change.

Women backing women

Women 'having each other's backs' makes a tangible difference to how women are viewed in the workplace, according to a 2017 US study,[126] which found that women's contributions in meetings are often ignored, while men are not only heard but often rewarded. In the workplace it's more 'legitimate' for a man to engage in these more assertive behaviours, and less so for women, according to the study's lead author Elizabeth McClean, Assistant Professor at the University of Arizona's

Eller College of Management. But when women endorse one another's ideas — both in the boardroom and beyond — they gain an extra measure of legitimacy in their colleagues' minds, her study found.

Using strategies such as 'amplification' with a group of colleagues, both male and female, can help women cut through, agrees Margaret Neale, a management professor at the Stanford Graduate School of Business. At Stanford, Professor Neale has a 'posse' of male and female colleagues she can count on to back her up:

> **When we are in meetings and we see a woman have an idea and it's not heard ... somebody else says, 'I've been thinking about what Kathie just said and I think she's got some real insight here.'**[127]

And with so many women using social media, this is another avenue for amplifying women not only within organisations, but across the country and even the world. Kirstin has become particularly focused on using social media to help other women shine, quite apart from the #CelebratingWomen campaign. If she sees a post on LinkedIn about a woman's achievement, whether she knows her or not, she will often like or comment on the post, knowing that this can potentially elevate the woman's achievements to a new network of people. The same applies to retweeting or liking tweets featuring the stories of women who might be looking for support in a project they want to start, or who have been recognised for something in their community. Sharing the post with others can help to spread that news.

And it doesn't take much time or effort to take part in this kind of amplication, which can be effective, positive and helpful for those who benefit.

While 'amplification' may sound like a new idea, women have long had each other's backs at the office, shop or factory — but in an informal way, wary of drawing attention to their mutual support. This 'behind the scenes' sisterhood flies in the face of the pervasive myths about back-stabbing women. Catherine recalls a range of women making an effort to help her during her career in journalism, including giving credit for her ideas in front of senior editors and in meetings, and taking a hands-on approach to problems — such as the time a senior woman journalist found Catherine crying in the bathroom on the day her twins had started school. Catherine had been called into work at the last minute — after ensuring she would have the day off to pick her twins up — and then loaded up with a virtually impossible task to complete in time to get back to the school gate to collect her girls. Her senior colleague — one of Australia's most awarded journalists — asked what was wrong, then told Catherine to stay put while it was sorted out. Sure enough, a few minutes later Catherine's colleague returned to the women's toilets (a place where much female bonding occurs) and told her it was all resolved, and she was free to head off to the school. It was a perfect example of using power and status to support, rather than undermine, a woman colleague.

The 'whisper network'

Such support wasn't confined to domestic emergencies, of course. In Catherine's career women regularly offered each other a hand in much more risky settings such as meetings (using a basic version of amplification), putting in a good word for female colleagues, and warning each other about potential problems with certain men (either because of harassment or old-fashioned sexism) by informally swapping notes. The so-called 'whisper network' has been described as:

> ... an informal chain of conversations among women about men who need to be watched because of rumours, allegations or known incidents of sexual misconduct, harassment or assault. It's a way for women to protect themselves, and to do so under the radar. In one way or another, in every major industry and institution, there have been whisper networks helping women to watch out for each other.[128]

Although the behaviour of some perpetrators is hardly a secret, the #MeToo campaign — built on unprecedented levels of support and sharing between women — has revealed that despite the extent of the harassment problem in workplaces, and the fact women have spoken up, it has been incredibly difficult to get complaints taken seriously. A US report notes:

> ... when women told *The Washington Post* about their alleged experiences with Alabama Senate candidate Roy Moore, they said it was well-known that he was a regular visitor to the local mall, where young girls were advised through the whisper network to hide themselves when the former judge roamed.[129]

The wave of online campaigns has raised those whispers into a shout, because the process of women finding their voice always needed to include a vital ingredient: being heard.

It makes a huge difference when your voice or testimony isn't penalised, of course. Until recently, such examples of women's solidarity were deeply appreciated, but generally kept confidential because of the backlash that often occurs when women do step up for each other.

Collective impact

Part of the individual motivation for the participants of #CelebratingWomen was, in fact, adding their voice to others to ensure maximum impact. The appeal of joining a collective made Dr Muneera Bano (profile #553) send in her profile because she wanted to be part of a movement to combat the denigration of women on social media:

> I found that having people who openly express positive thoughts and opinions matters a lot to cancel the negativity on social media. Building a community of women who volunteer to support other women (whether expressing opinions or actually taking actions) can make the cyber world a better place for women.

For Melissa Pouliot (profile #674), the incentive to join was about paying back the support she herself had received:

> Since I started my own media company when I was in my late twenties (after having my first child in 2000), the first of its kind in regional Victoria, I have been fortunate to have some incredible women mentor me along the way. In the 18 years since I have been given incredible opportunities by women, all of whom I still keep in touch with. They have believed in me,

nurtured me, encouraged me, challenged me and taken me outside my comfort zone. Most importantly, they have made me believe in myself.

The shared power of the group can help in practical workplace interventions, too. As seen in chapter 2, women comparing details about their pay can identify anomalies. Writing about pay negotiations, journalist Georgina Dent (profile #128) noted the way Sheryl Sandberg's *Lean In* suggests women:

> ... refer to the collective efforts of the team in their business case because it demonstrates their regard for organisational relationships. This can neutralise the backlash that can be associated with women asking for more. It is why she also advises women to explain that they are negotiating for a higher salary because women in general are often paid less than men. She says it shows concern for all women, not just themselves.[130]

As Georgina explains, it's a shame women still have to modify their behaviour due to backlash from stereotypes, but sometimes change is about pragmatism.

The more story-telling among and about all kinds of women, the better. It has had a very real impact by showing to business leaders and institutions both the potential of women, and the barriers they still face. And it helps in shifting social norms about the value women bring, as Australia's Sex Discrimination Commissioner Kate Jenkins (profile #466) says:

> We are getting better data and stories, and it's more accessible through social media. The stories are so important to stop complacency and to ensure

workplaces understand the real experience of women, and the opportunities for progress that remain.

The lack of obvious leadership models and women in authority at all levels in many workplaces has been highlighted by #CelebratingWomen's abundant supply of them. Lots of women have been playing a role in making this powerhouse visible — and encouraging others by celebrating their achievements loudly, often, and publicly.

UK-based Bijna K. Dasani (profile #81) has been presenting a series of videos, for a mentoring-on-the-go app called Cajigo, to encourage women into leadership, and help them set and develop their goals. The first video was released on International Women's Day 2018 at Amazon's London headquarters. Simultaneously, Bijna has also been co-presenting a 'Women in Business' TV show, produced by an Australian serial entrepreneur. 'These are small incremental components that attribute to some significant greater milestones and changes across my circles,' she says.

Empowering capable women in leadership roles provides tangible role models, participant Megan Welch (profile #420) says. But while she understands the need for such visibility in the workplace, this shouldn't come at the expense of women by treating them as tokens, or spotlighting them to boost corporate diversity credentials:

> I feel artificially promoting young women (by using them extensively in advertising campaigns where they appear older, or in roles other than that they hold in the company) can undermine their own worthwhile achievements.

The impact has been discernible at senior levels, too, Holly
Ransom (profile #90) believes:

> It's built up a community of people you feel you can
> reach out to and get advice from — women I deeply
> admire and respect. In board situations, it feels like
> you are on your own, but there's broader support now,
> and we are part of a bigger movement and get the
> benefit of not feeling isolated. Even though it will
> take a long time for parity to catch up, it's important
> knowing there is a community of female leaders
> going about advocating this day in and day out;
> it's collective courage.

A matter of policy

Powerful teams of women have been leading key changes in
policy, too. For decades, Catherine has called regularly on the
gender and work expertise of Professor Marian Baird, and more
recently her colleague Professor Rae Cooper (profile #173),
both at Sydney University Business School. In 2005 Marian
managed to get $5000 to start up her Women and Work
Research Centre to focus on pulling together research on core
issues in the area:

> I was looking around and thought there are a lot of
> people doing great research at Sydney University with
> little opportunity for collaboration. You do this sort
> of thing on top of your job — you never get paid for
> the time it takes. I was determined to get it going

because there was a need for it. Then we brought
the practitioners together and the debate influencers.

The name was changed to the Women Work and Leadership
Research Group, and Rae became involved as a co-director
after Marian encouraged her to join:

> We were working together anyway and would talk to
> each other and build alliances. Rae has tremendous
> energy for creating change. It was a good example
> within the academic community of women really
> supporting each other and using that to drive the
> policy debate.

The work by the group was instrumental in gathering enough
support to finally succeed in creating Australia's first national
paid parental leave scheme, introduced in 2011. Says Rae:

> I think the reason it was successful was the network
> Marian pulled together across really different
> disciplines, and the impact that had on the paid
> parental leave debate. They were the intellectual
> driving force that had a massive impact. She had the
> intellectual respect to do that, and the capacity to
> pull together policy makers, trade unionists, senior
> businesswomen and workers, and it created
> momentum. And it was Marian's voice.

It's a fitting tribute from another woman who has herself
been a significant leader in research and thinking about
women's workforce participation. Rae also credits Marian
with handing on plenty of good counsel over the years. These

joint efforts are about shared success and effectiveness when women are at the helm in addressing problems they have in-depth knowledge about. Encouraging women to collaborate on issues that matter to them can move mountains, as Rae and Marian's experience confirms.

And Holly Ransom (profile #90) sees the effect these shared efforts and leadership are having on a new generation of women. There's a tangible shift in attitude from younger women who are finding their voices and crucial female role models through this community and in a medium they feel comfortable using, says Holly. 'I see it in young women who I mentor and the questions they are asking.'

Being heard

The clout of collective campaigns may have double benefit for women struggling to be heard. We know that women have always joined networks, as the history of female solidarity makes clear. What has been shifting recently, thanks to social media campaigns, hasn't been the calibre or enthusiasm of women who participate, but the fact that they may be listened to, their influence recognised, and their advice taken seriously. At last. From our years in the workplace, if there's one thing we both know it's the importance of not just using your voice, but ensuring it is heeded. It's no easy task for many women, and comes with extra hurdles and a sometimes-hostile reception.

A woman lawyer once told Catherine she was asked by a male colleague to talk more quietly in the office because her voice reminded him of his wife. And most women have a story about offering a suggestion in a meeting to little reaction, only to have it repeated by a man who gets a pat on the back. At a launch event for her book *Stop Fixing Women*, Catherine spoke to an audience with just one man attending. He then dominated the question session by explaining in excruciating detail what he knew about women in the workplace until he was asked to let someone else speak (this syndrome is commonly known as 'mansplaining' and can apply to any topic, including how it feels to be a woman). He didn't seem to appreciate the paradox of dominating such a discussion, and certainly didn't like being told politely to put a sock in it.

The clout of collective campaigns may have double benefit for women struggling to be heard. We know that women have always joined networks, as the history of female solidarity makes clear. What has been shifting recently, thanks to campaigns such as #CelebratingWomen, hasn't been the calibre or enthusiasm of women joining these groups, but the fact that finally these groups may be listened to, their influence recognised, and their advice taken seriously.

Numerous studies have found women are routinely interrupted and speak less than their male colleagues in meetings. As *New York Times* journalist Marie Tessier points out, 'women take up just a quarter to a third of discussion time where policy is discussed, and decisions made, except when they are in the majority'.[131]

The common default explanation for this lack of women's voices is poor confidence. But Tali Mendelberg, a Princeton University professor and co-author of *The Silent Sex: Gender, Deliberation, and Institutions*,[132] published in 2015, found it's not that simple. Women are often confident of their views — but they're not confident that what they have to say is valued, and that in turn shapes how willing they are to speak, and what is discussed. Society signals that the domains of power are still reserved for men, Professor Mendelberg says; women speak more and express their opinions when the group signals that it welcomes their voices. She adds:

> It also helps when the group uses a lot of positive interjections. This creates a group dynamic of mutual acceptance that allows everyone to express what's really on their minds with less fear of social rejection.[133]

Research has also shown that women have often been penalised for talking about their achievements, and aren't seen as being as accomplished as their male peers, notes an article in *Quartz*.[134]

As the article points out, back in 1949, Simone de Beauvoir wrote in *The Second Sex* about how:

> … the *woman* must ceaselessly earn a confidence *not* initially granted to her: at the outset she is suspect; she has to prove herself. *If* she is any good, she will, people say. But worth is *not* a given essence: it is the result of a favourable development.[135]

And there is still an 'insistence that women provide ample proof of their skill before we trust that they know what they're talking about, combined with the presupposition that men belong and are capable until proven otherwise.'[136]

Being listened to and respected are key factors that can make women feel more confident their views are valued. 'Women and the Future of Work', a major Australian study of more than 2000 working women aged under 40 years released in early 2018,[137] found less than half the women surveyed said they had the capacity to be heard and have an influence at work, and 56% felt valued at work. About two-thirds reported being respected at work, although 80% placed most value on having a job where they were respected. While most employees want to be listened to, this was a group who were highly qualified and keen to be involved.

Collaborating once again, Professors Rae Cooper and Marian Baird, two of the study's authors, told us women realise they have shared problems around having children and in workplaces, and were not having their voices heard. While the participants were not asked specifically about support from other women, they talked about good and bad bosses and that older men could be a challenge. 'There's a real sense of a good boss who "gets it" about what women need, and the desire to be valued and heard,' Rae adds.

IAG's Suzanne Young (profile #245) has picked up a few tactics that can help ensure your voice cuts through. She is much more strategic these days about where she sits in a meeting, and tells other women to do the same — think about your role in the meeting, and the best place you can be in, who you sit next to for relationship building, and even discussing other things outside the core meeting agenda that you need to catch up on. Also think about how you can leverage others in the meeting for support, and where you need to be to be in the flow of the conversation. But when it comes to being heard, she has found the direct approach is best:

> I was the only woman in a finance leadership team
> meeting and a particular man would frequently talk
> over the top of me, even when I was presenting. So
> in one meeting, in mid-stream when he interrupted
> again, I said 'Stop, I have not finished speaking' and
> stuck my hand up like a stop sign! He apologised later

and said he didn't realise he kept interrupting me and he didn't do it again.

As she points out, another woman (or man) in the meeting could have drawn attention to his interruption, which would have also been effective.

Practice makes perfect

#CelebratingWomen was an exercise in female empowerment that quickly caught on because it created a platform for women to articulate their value, demonstrate pride in their accomplishments and inspire others, says Kate Barker, Vice President and Global Diversity & Inclusion Fellow for the multinational software company SAP, who first came across the campaign in October 2017:

> I believe [#CelebratingWomen] is so ground-breaking because it demonstrates what starts small as the voices of local community of talented women can quickly become a global tribe of hundreds of thousands of inspiring women, overcoming fears and sharing their own stories to create real change and is new territory.

The campaign, which gave women the opportunity to contribute and hone their stories, has helped influence the agenda within SAP, which has its own business women's network, with 60 chapters globally and 10,000 women involved across the company. It is open to men, and when the Singapore network recently announced a mentoring scheme, 20% of the participants were male. To push it faster and further,

Barker says they are looking at how women are supporting women globally, and the role this plays in motivating others.

While the company has 25% women in leadership, there is still some way to go, but Kate is an optimist and says the actions of a few can create a butterfly effect. And she can attest to the power of women's networks, having received support from leading women during her own career:

> As a Gen X I'm very grateful to women before me who have worked hard and created the opportunities we have now — they are the trailblazers and have given us greater opportunities now to secure senior leadership positions.

Participant Georgie Somerset (profile #703) says she helps give women opportunities to learn and practise their skills, by being a confidential sounding board, which along with regular mentoring, helps provide some 'scaffolding' for emerging and established leaders.

Catherine Cahill (profile #354) found putting her profile into the campaign made her think about practising, more than just providing, support:

> I always felt that I was a 'supporter' of women, but I have now included a focus on 'celebrating' what we do. I encourage other women to celebrate our successes — which they usually immediately minimise — and then I ask them again to take the positive feedback on board and be proud of it.

Cracking the confidence myth

Women's enthusiastic tweeting challenges the idea that the best way to be heard is to sign up for another confidence building workshop. As the various online campaigns of 2017 show, despite the trolling, social media has paradoxically provided a forum where women have increasingly felt they are heard and valued without their views being moderated or shut down. Yet the blunt assumption that all women lack a crucial confidence gene has been pervasive, despite increasing analysis showing a different story.

The reliance on this thinking to explain workplace inequity recycles a tired rationale that women are responsible for their own marginalisation once they walk through the door to paid work (wrangling a toddler or bargaining at a market requires plenty of confidence, which most women seem to effortlessly exhibit).

Efforts to fix the confidence bypass have spawned reams of well-intentioned advice, which has been increasingly popular as women streamed into paid work, only to hit the glass ceiling. Blaming women for an unfortunate innate lack of skill and aptitude is much easier and less confrontational than blaming messy, upsetting sexism and bias in organisations designed by and for a male breadwinner.

The collective women's campaigns, where thousands and thousands of women around the world joined together to show their strength, have done more than scupper the Queen Bee, by managing to also deal a heavy blow to the female confidence myth. Stepping up with purpose and courage to join a social movement wasn't the result of an overnight injection of confidence serum for most women. It was the creation of a safe place where their efforts were seen and valued that triggered these gutsy efforts. While many women recognised the impact of imposter syndrome when they first heard about #CelebratingWomen, they overcame it fairly quickly when they felt the conditions and company were right.

It became evident that women apparently suffering from a lack of confidence have often been using coping behaviour to deal with tough environments and double standards, while being also fully aware they had strong skills and qualifications.

Having their profile celebrated and inspiring others has allowed that pride and confidence to surface. Leith Mitchell (profile #49) says seeing women achieve so much disrupted the myth that women are not confident or there is a confidence gap. As Catherine often tells women at speaking events, the best way to boost anyone's confidence is not to berate them for a perceived weakness, but focus on their strengths and what they have achieved.

Answering the four questions for #CelebratingWomen had a similar impact on the women involved by reminding them that what they had done mattered. At IAG, an internal program that highlighted women and their careers also made women feel more valued and included. It's not the answer to the bias that riddles rules and practices in organisations, but it offers a potential way of mitigating the potent messages that make women feel excluded.

How any woman can amplify

From the moment we started researching and writing this book, we uncovered a goldmine of information on how every woman can build on the support she already offers others. And it snowballed. We discovered almost daily evidence of how women were taking it to the next level at work, at home, with friends and in the community. And while #CelebratingWomen was simply one example of using social media to amplify others, there are much more straightforward, personal and simple ways women can have the same impact on the women around them.

Any woman, we found, can amplify another's contributions by backing them up and repeating their points in meetings and conversations. But it doesn't stop there. We can all draw attention to the input and impact of women, from helping a neighbour to coming up with new ideas for the school community. The more women use these examples of mutual support, the more they get repeated and appreciated.

Any woman can make it a mission to celebrate what women are doing around them whenever they can. A retweet or a 'like' on social media takes seconds, but packs a punch and inspires others to do the same. And a simple text to another woman when the chips are down to let her know you have her back can make the world of difference.

Any woman can make a point of spreading the word about the often unpaid work they do in setting up and maintaining networks with colleagues, groups or friends. In workplaces, women can compare notes on their pay or progression, and make sure their networks move in from the sidelines and are acknowledged and properly funded.

And they can go as a group, using their organisational connections, instead of undertaking risky individual lobbying to get change happening — through gender pay-gap audits or identifying bias in recruitment and promotion, and tackling bystander behaviour.

Any woman can make a point of recommending women for new opportunities or connections whenever they see a chance.

And when women benefit from a referral, they can immediately pay it back by doing the same thing for someone else.

Any woman can write about these support systems and sow the seeds for more action: using local newsletters, online forums, in workplace updates — wherever and however the message can be spread.

And any woman can show her gratitude to the women around her for their support. They can challenge the putdowns about 'ladies who lunch' or 'girls' coffee mornings' by having more of them and proudly spelling out why they keep many of us sane and mentally robust.

Any woman can hold a 'manless dinner' (or morning tea or lunch), and tell the women around the table why they matter and how to pass on the goodwill. And they can be gratified rather than embarrassed that they often build personal connections across all sorts of boundaries, in and out of their workplace, geographically and through shared interests.

The scope and impact of what women, together, are showing they can do is fast becoming a powerhouse for social change. It is rapidly overturning traditional ideas about power, decision-making and who is in charge.

And it has profound implications for those at the top.

7

LESSONS FOR LEADERS

#CelebratingWomen's original aim had little to do with offering guidance on how to be a leader or tackling workplace diversity. This is, after all, well-trodden territory. But posting hundreds of women's profiles and speaking at a wide range of corporate events, combined with her hands-on experience as a CEO and company board director, revealed a new picture to Kirstin of the campaign's impact on gender dynamics in workplaces. As the year progressed, more people began taking notice of this alternative approach, and what it could mean for employers and leaders everywhere: leaders of all kinds of organisations, women and men, who were looking at what was happening and wondering what it meant for the future.

The campaign uncovered the efforts and contributions by women in all walks of life, which until then had been largely unacknowledged. The simple process of recognising women as role models online dispelled many of the negative stereotypes that had kept them in the shadows, and revealed the tenacity of traditional ideas about who makes the best boss.

The enthusiasm from hundreds of women who grabbed the platform to showcase their experience proved they were not deficient in chutzpah or aspiration, or innately bitchy. Many already knew what could be done through collaboration to make workplaces fairer. And international shared activism means the powerful are listening like never before — offering leaders, both men and women, a major opportunity to learn from the compelling lessons of women's support.

What does a leader look like?

For many of us, the idea of a leader still conjures up an image of a powerful man. When a high-profile woman displays exactly the same qualities — decisiveness, risk taking, ambition — she is often pilloried because she doesn't conform to female stereotypes. When a personality test early in her career revealed Kirstin had many of the qualities associated with masculine leaders, her first reaction was dismay at being 'found out', as she had tried hard to disguise those qualities. Facebook executive Sheryl Sandberg has written about being labelled 'bossy', which is clearly not a compliment, and led a campaign to ban the word, which is so often used to denigrate girls and women.[138]

And bias affects us all. Both men and women tend to draw a male figure when asked to picture a leader, according to a 2018 report on US research.[139] When we 'process information through the lens of stereotype', our interpretation may be 'consistent with stereotyped expectations, rather than objective reality,' explains Nilanjana Dasgupta, a Professor of Psychological and Brain Sciences at the University of Massachusetts. 'When people are consistently exposed to leaders who fit one profile, they will be more likely to notice leaders who fit that same profile in the future.' Overcoming this problem means seeing more women as leader-like and, of course, in leadership positions.

Even today, women's leadership remains largely invisible. This vacuum can be traced back to the ancient world, as UK classics academic and historian Mary Beard points out in her book *Women & Power: A Manifesto*.[140] Challenging this stranglehold in the collective thinking about power and leaders — which she notes has meant we are doing without critical expertise from half the population — requires more than telling women to lower their voices and fit into the existing model, which is already 'coded as male'.[141] She suggests it requires a new way of defining power, by 'thinking collaboratively about the power of followers and not just leaders',[142] and treating power as an attribute rather than as a possession.

> What I have in mind is the ability to be effective,
> to make a difference in the world and the right to be
> taken seriously together as much as individually. It is
> power in that sense that many women feel they don't
> have — and that they want.[143]

The reason we want more women in power, Professor Beard adds, is because:

> ... we simply cannot afford to do without women's expertise, whether it is in technology, the economy or social care.[144]

Women have often had no choice but to lead in a different way to men — with many positive outcomes. This alternative style hasn't been a function of biological predisposition to kindliness or collegiality, but due to a long exclusion from traditional power structures, says Alyse Nelson, the CEO of Vital Voices Global Partnership:

> Restricted access to resources has made ingenuity a matter of survival for many; frustration with impenetrable oligarchies and inherited bureaucracies has instilled the value of transparency and creative, practical thinking in others. Women have been forced to operate from outside closed networks, which means they've had to adapt by creating their own worlds; they've learned to unite peripheral, disenfranchised communities into collectively organised and governed microcosms.[145]

She adds that the World Bank's 2012 World Development Report found:

> ... women with decision-making power accelerate positive development outcomes, and studies from the World Economic Forum confirm a strong correlation between an increase in gender equality and an increase in gross domestic product per capita.[146]

Out in the community, women have always been leaders. Quentin Bryce, Australia's first female Governor-General, saw women constantly stepping in to lead community movements and lobby for childcare and health outcomes. She remembers the role model her mother provided when she was growing up in rural Queensland, and was surrounded by many women leaders in the community.

The upside to this shared style of leading is becoming clearer. The models aren't new — management literature has long extolled the virtues of distributed, diffuse and collaborative leadership, which operates across ranks, and through uniting people towards common goals. It's the opposite of rigid 'command and control' leading. Women are often seen as 'better' at this style because it fits with female stereotypes, yet working collaboratively usually also happens to deliver better sustained results — if given the chance.

Of course, much still remains to be done to tackle the formidable structural impediments for women in political and business leadership, former Prime Minister of New Zealand Helen Clark told a conference in early 2018. Despite progress in many places, glass ceilings remain, and women in leadership positions globally are still a rare commodity. There are many proven ways of breaking through those glass ceilings. Addressing basic structural issues is a precondition, says Helen Clark — women can't even get near the glass ceilings if they are denied equality and protection under the law, and cannot determine their own destiny.[147] This is where leaders, men and women, currently holding the power to change the norms and structures, play such a crucial role.

To sustainably change leadership norms requires a mainstream shift in gender beliefs and attitudes. This cannot rest on women's shoulders alone — no matter how adept women are at garnering and leveraging support for each other. As Hillary Clinton told an audience of nearly 7000 in Sydney when she appeared with former Australian Prime Minister Julia Gillard:

> The research shows the more successful a man becomes, the more people like him. But for women it's the exact opposite. Women are seen favourably when we advocate for others, but unfavourably when we advocate for ourselves.[148]

Delivering the goods

It can be exhilarating, nevertheless, to hear directly how a woman's different leadership style works in practice. Christina Matthews, CEO of the Western Australia Cricket Association, told an audience in Perth for the 2018 Australian Women's Leadership symposium that for her, leading was all about watching and learning what *not* to do. As a woman in a very male-dominated sector, she saw how an authoritarian and adversarial approach didn't get the best outcomes. She decided she didn't need to do the job that way and took a more collegiate path, changed the format of events, and started asking more women to functions and featuring women speakers. When she stepped into her role, the WACA was the 'biggest boys club' in Perth, but she refused to be bullied out of a role she loved, using a cohort of strong women in the local community for advice and counsel. Under her leadership, the organisation's revenue grew from $24 million in 2012, with $38 million in revenue expected in 2019.

The variety of leaders and role models reflected in #CelebratingWomen also challenges deeply embedded ideas about who can lead — and whether it must be an individual enterprise. As the campaign snowballed during 2017, so too did the interest in its effect. It was a lightning rod for celebrating diverse examples of success, says one avid follower, Dr Darren Saunders, Associate Professor of Medicine at the University of New South Wales. #CelebratingWomen was a simple but incredibly effective way to give a voice to women performing in all spheres of life. He saw the qualities reflected in these women — vision, determination, originality, creativity, empathy — as universally human, resonating equally with men and women. Importantly, he says, they showed a uniquely female context to leadership. When we are so accustomed to our loudest voices and leaders being male, it was refreshing to hear insights from a female perspective.

Organisational leaders motivated to address gender inequity could see the potential of an inclusive shared power model. Several found the strength of the campaign an eye opener, saying it provided further proof of the need to move beyond worn-out arguments about women's lack of skills and ambition. For some, there was strong validation for their work in fostering diversity and confronting backlash. For many, it has dragged the issue of gender at work further into the mainstream, and offered evidence that redefining and opening the path to leadership is the actual problem, not the supply of women.

Timing is everything

The assumption that the lack of women in executive ranks would simply resolve itself has been upended in recent years, according to Kathryn Fagg, Reserve Bank board member and President of Chief Executive Women (CEW). A wealth of research (some commissioned by CEW) documents how many qualified women are failing to reach senior jobs at the same pace as men, because of bias and adherence to the sexist norms used to define 'merit'. Having been deeply involved in efforts to boost women's leadership for many years, Kathryn knows that business attention to breaking down barriers is cyclical. But for that to change, leaders need to step up and get involved — and that means men, too. Thankfully, many male leaders are recognising what's needed to bring about change, Kathryn adds.

One example of how to get leaders to talk to each other and find ways of addressing the problem emerged from a CEW program called the CEO Conversation, where members discuss how to make progress towards gender equality with the top team of various organisations. As a direct result of this particular conversation at a professional services firm, the company implemented a formal sponsorship program for women, which a few years later saw an increase in female leaders. Kathryn says the success of this example came down to leaders saying, 'Here's a few things to make a difference'; the really big step is for senior leaders to engage, to measure and review what they are doing, and take note of what the top team looks like.

The campaign reminded Kathryn that leading change doesn't need to be complicated. It needs to be *accessible* — and timing is pivotal.

Really, who would have guessed this era made things easier because people are thinking it's intolerable to go backwards? And there's a real threat of that. It's

so important to see women in leadership roles
across the community being effective. We do want
a different leadership model.

The unfolding social movements have created a moment,
Kathryn says, and now we need to run with it.

Pressure from waves of activism — as well as reporting
measures such as the UK's gender pay gap legislation (which
requires organisations with over 250 employees to publish the
average salary and bonuses of male and female employees) —
has put more onus on leaders to act, says UK gender specialist
Avivah Wittenberg-Cox.[149] In this brave new world of
transparency, many don't feel equipped to lead through this
kind of publicity, and the issues surrounding gender in business
are complex. However, smart corporate leaders will minimise
the risk to their brands and reputations through strategic and
skilled management.

The good news is, according to Libby Lyons, the Director
of Australia's Workplace Gender Equality Agency, we are seeing
more organisations take action to address gender equality.
According to Libby:

Through annual employer reporting, Australia is
building a gender equality dataset that is the envy of
the world for the breadth and depth of insights it can
deliver. The clearest insight is this: that when it comes
to workplace gender equality, good intentions are not
enough. After all, employers generally do not set out
to purposely pay women less or stymie their careers.

Workplace cultures and practices, however, have not kept up with the pace of social change, she says:

> Unless employers actively and systematically set out to remove barriers to genuine gender equality in the workplace, the data tells us that pay gaps and under-representation of women in senior roles will persist. Systematic change in organisations requires data and evidence, a strong internal business case, support for flexible working for women and men, and leadership accountability that must be driven by the board and executive team.

Business leaders simply can't afford to ignore the pressure for transparency across society. Recent movements such as #MeToo have had a dramatic effect on uncovering inappropriate behaviour that has been long overlooked, says financier, philanthropist and senior company director Simon Mordant — and while there is always a risk that community sentiment can sometimes swing too far, business leaders would be wise to take note. Change is needed, he says, and starts from the top, so boards need to reflect the community and their customer base, which means addressing issues around gender and cultural diversity.

There has already been a discernible change in the way diversity and leadership are being discussed in workplaces, says Jacqui McGill (profile #66), head of BHP's Olympic Dam, which is South Australia's largest mine, with 3500 employees. Watching the #CelebratingWomen snapshots showed how many women were leading under the radar:

> I think often women are out there doing a range
> of things, but are invisible, and young women don't
> know. But they need to know they can have a job
> and family, and your life is yours to define.

In organisations, there is a new legitimacy around the topic,
adds Jacqui:

> I've been engaging people in the conversation for
> some time — it might be #MeToo and the women's
> movement — and it's easier for women to discuss and
> engage on feminist issues than before. It's in the
> paper and we can talk about it. It started to make us
> think about it. I found that there are really interesting
> conversations around the water cooler and they have
> broader participation. And it's at senior levels.

In the broader business community there's a different
conversation among leaders, too. In late 2017 Jacqui attended
a women and leadership forum, not long after allegations over
inappropriate behaviour had seen a high-profile partner at a
local professional services firm stood down. A senior partner
from the firm was speaking that day, and had a conversation
with Jacqui in which he was clearly concerned and candid
about what had happened, and the need to address the
problem, which Jacqui applauded. That simply wouldn't have
happened two years before, she says, and was so different to
the 'don't say anything' attitude of the past. 'When you see
senior male leaders step up and do that, they can't just do the
lip service anymore,' she adds. As it happened, the woman who
had experienced the harassment was also at the event and
made it clear she had nothing to be ashamed of, which also

impressed Jacqui, and makes her hopeful that the shame that's been attached to speaking out about such issues has receded.

BHP has undergone a radical change in its diversity strategy, declaring a goal of having women make up half its workforce of about 65,000 employees by 2025. It's a big challenge, Jacqui admits:

> But I've got a gender-balanced leadership team — you only have to ask your head hunter once and they will put [women] on the list and you never have to ask again. It's to get very rare individuals, and it's amazing the difference it makes. People say you can't find them, but you can.

While other barriers remain, the validation of women from more mainstream recognition and online campaigns is not about to disappear, says Jacqui:

> I'm very optimistic. What I see is women's support and better conversations in business around ethics and behaviour — that's the piece we look at to create a different world. But we can't forget there are many pockets that will be slow to change.

The mere process of asking questions was often enough to force difficult conversations and provide the impetus for change, suggests diversity champion and Associate Professor of Medicine at UNSW, Dr Darren Saunders — but leadership is also about fostering an environment in which those questions can be asked. Listening to ideas, and resourcing and supporting those driving change, are key.

How organisational networks operate

Understanding the dynamics of an organisation, and the interactions between men and women throughout the business, are crucial for any leader. An Australian HR tech company uncovered astounding results when it ran an 18-month study of feedback between 650 staff in a UK professional services firm with a relatively equal gender split (45% women, 55% men).

Like so many stories in this book, it came to light through Twitter, in a thread discussing the power of women supporting women. Kirstin came across a tweet from David Perks, the CEO of Pay Compliment, which measures culture and other dynamics, and conducted the study. David had tweeted an image of the results, Kirstin was intrigued, and phoned him the next morning to understand more.

The research[150] by David's company found that women's networks within the UK professional services firm operated four times more effectively than men's. Or more specifically, that women demonstrated four times the propensity to share feedback with other women compared to any other gender combination (women sharing feedback with men, men sharing feedback with men, or men sharing feedback with women). While anyone who has attended a women's networking event will not be surprised at this result, the magnitude of the variation was surprising.

Another compelling finding from the research, which has clear implications for leaders, was the effect of seniority when combined with gender. Women will provide feedback up, down and across all levels of the organisation to other women, and from the most senior female leaders to the most junior women in the firm. In contrast, men followed a strict hierarchy in their feedback interactions with other men, and there was not a single occasion where feedback from one male went more than one level up in the organisation, or more than one level down. Interestingly, men did show a much greater propensity to interact with less senior women, while women tended to initiate feedback generally only with male peers.

Another significant finding for leaders was that women used different language when giving feedback. When providing feedback to men, women tended to use affirming language, which reinforced a fixed mindset of 'confidently powering through'. When providing feedback to women, more celebratory language was used, with greater undertones of a growth mindset, of flexibility, and of overcoming adversities to get results.

The research highlights that leaders need to better understand the gender dynamics at play within organisations. And there is an opportunity for women to provide feedback to men at all levels — which rarely happens because most women limit their feedback to other women — and for men to provide feedback throughout different levels to both men and women.

Stop fixing, start promoting

Leaders can use this kind of information to provide much-needed encouragement and improve promotion opportunities for women. A simple imperative to emerge from the recent reboot of the women's rights movement and its impact on the workplace is the necessity to have more women in decision making, in all kinds of institutions.

Women have the skills, and given the right environment are happy to own their achievements — and they are leveraging their connections for impact like never before. But this new era of transparency has only come about because there have finally been some women in positions of power to lead the charge. Women are increasingly bypassing the blockages and the old boys' club, and as this book clearly shows, are using their own networks and support to advance their careers. But it's not enough. Much more needs to be done to more accurately reflect and amplify women's contributions and leadership skills in workplaces.

Until now, the business rhetoric about how to get more women around the table focused on what women need to change to enjoy better outcomes. That could include their name, according to Australian gender researcher and consultant Conrad Liveris. As he told the Australian Broadcasting Corporation in 2018, data on the CEOs and chairs of Australia's largest 200 companies showed that as a captain of Australian business, you are 40% more likely to be named Peter or John than to be female.[151] Straight, white, able-bodied men aged 40–69 years represent the majority of Australian leadership, he explained, yet make up 8.4% of the population. And the number of women in key leadership positions in top companies actually fell in 2017.

The activism unleashed that same year challenges traditional advice on how to change this dismal picture. Women's collective testimony proves that barriers exist — but it's not their job to constantly make the case for change. The focus must move now onto men's behaviour — and their role in supporting and promoting women.

This is not about fixing women, or berating men, but listening to what women have experienced, and investing genuine time and money into boosting the ways women are already collaborating, given that campaigns and networks for women have revealed how effective collective support can be. Many employers have neglected, sidelined or ignored the mechanisms already working under the radar in their own organisations, yet these have the potential to produce better outcomes by drawing upon women's knowledge, referrals and connections. It is time to recalibrate those traditional diversity tools.

Given men are still overwhelmingly in charge of running many organisations, we asked a range of leaders, CEOs and directors about what they were already doing to address the gender gap in their organisations, and the impact of #CelebratingWomen and the wave of women's campaigns on their current efforts and outlook for the future.

When Dr David Cooke, Managing Director of Konica Minolta Australia, and a strong advocate for gender equity, intervenes to address gender imbalances, he always explains why change is needed. He is a Male Champion of Change — a group of Australian leaders committed to seeing more women in leadership, set up by former Sex Discrimination Commissioner, Elizabeth Broderick. When David became the first non-Japanese Managing Director of Konica Minolta in 2013, his aim was to make the business a place where all employees could access the same opportunities. While it is a work in progress, it has become a far more equitable company to work for when measured against age, gender and ethnicity criteria. Of the 150 field service engineers at Konica Minolta, only one was a woman, so the business now seeks to recruit women directly from TAFE. David has also promoted women into senior roles — and understands the need for younger women to see these senior women's careers progressing, realising they, too, can have careers throughout the business.

When asked how he justifies these interventions, David says without women, the company would still be thinking like a bunch of middle-aged white men, and this lack of diverse thinking compromises its ability to compete. His diversity strategies are backed by a strong belief in a core moral and ethical need to change the mix; equally, he believes it is an agenda that is not a 'nice to have', but an imperative. Inclusiveness is more than a buzzword, it's a business necessity, he states.

Banish the bystander

The global online campaigns have been a catalyst for men in leadership to also speak up and call out sexist attitudes. Company director Andrew Stevens, a Male Champion of Change and a member of the Australian Defence Force's Gender Equality Advisory Board, sees the rising tide of activism as a tipping point for change over the next decade:

> Community expectations have moved first, then regulation will follow … The things that were going on in the 80s and 90s it's clear today were totally unacceptable. That's changed and that's a really good thing.

The imperative for men to act, and to avoid bystander behaviour when they see sexism, is a strong driver for Andrew. When he hears old-fashioned sexist attitudes or confusion about the need for change on boards or in discussions, he doesn't hesitate:

> I go in for it and say, 'I don't think that's right'. This is the new normal, and the steps being taken are not going too far. It's about countering everyday sexism,

and once you really listen you know what to do.
When someone says 'women are getting favoured',
I ask what numbers are they looking at? And that
then takes them down a path.

The effect on women from increased awareness has also been galvanising, he adds, with many feeling they have enough 'air cover' and support to go forward with their stories and testimony. His tactics to actively bring about change by directly challenging sceptics shows men talking to men can really make an impact.

Consistently tackling poor behaviour prevents long-term damage from it going unchallenged, says Dr David Cooke. He doesn't let backlash or casual sexism go through to the keeper:

If a person is called on for behaviour early and often,
they get the message. If they are not, there's a licence to
take it further. Every male needs to ask where they draw
the line before they get uncomfortable and outraged,
and the bystander effect. I see that dynamic a lot.

Men in power must step up by setting standards for what is acceptable, he adds, having seen plenty of occasions when 'bystander behaviour' has allowed norms to go unchallenged.

Leaders play a key role in tackling the tricky area of casual sexism, too. At a Sydney panel discussion on inclusivity in 2017, Catherine met Gavin Fox-Smith, a senior regional executive with Johnson & Johnson, and another Male Champion of Change. He spoke about the informal sexism among some of his friends due to stubborn social gender norms. While he said it was a tough issue to tackle with friends you have known for most of your life, as a business leader you can take action to change the picture — and that's what leaders are there for:

> #MeToo shows the bias, and you would have to be
> a Neanderthal to think there is not an issue — but I
> think there are people who don't see that. A man who
> worked for me, when a woman was appointed to a
> senior role, said 'I'm obviously the wrong sex.' I wasn't
> prepared to let that go, and didn't want him to think
> I am sympathetic to that view. But I needed to
> reinforce the reasons the woman got the job. Some
> people can't get their heads around the fact that
> a woman cannot get a job because she is female.
> I struggle to understand it. But we have busted the
> myth of who can be a senior executive.

Gavin has seen the support among women in his own workplace — after announcing the appointment of the new woman executive, nearly all the responses were from women employees delighted by the news. And he found the leadership displayed in the #CelebratingWomen profiles inspiring, particularly as they bridged the gap between very privileged lives and those in developing countries.

While progress like this is definitely being made, Gavin still regularly encounters push-back on diversity measures such as ensuring there are women on recruitment lists and interviewing panels, and using inclusive language when posting job descriptions. But that certainly hasn't stopped his efforts.

Taking stock

For leaders keen to make a difference, taking stock of progress brings perspective and clarity on what still needs to change to ensure better sustained outcomes. Given the rhetoric in business about embracing innovation and disruption in the digital age, it's surprising to encounter conversations about gender that hark back to the way things were 'always' done, and the need to adhere to traditional concepts of merit when it comes to advancing women.

Company director Ming Long (profile #468) says the dinosaurs in leadership need to go, and is concerned they are setting an example and role-modelling to younger leaders. Some men on boards have never had to think about having women share equal power, Ming believes, and their inability to adapt to change or deal with disruption to see new ways of doing things has left them like rabbits in the headlights. Many women meanwhile are consistently rising up and showing they have great capability — as #CelebratingWomen made clear. Women's lives have changed significantly in most parts of the world in recent decades, but there's been far less of a shift in workplace norms.

There have been some key steps forward. Two decades ago, for example, the absence of women around a board table simply wasn't an issue, says Peter Warne, Chair of Macquarie Group Limited, as it wasn't consciously thought about. One board he was on during the late 1990s was all male, and only after eight years did the Chair decide they needed a woman. While that wasn't unusual then, a lot has changed in 20 years.

That shift, which has been reinforced by the collective voices of women, has led to a growing understanding of what is at stake among many of the business leaders we interviewed. Peter Warne says leaders are realising they need to ask how they can encourage women to join an organisation, and stay with it as they gain experience and become more senior. This includes examining the way people work, and their working conditions — especially long hours, such as working until 10 pm every night.

Quite apart from the moral rationale for a better gender mix, there are sound commercial reasons to reflect what your community and your clients look like, Peter says. These days, you should automatically be seen as less qualified to do a good job for your client if you don't have a diverse team, he adds.

The impact from renewed attention to gender issues is equally apparent to Angus Armour, CEO of the Australian Institute of Company Directors, whose members include some of the country's most influential decision-makers. The big challenge has been creating the momentum and environment where positive conversations about diversity keep radiating out, penetrating into elite business spheres like the Australian Securities Exchange (ASX), he says. The AICD has called for all boards to ensure that 30% of their directors are female and urged ASX 200 companies to meet this new target by the end of 2018, which allows them to measure against a peer group.

On a national basis, Angus observes, it's clear that equality is where our society is going:

> It's a transition in society, and it will be stop-and-start, and require reinforcement to emphasise the impact, which I do see increasing.

The #CelebratingWomen campaign was a healthy sign that there is female leadership at every level, a diverse range of women are collaborating, and it's time to use all this potential, Angus says. And the message is resonating through all kinds of organisations:

> Are leaders listening? Yes. And it's profound. I spend more time convincing, but I'm still optimistic — it's a fundamental, core belief.

Allied forces

When she set up #CelebratingWomen, Kirstin was clear that the campaign was not about men. Although an advocate for programs such as Male Champions of Change — which does so much to ensure leading men in business focus their organisations on diversity issues — they were not her priority. She didn't make a conscious decision to exclude men, they simply didn't factor into her thinking when the idea emerged that day on the beach. This was all about women. By women, for women, supporting women.

That said, the level of support from men for the campaign has been huge, which is crucial — as men, who support women supporting women, can have such a powerful impact.

The men who contacted Kirstin during the campaign wanted to support the women in their lives — whether at home or in the workplace. Male leaders wanted to know how they could encourage women who worked with them to put themselves forward. Fathers said they were showing their daughters the profiles to encourage them to see different role models for their future. Partners would write to Kirstin saying how incredible the women in their lives were and why they deserved to be celebrated. Kirstin's father read every single profile, 'liked' them on Facebook and then talked to her about the ones he'd found particularly fascinating.

The role of men in #CelebratingWomen wasn't about providing a channel for male voices, but in supporting women to have theirs. This made all the difference, and was an important aspect in helping women to support other women and empower themselves.

Since the campaign finished there has been time to analyse how and why it struck a chord, and the implications of its impact. While the commentary at the end of 2017 and into 2018 mostly covered the fallout from #MeToo, both positive and negative, some of it has looked at what men are thinking, and what they see as their role in this social shift — particularly in the world of paid work.

Become allies

Men have a key role to play in shifting the gender balance, according to Kate Jenkins (profile #466), Australia's Sex Discrimination Commissioner:

> The emerging trend is that men have recognised the benefits of gender diversity and started to engage more in the barriers to equality. They now recognise they have a role to play in changing the status quo, a status quo that has delivered them to positions of power. Men can use their position of power and their voice at the grass roots to step up beside women to change workplaces for the better. Even if we have every woman supporting it, we don't have enough in positions of power to pull us all up. Women are being listened to, but even the #MeToo movement shows us that we have needed multiple women to complain about harassment and abuse before their allegations are taken seriously. We need men to notice this, too.

Many men are indeed thinking about their role since the wave of women's campaigns, says Dr Graeme Russell, academic and consultant on diversity, flexibility, fatherhood and leadership. For many years he has been a leading thinker on how to restructure traditional workplaces, introduce flexibility and challenge masculine norms. The reaction from the men he has asked has been of reflection and surprise, and thinking about what they need to do. For Graeme, the lesson was to listen and understand — and to engage in conversations around the kind of behaviour that is acceptable, and the behaviour that isn't.

Besides listening and talking to each other and supporting women, it is crucial that men set standards and role-model to boys. A frequent question parents of boys ask is how they might raise sons to understand the importance of gender equality, says Claire Cain Miller, who consulted neuroscientists, economists, psychologists and others for a *New York Times* article in 2017.[152] Their advice was to provide boys with a range of good, strong role models — both male and female — since 'boys are particularly responsive to spending time with role models, even more than girls'. Boys should also be encouraged to do their fair share of chores, which isn't currently happening. In America, girls aged 10–17 spend 2 hours more on chores each week than boys, and boys are 15% more likely to be paid for doing chores, the article notes.

To raise feminist sons, parents need to teach boys to care for others. This means giving them responsibilities for caregiving — have sons care for pets or younger siblings, or become local babysitters, coaches or tutors. Parents can resist gender roles in childcare, which also means sharing the breadwinning, where possible, between the mother and father. Parents can also teach young sons about respect and consent early in childhood, and teach boys to call out teasing or harassment — and to understand that 'Boys will be boys' is not an excuse for bad behaviour. Finally, raising boys is not all about ruling out gender differences altogether. It is about how to:

> … teach boys to show strength — the strength to acknowledge their emotions. Teach them to provide for their families — by caring for them. Show them how to be tough — tough enough to stand up to intolerance. Give them confidence — to pursue whatever they're passionate about.[153]

Listen up

As #MeToo gathered pace, a number of campaigns have emerged to get men actively involved in change,[154] including #IDidThat, #AskMoreOfMen and #HowIWillChange.

Movements focused on men show a different way of changing gender dynamics and where the onus for action lies, says Dr Graeme Russell. The 2017 report for the Diversity Council he wrote with Dr Michael Flood, *Men Make a Difference: Engaging Men on Gender Equality*,[155] outlined a variety of approaches to reposition gender equality as a core workplace concern, rather than a women's issue. Crafting messages that men will hear is key, while emphasising the role they can play as allies and in talking to other men about the agenda.

The women's campaigns that launched in 2017 have made a difference, Graeme says. But tackling sexism and harassment will need more than a re-education program:

> To me, one of the most powerful things is it's made [sexism and harassment] visible. For those of us who work in organisations, you come across the conversations, but often it's not visible, and people don't make a formal complaint. And that makes me

reflect: is there a way to change the way we go about challenging this? Are the processes in organisations really changing behaviour? And the answer is no.

While it is vital that men listen and learn, a number of myths about where change could emerge also need to be challenged, says Graeme. We can't assume that young men will suddenly transform societal norms and usher in different behavioural codes overnight. Graeme is part of a group called Men Advocating Real Change (MARC), set up by non-profit US research and advocacy firm Catalyst; research has reported that younger men have quite traditional views about gender issues, and do not reflect a major generational shift.[156] Other evidence confirms that age is no guarantee of awareness — Graeme points to reports revealing systemic hazing, bullying and ridiculing by young male students of their women peers (and some men) in university colleges in Australia.[157, 158]

Own it

History reveals an important lesson on how to accelerate social change — by building a case that shows benefits for all, according to Facebook executive Sheryl Sandberg and academic Adam Grant:

> To make gender parity a reality, we need to change the way we advocate for it. The usual focus is on fairness: to achieve justice, we need to give women equal opportunities. We need to go further and articulate why equality is not just the right thing to do for women, but the desirable thing for us all.[159]

Many men who support equality hold back, they suggest, because they worry it's not their battle to fight. 'It's time for men and women alike to join forces in championing gender parity,' they urge.

Everyone has a role to play in supporting gender equality at work, says the director of Australia's Workplace Gender Equality Agency, Libby Lyons. An important way leaders can support women is to give them experience in the operational roles that will help them progress through the leadership pipeline. But men also deserve support in the workplace to be recognised as parents, carers and valuable members of the community outside of their breadwinning role. True gender equality must lead to everyone having the same opportunity to make genuine choices about how they live and work.

Understanding how some men think about gender, both personally and professionally, can also help get more involvement, suggest Dr Graeme Russell and Dr Michael Flood. Men often assume that the men around them support sexism more than they do; some men fear being judged by their male peers if they intervene, and other men simply don't know what to do or say.[160] Men, they point out, are part of the problem and the solution. Their 2017 report includes a number of recommendations, including treating gender inequality as a business issue, educating men about how to take action both in their personal behaviour and in changing rules and practices, and getting men and women involved in initiatives as equal partners.

Dr Darren Saunders, Associate Professor of Medicine at UNSW, says he notices that when men share the message about these issues between themselves it gets attention, whereas messages from women are often ignored or greeted with hostility. He tries to frame the topic in terms that are relevant to men, and show that action doesn't represent a threat to competent men:

> I use language that is familiar, and base my arguments on evidence. Of course, the most effective way of speaking to men is not using words at all, but through action and leading by example.

Male Champions of Change has been addressing systemic responses to #MeToo, and has involved men learning from each other's experiences, says Gavin Fox-Smith. It's not about speaking for women, but getting the system sorted out, because if you don't get commitment from people leading then it will never change, he says. The members of the Male Champions of Change STEM group have each conducted focus groups of their employees, covering issues such as harassment, and have then used the data to formulate strategies.

A number of men we interviewed said there was also a need to change the perception that closing the gender gap is about winners and losers. Fear of loss drives resistance by some men — particularly in the middle management ranks — which often manifests in the complaint, 'you have to be a woman to get ahead'. Making the reason for these appointments crystal clear, as Gavin Fox-Smith did, helps counter this idea.

Act on it

The impact of #CelebratingWomen, and the opportunity for men to support women's advocacy for each other, made Dr Darren Saunders think about his own role and the need to do more. He says his effort had been stereotypically masculine, and directed at solving problems through his own action — demanding and enabling equity at conferences and panels, and on peer review committees, through direct action as an organiser, and by highlighting events or organisations where equity has not been achieved:

> I aim to achieve equal representation of male and female scientists in the science stories I cover on radio, and will usually suggest female colleagues when journalists and producers ask for help finding experts. As a member of the Science & Technology Australia executive, I advocated adoption of best practice in supporting gender equity and diversity in the board appointment process, and supported establishment of the Superstars of STEM program to help raise the profile of women in STEM.

The founder of the Male Champions of Change, former Sex Discrimination Commissioner Elizabeth Broderick, has seen the impact of men legitimising women's own support efforts:

> I went into a global law firm where they brought together all their global female partners and the Managing Partner had made that happen. He had to justify it to the male partners who said, 'Why are we going to the expense of doing that? Why can't they come to the partners meeting?' But women need safe places to come together to discuss and share stories of success and challenges, and how they have navigated and found their way through, and the general partners meeting wasn't a safe place to do that. It was important to have carved out the safe space.

The Managing Partner lent his power and authority to make that happen, and it's why you need powerful men to do just that, Elizabeth explains. Men can make a difference when they listen deeply to women, and that's why Male Champions of Change has its core areas of listen, learn and step up beside women to get to gender equality. They listen to what women need and what kind of support they need, and then men can use their power and influence to make that happen as male allies, she adds.

In the United States, some analysis about men's role in standing together with women after the recent wave of activity has focused on the steps they can take right now. In the post-Harvey Weinstein era, according to Kim Azzarelli and Deanna Bass, men:

> ... are the greatest allies women can have. Time and again we've seen men do the right thing: stand up for women, fire miscreants — and in some instances put women into the leadership roles vacated by men.[161]

US sociologist Michael Kimmel agrees men can take concrete steps to be allies in the wake of #MeToo:

> After decades of accepting sexual harassment as the status quo, we have to take some of the weight off women's shoulders. It's simply not their responsibility alone to talk about and enforce workplace equality. We must call out the sexist behaviours of other men because it's wrong and because it undermines women's confidence and effectiveness in the workplace. This is what it means to be allies, men. To stand up together and do the right thing. We

> know how to do it, and we're good at it most of the
> time. Brotherhood, teamwork, and camaraderie are
> the essence of the fraternity, the foxhole, and the
> sports team. Now we have to learn how to come
> together at work — and on the right side of things.[162]

Men can amplify the voices of women in their companies — in the same way women are doing — by recognising women's contributions and making sure they get credit. Some male leaders make a practice of passing professional opportunities on to women colleagues, such as invitations to speak or participate at conferences. They can also make a difference by alerting others to gender stereotypes.

Another suggestion is to implement the Plus One Pledge, where men at all levels pledge to add at least one woman to their team when roles become available. Significant numbers of men have taken this pledge, resulting in an increase in the number of women in senior roles in participating organisations.[163]

The Hon. Philip Dalidakis, Victorian state government Minister for Trade and Investment, Innovation and the Digital Economy, said it became abundantly clear early in his term that many companies within STEM industries had a problem with gender equality. The issue became personal, he says, as he found himself being challenged around what he would do to fix it. He made a commitment to the 'Panel Pledge', which has led to very practical outcomes for women:

> I won't sponsor a conference that doesn't agree to
> have as a minimum 50% female speakers/panellists.
> We have walked away from one high-profile
> conference that wouldn't agree to meet such gender
> equity measurements, we've challenged some to step

it up under the threat of pulling funding, and have
been pleasantly surprised to hear others publicly
adopt the policy as if it was their own.

Philip says the issue is important to him because leaders need
to start taking action and setting an example:

For some, gender equality on its own speaks for
itself. For others it's acknowledging other forms
of discrimination: sexuality, religious, disability,
socioeconomic, amongst others that we need to
constantly work on to minimise …. It's 2018 and
#MeToo and #Equalpay should not be hashtags,
they should not be things. So, if they are we need
to work twice as hard to change them.

The survey of #CelebratingWomen participants offered other
ideas for engaging men and encouraging them to be allies.
This means addressing the fear of men 'who no longer know
what is acceptable, and are scared to be themselves around
women for fear of offending in some way', suggests Rachel
Scanlon (profile #253).

Let's help raise men's awareness of the systems and norms
at work that are difficult for women, says Monique Beedles
(profile #50):

Most men are individually supportive of women,
but often fail to see how their organisation, or the
system as a whole, might fail women. If they have
not experienced exclusion themselves, they may not
recognise the subtleties of how it manifests.

And amplifying the positive also helps — there are 'plenty of decent men who have been excellent role models and mentors and should be celebrated', points out Jane O'Connell (profile #290).

Even with the momentum from women's social media campaigns, says Cheryl Hickey, who responded to the survey about the impact of the #CelebratingWomen campaign:

> The reality is it's going to be a long, hard road unless husbands, fathers, really step up in a constructive, practical and genuine capacity and support the women in their lives. I don't believe women supporting women can, solely, improve the plight of women globally, and men must make a genuine, long-lasting and meaningful contribution to the cause.

Gender equity progress means combining individual and structural change across society. Swedish commentator Gary Barker suggests we need to stop thinking simply about 'engaging' men, as if it were an end in itself, and to think more about men and women working together — 'resisting, changing, envisioning, and creating societies where social justice thrives'. He adds:

> The most successful force in changing men's attitudes and practices related to gender equality is obvious. It's called feminist activism, or the collective women's rights movements. More than any other social force, policy or program intervention, the collective civil society and political efforts to promote women's empowerment — socially,

politically and economically — are the leading
driver of change in men's attitudes and practices
in terms of gender equality.[164]

We'll know the chance of accelerating progress into success for women's rights, with all its many economic and social benefits, is imminent when men routinely, overtly and enthusiastically join with women and urge them to say more, not less, about this agenda. In the home, the community and, of course, at work.

8

OPPORTUNITIES FOR ORGANISATIONS

Before diversity was even coined as a management term to describe the lack of it in many workplaces, quite a few businessmen and organisational leaders assured us that women just didn't want to climb that notorious ladder or stay in the workforce long term. Had they actually asked women if this was what they wanted? The answer, frequently, was no.

Times have changed of course, and diversity programs are ubiquitous, but the campaign pointed to a much more powerful and effective framework for delivering results, while saving time, money and frustration levels from rocketing. It starts with a simple step: ask women and listen to what they say.

Many popular diversity programs are actually not very popular with employees or bosses. In fact they have proved not only expensive and time-consuming, but actually become part of the problem rather than the solution, by increasing resistance to reducing bias. No wonder there has been an outbreak of what *The Economist* has dubbed 'diversity fatigue' — nominating 12 of the most terrifying words in the English language as: 'I'm from Human Resources, and I'm here to organise a diversity workshop.'[165]

We can relate to that fear. These efforts often seem to miss the mark and only increase irritation levels.

#CelebratingWomen showed there was, in fact, a wealth of successful, inexpensive diversity in action already well underway. Instead of wheeling in a consultant or company trainer spouting those dreaded words about yet another workshop, organisations could benefit from asking more women about what they need, and how women themselves are often working on the fringes to provide support that delivers outcomes. This isn't to suggest any woman can provide 'the answer' — or that the responsibility for change rests only with women, when men make up more than half the workforce and are over-represented in power.

Attention and expertise is, however, needed to draw upon and invest in the work women have done with each other and incorporate it into mainstream business practice.

Organisations have often, in fact, confused being a woman with having gender expertise, points out Australia's Sex Discrimination Commissioner, Kate Jenkins (profile #466). And while employers need to increase the numbers of women in key roles, and gain gender expertise, they are not the same thing. As regular speakers at diversity events, it is clear to us that many women feel confused about the complex topic of tackling inequity, but many feel patronised by the remedial programs they are sent off on, such as confidence-building courses or sessions on how to negotiate. Catherine regularly tells audiences of women that if they can handle a sulking teenager and buy shoes at a sale they already have pretty good negotiating skills. And the same goes for confidence, as we have examined, with many women well aware of their own skills, but reluctant to speak out because of penalties or backlash. And anyway, who decided bombastic, chest-thumping behaviour is the best indicator of whether you are confident?

One factor that bonds many women, however, is irritation at the assumption they can't speak up for themselves or identify opportunities for change. Many of those we interviewed who are running effective women's networks — such as Kimberley Cole at Thomson Reuters and Suzanne Young (profile #245) at IAG — had developed sophisticated, thoughtful approaches to address diversity problems, such as an active and well-financed women's network, which can be a great place to start making headway while affirming and elevating women's experiences. And it seems those classic female 'flaws' disappear in these environments.

Despite significant spending by employers, efforts to address the gender gap in organisations have had varying levels of success. In the United States it is estimated firms spend as much as $8 billion a year on diversity programs and training[166] — but much of the money, analysts have concluded, has been concentrated on raising awareness, rather than skills or action. As US researchers Frank Dobbin and Alexandra Kalev reported in 2016, it isn't surprising that most diversity programs aren't increasing diversity — many companies are relying on outdated approaches used since the 1960s which, they concluded, often make things worse, not better.[167]

The diversity menu that is often relied on includes reducing bias on the job, looking at complaints systems, hiring tests and performance ratings to guide recruitment and promotion, but are 'mostly designed to pre-empt lawsuits by policing' the actions of managers, the researchers explained. However, studies show that this kind of 'force-feeding' can activate bias, rather than stamp it out. As social scientists have found, people often rebel against rules to assert their own autonomy.[168]

Small wins are still wins

The amount of spending and lack of results from many current diversity programs may have also resulted from an understandable, but unrealistic, goal to find the 'right' solution for a complex problem. Along with a team at the Clayman Institute for Gender Research, Stanford Professor of Organisational Behaviour Shelley Correll has come up with a 'small wins' approach to reduce the stereotypic biases that are disadvantaging women in workplaces.[169] Understanding a problem is not enough to generate a shift, and the changes we can realistically make are often small and imperfect:

> I have decided I can live with that. We have to start
> somewhere … We have seen that both unconscious
> bias training and formalised organisational processes
> have led to some decrease in gender biases, and some
> improvements in gender diversity. Yet neither has
> been the great leveller. Bias training can backfire,
> increasing bias; and formal procedures can be
> misused by decision makers or, worse, have gender
> biases built into their design.[170]

Small wins are concrete actions that produce visible results, and have the advantage of being seen as doable by supporters, while often flying under the radar of detractors, Professor Correll explains. It means going beyond training managers, to changing organisational processes — which could involve strategies such as writing clearer promotion criteria or job descriptions that avoid bias.

As one example, Professor Correll says, a tech company introduced training about the double standards that make it difficult for women in leadership to be seen as simultaneously competent and likable.

> A hiring committee at this company had settled on a woman as their top candidate, but when this woman negotiated for a higher salary, the hiring manager said he was 'turned off' by her strong negotiation style, that she seemed 'high maintenance', and, consequently, that he was considering rescinding her offer. A woman who had been at our training saw this reaction as an example of the double bind. She asked the hiring manager to describe how he had negotiated for his job, which led him to see that he was holding the woman to a different standard. This conversation led to the successful hire of the woman candidate and at a higher salary.[171]

Employers can also intervene to give women a different sense of their value and close performance gaps, particularly in male-dominated workplaces. A few years ago, INSEAD Business School addressed the problem of women MBA students consistently lagging behind men in grades. Professor Zoe Kinias:

> ... had all students, male and female, do a written
> exercise to affirm their core values — and managed to
> narrow the grade gap by 89%. While the exercise had
> no effect on men, grades for women MBA's rose to
> men's levels ... The exercise turns out to give women
> 'an invisible shield' against feeling undervalued in
> environments where there are majority men.[172]

The exercise involved incoming students being given a list of
10 values, asked to pick three, and then explain why the values
were important and how they were being implemented in daily
life. It has also been used by a Singaporean bank, with other
organisations interested as well.

Professor Kinias explains:

> Thoughtful introduction of this type of intervention
> has potential to improve gender balance anywhere
> women are under-represented and there are beliefs
> that men are more suited to the job, including
> leadership within competitive global business.[173]

This was particularly true in companies where 'women are
doubting whether they're valued, and they belong, and they're
going to be taken seriously, and they have to work that much
harder to prove themselves,' adds Professor Kinias.[174]

Interventions like this and small wins sound very much like
some of the informal tools women have been using and sharing
through campaigns and in networks — including accessing
career advice tailored by and for women, using connections,
'amplification' and referrals. Some of these tools bypass
roadblocks for women at work, and may even help change
organisational processes, with several #CelebratingWomen

participants encouraged to identify and challenge biased practices in their workplace.

Assessing the impact of the campaign has revealed some specific areas where organisations could reap small wins that can add up to large shifts.

Reframing women's programs

Over the years, we've seen a few of the ubiquitous women's training programs (as distinct from networking groups) in operation — and while they can provide some nuggets of good advice, the framework often hinges on trying to fit women into masculine models of success.

Women are berated for not being tough enough, or conforming to cookie-cutter ideas about professional behaviour, while their own experience and pathways are ignored. Many women have told us they find them far too remedial, and the messaging implies women have never tried to lean in or ask for a pay rise, while ignoring the impact of difficult workplaces and backlash from their male peers.

At one session Catherine attended, women were asked to describe their positive qualities, and it emerged loyalty was near the top. The program convenor told them if an employer wanted loyalty they would get a dog. Not an uplifting message.

Much of the effective work around diversity hasn't been integrated into organisational change processes, so it stays on the periphery, explains researcher Dr Graeme Russell. Women's programs — such as leadership or negotiating workshops — have often been a company box-ticking exercise, so any recommendations or work they produce is generally ignored:

What we haven't done is to listen to the experience
women have in organisations and to legitimise them.
I'm a strong believer it's about men and women
working together to solve organisational problems,
with men listening to women's experiences, and we
don't do that in organisations now. They need to
engage with the evidence base around gender. I think
#CelebratingWomen was very powerful because it's
about doing the positive, and the profiles are open
and out there — so it's taking control. We have to
look for opportunities to change.

Graeme believes there's a need for more open conversations
about the nature of the behaviour within organisations, and to
review the policies their training leaders have put in place that
haven't delivered. After many years of consulting to leading
companies in this area, he says the evidence is telling us that
much of the old approach hasn't worked.

For leaders of organisations thinking about the ways gender
equality can be enhanced, these kinds of factors require a more
nuanced approach. As Dr Jessa Rogers (profile #224), Project
Director for Indigenous Research and Education Strategy at the
University of New England, points out, it isn't enough to just
have an Indigenous quota for 3% Indigenous staff if, for example
on a university campus, all of those Indigenous staff are women
working in administrative roles. And it is also not enough to have
four senior Indigenous university professors if all of them are
male. This may mean organisations need to review the processes
they have in place for gender parity, and ensure Indigenous
women and women of colour are not lost in the diversity narrative.

Australia's Sex Discrimination Commissioner, Kate Jenkins
(profile #466), agrees it's certainly time for a revamp of the

standard women's leadership programs in many organisations. As a lawyer who was employed for some years at a large law firm, she realised that she had seen or been involved in many 'women in business' programs, and while they had real value for her career, they also need to evolve. Traditionally the 'Women in XX' programs were generally arranged by women, for women, and often with acquiescence — but not a lot of support — from the organisation, or from men. While it's important for programs to build women's skills and offer mentoring, many of these programs have not been integrated into the bigger business picture, and were supported not by proper resources, but by women in their spare time, without pay. Although well-intentioned, the focus was on fixing the women — and off to the side — while the main organisation remained unchanged. Says Kate:

> There was a lot of backlash for it then and there still is. Women's programs are viewed as special treatment, which many men and some women think women shouldn't get. That's the main argument. In reality, they are often programs to give women access to networks, as they are less likely than men to have access to same-sex mentors or role models in their daily working lives.

As women's support goes mainstream, organisations now have the perfect opportunity to reassess these programs, and to be clearer to everyone about why they are needed. It's time to look at this differently, Kate adds, and define clear purposes or goals for what they are meant to achieve, and properly resource them to be successful:

> The time is right, it's a really good moment to take stock and realise that these are women supporting women, to help them survive a system that doesn't want them to succeed. These networks provide women access to other women as role models and mentors. They need to become more legitimate.

Reviewing the programs requires expertise, but clarifying the goals and expected outcomes can help make such efforts more effective, and reposition them as mainstream business training to reduce backlash and provide legitimacy. Until more progress is made to close the gender gap, support for women in most workplaces is still needed — but siphoning women into poorly constructed courses seems doomed to fail, and can even attract more backlash from a perception these measures are 'unfair'.

Once progress emerges, the need for dedicated women's programs reduces or even disappears. Rachel Argaman, CEO of TFE Hotels in Australia, explained to Catherine in an interview for an article in Virgin Australia's *Voyeur* magazine, that when she was able to achieve a roughly 50/50 workforce throughout the business, it changed how they approached leadership development:

> I don't want special programs for women or men in our business, because we don't need it, and don't want that messaging. We have great leaders and we have diversity.[175]

Create your own #CelebratingWomen effect

Imitation is the highest form of flattery, as already explored in chapter 2, and Suzanne Young (profile #245) from IAG lost no time in setting up an internal version of #CelebratingWomen when she saw the impact it was having. Her own program was enthusiastically received, particularly by younger, mid-career women. One spin-off from this internal campaign at IAG was a kind of mentoring forum, which offered junior women the chance to interview senior women who had navigated the same gender issues within the organisation. And the interviews, which were available on the company's digital news page, were unscripted, so the result was natural and authentic, which added to their impact, Suzanne says. Younger women found the profiles of their more experienced colleagues fascinating and motivating — and often got to meet them for the first time, connecting with each other across divisions and job types. Network events were also held in family-friendly hours.

Suzanne is continuing to work with the diversity team to prioritise initiatives that will make a significant difference, including plans to establish a Male Champions of Change cohort for the insurance industry, and work with The University of Sydney Business School to research issues and approaches to mainstream flexibility, to build pipelines of women for more senior roles in the future.

Suzanne says that will mean encouraging senior men and women to use the current momentum to get more support for the program:

> **We as senior women can do more, and need to ask for what we want and what is going to make a difference**

for those who follow. The time to ask is now — but if we don't, I'm concerned it will not change.

While there have been some concerns raised over the IAG events — even though it has been clear that the events are open to men and women and all are welcome — Suzanne says there are signs that the culture of the organisation is shifting, with the board and senior leadership teams spending more time on this agenda.

Many #CelebratingWomen participants also nominated a women's networking or mentoring program as an effective way of connecting with and supporting women beyond their own workplace or across a sector. This isn't the kind of traditional mentoring that pairs more senior managers (often men) with a narrow cohort of 'high talent' women, but linking a broad range of women to share ideas and learn from each other. When Sharryn Naylor (profile #531) worked at Wenona, an independent girls' school in North Sydney, she was part of a network for women teachers called the Renaissance Women Leaders' Network, founded by the Principal, Dr Briony Scott (profile #23), and Dr Nicole Archard, now Principal of Loreto Adelaide:

> We met once a term to hear a high-profile woman
> leader speak, and for networking. It was a brilliant
> project. Like the #CelebratingWomen project, as
> a participant experiencing the benefits, you asked
> yourself 'Why hasn't this been done before?' So
> simple — yet so powerful and effective and positive.

Kirstin was invited to speak at a Renaissance Women Leaders' Network event in Sydney in 2018. The beautifully restored Art Deco theatre in North Sydney was filled with more than

200 teachers from public, independent and Catholic schools keen to hear about the #CelebratingWomen campaign, but also to learn from, celebrate and support one another. One of the female teachers told the assembled crowd how she had overcome her initial trepidation (by silencing the imposter syndrome) to apply for a professional development scholarship. To her great delight, she had just found out her application had been successful. The theatre spontaneously erupted in cheers and applause for this teacher, demonstrating the level of informal yet incredibly powerful support such gatherings can offer.

Lawyer Fay Calderone (profile #6) also found mentoring programs within her firm and through the Law Society of New South Wales helpful for supporting younger female lawyers:

> I have enjoyed working with the Western Sydney Wanderers W League mentoring program, and feel as business leaders we have a lot to offer young female athletes to help them gain life skills, to ensure balance and success on and off the field.

Georgie Somerset (profile #703) suggests organisations should provide formal and informal mentoring — and in male-dominated environments, a forum for women to support each other, both peer to peer, and at diverse levels, along with shadowing (where younger women follow and learn on the job from more senior women) and sponsorship.

Bijna K. Dasani (profile #81) says creating 'communities' for women within organisations allows women to network, collaborate and exchange ideas, and also open doors for one another through sponsorship, mentorship and various support systems. Bijna explains:

> In my current workplace, we have various
> communities around flexible working, work-life
> balance, mental-health, returning to work after
> childbirth and career-breaks for raising children.

Taking the message to the corner office

The tsunami of support for women's rights campaigns has delivered more attention to the agenda than we've seen in decades. That's an opportunity too good to waste.

Now is the time to press home to top leadership teams the need to think differently, says Sabina Shugg, founder of Women in Mining and Resources WA (WIMWA), which has more than 2500 members. Showing senior management the breadth of women's capabilities is a key step, as leaders are definitely listening now — and the diversity agenda is no longer about proving the business case, but being part of the licence to operate. Leaders need to move beyond lip service and start serving up change.

Opening the eyes of the senior ranks at male-dominated resources companies to the deep reservoir of skilled women and potential employees can have a direct effect on who gets appointed to jobs — as Sabina knows. Since WIMWA launched in 2003, the picture has definitely changed:

> We just signed a three-year agreement with
> Rio Tinto, so I think from that grassroots level
> in the early days at WIMWA — of asking a manager
> if you could have some money to take people to
> an event — to signing up these agreements with

major corporates is a sign of the change. We get
engagement from the most senior levels in resources
companies. Before the 2017 WIMWA Summit we
had the mining company South32's board members
from across the country at an event mixing with our
mentors and mentees, and it was very powerful.
A lot of these board members at such a high level
have no idea of the women working in the roles they
do, so to meet them face-to-face — maintenance
managers and engineers — and see these people are
women General Managers is a really powerful thing.
These board-level people are seeing that when
there is a job to fill, they need to buck the idea
that everyone has to look like them.

The momentum of online women's campaigns has also offered
a chance to have deeper and wider conversations about
sensitive topics. Ensuring the behaviour and bystander
responses that deter women in the workforce are acknowledged
and addressed at all levels is essential for organisational
progress, says Fay Calderone (profile #6):

The only way we can achieve transformational
cultural change is to discuss these issues, for people
to understand how damaging they can be, how
important they are to address, and for them to be
pulled up — not just online, but in workplaces and
everyday interactions around the world. The standard
we walk past is the standard we accept, and finally we
are starting to see bystanders more actively addressing
these issues.

Copy the leader

Organisations can make practical and effective changes to close the gender gap that don't involve dreaded diversity workshops — and many of these were suggested by women involved in the campaign who had seen them in operation. It helps to ask, of course. A key element to emerge from surveying women after the campaign ended was the efficacy of finding out what *women* think their employers can best do to make the most of their skills and experience — an underused cache of wisdom.

When we asked women to nominate the key steps organisations can take right now, they often mentioned removing bias from recruitment, promotion and pay processes, along with offering better flexibility, training and sponsorship for women — and education on discrimination for men. The good news is a range of workplaces have been making headway in some of these areas, with initiatives that can be easily emulated.

Some employers now offer far more comprehensive parental leave than the basic national scheme that was introduced in Australia in 2011, including Westpac and GE Australia and New Zealand. This includes paying superannuation (or pension contributions) while employees are on unpaid leave, and increasing the amount of paid and unpaid parental leave partners can take.

At professional services firm PwC in the United Kingdom, there is now a ban on all-male shortlists for jobs, and plans to ban all-male interview panels, too. Reports suggested the move was prompted by a pay gap report showing men on average earned 43.8% more than women.[176]

A range of well-known employers have offered flexibility to all their workers, sometimes known as 'all roles flex'. Pioneered by telecommunications company Telstra, the approach means everyone has the chance to negotiate flexible options, such as adjusting hours, working part time, working from home, job sharing and taking extra leave to cover school holidays.

Engineering firm AECOM launched school term-only contracts in 2017 for a number of roles in Australia and New Zealand. According to one article:

> Currently on a first-year trial, the initiative, which sees parents take up to 12 weeks annual leave to coincide with school holidays, is AECOM's way of upping the number of females in the workplace. Today, women make up less than 12% of all qualified engineers in Australia.[177]

When it comes to the gender pay gap, increasing numbers of companies are running audits to identify the problem. And some have actively addressed the pay gap. Energy Australia announced in early 2018 that it had eradicated the gap by spending $1.2 million, to:

> … boost the pay packets of 350 women who were getting less than their male counterparts, and promising a review in five years to ensure men have not negotiated their way back on top.[178]

Women of the future

Young women are not just keen to see these kinds of options, and many others, in their working lives: they expect them.

More than 2000 Australian women surveyed in late 2017 for the 'Women and the Future of Work' report[179] were not backward in coming forward with plenty of ideas, according to two of the authors, Professors Rae Cooper (profile #173) and Marian Baird, of Sydney University Business School. Their study findings attracted plenty of attention. The women participants, all aged under 40, showed great enthusiasm and ambition for their working lives, which they expect to be sustained; they don't assume they will be out of the workplace for extended periods of time. Young women want to be working long term, in employment that's interesting and well paid, and with the capacity to influence decisions.

The other key finding from the study was half the women thought the workplace was unequal. Women in the focus groups actually said they would change employers — and would make the effort to seek out employers who are offering the career and jobs they want. And they will also change sectors to seek that out.

This highly qualified cohort of women were clear about what they needed in order to do the best job possible: the right skills and qualifications (92%), access to flexibility (90%), paid leave to have and care for family (84%), and support and mentoring to develop leadership skills (83%). These were seen by women as the most important factors to facilitate career progress.

This is not some little diversity blip happening, but a major shift in the workforce, Professor Marian Baird says. Employers need to consider whether they are ready for it, and actively address these areas if they want to attract and retain skilled workers in the future.

Our own analysis, research and the feedback from women of all ages involved in #CelebratingWomen shows there is no shortage of robust advice or proven ideas on how to make progress in all kinds of organisations. The business case has long been made, as Bernard Coleman, the newly installed Head of Diversity & Inclusion at Uber after a range of harassment scandals emerged at the organisation, told *Forbes* magazine.[180] What's needed now is action:

> I'm often asked what we can do that's innovative and ground breaking in the D&I [diversity and inclusion] space, but I think that's the wrong question. Innovation isn't the problem, it is the collective intention or lack thereof. The No. 1 reason progress is not advanced is because it is not prioritised. It is fundamentally a lack of will and sustained follow-through.

And he goes on to quote Winston Churchill:

> Success is not final; failure is not fatal: it is the courage to continue that counts.

And courage, like confidence, is infectious.

CONCLUSION

For a tech-company billionaire, Jack Dorsey, the CEO and co-founder of Twitter, is pretty low key. He speaks softly and thoughtfully about the reach and impact of the social media behemoth he helped create, which has grown from modest beginnings in 2006 to attracting more than 330 million regular users, including the US President. During his jam-packed visit to Australia in 2018, Kirstin was invited to speak about #CelebratingWomen before Jack Dorsey was interviewed onstage at the Sydney offices of the company. What she had done was amazing, he told her, noting that while the number of social campaigns using Twitter has increased, very few have been able to leverage the same kind of positivity. And that's something we need to see more of, he added.

It was an endorsement that capped off a remarkable and unlikely trajectory started by a single tweet posted from a beach in Queensland. To have a campaign build such momentum that it inspired the founder of Twitter itself was well beyond any of Kirstin's expectations. It was particularly affirming to have the campaign recognised for its uplifting impact, given the prevalence of trolling and online bullying that had spurred Kirstin into action in the first place. As Gail Kelly, a former Westpac CEO, told an audience in Brisbane after hearing about the campaign:

> You may have all heard the expression from
> Madeleine Albright, the US Secretary of State, that
> there is a special place in hell for women who don't

support other women. I think there is a special
place in heaven for women like Kirstin who do
such wonderful work for women supporting women.
It is truly an important thing.[181]

Many participants felt the same, as Sally-Ann Williams
(profile #603), who works at Google Australia, tweeted:

[Kirstin's] specific contribution to making invisible
women visible through her own platform and
brand was, and is, a shining example of leadership
and generosity to developing others. That is
visionary leadership.[182]

Frustration may have been a factor in starting the campaign,
but friendship, connections and support fuelled it. While the
campaign formally finished after one year, as intended, its
impact continues to reverberate and inspire the women
involved, including Kirstin — and, it appears, Jack Dorsey
and Twitter. The daily profiles may have stopped, but the
sharing and power from women supporting each other has
energetically continued.

Something at the core of this campaign helped show the
momentum that can be unleashed when women have had
enough — putting their own stories forward and building a
platform of sustainable connections and affirmation that
hasn't faltered. So many women told us how they were
'paying it forward' and sticking up for each other in ways they
had never felt able to before.

They were creating the amplification effect by intervening
in meetings to make sure women colleagues were not
interrupted and their ideas were heard; recommending each

other for new opportunities, and using social media to spotlight women's contributions and achievements; publicly thanking their women friends and mentors for their support; and using strength in numbers to ensure their workplace networks were properly resourced and moved from the sidelines into the mainstream. And quite a few were planning a 'manless dinner' to celebrate the women they relied on every day.

All of this activity wasn't just about them, but for the next generations of women as well, and women everywhere were seizing the moment, loudly and publicly challenging the idea that women routinely pull each other down or have no interest in each others' lives. The campaign clarified and tapped into an urgent and unstoppable push for women's right to be heard and redefine society. Indeed, just as we finished this book the women of Ireland joined together, many returning to their homeland to show solidarity, to help overturn the Eighth Amendment, which had made abortion illegal.

Backlash has always accompanied steps forward for women, and there's no shortage of resistance to the recent renaissance in the women's movement. But these forces are also facing a very different style of distributed power — without gatekeepers, and beyond the control of traditional authorities. It's upending certainties at a time when news flows in a split second around the globe, and connections of all kinds are immediate and visible. The potential is enormous, and women are just beginning to realise the strength they now have to set a new agenda.

We've also learned so much from writing this book. That a relatively simple idea can make a significant impact. That you don't need permission from anyone to start a social media movement. That women are fascinated by each other's lives and stories. That women's friendships are powerful, not peripheral. That you don't have to be a high-flyer to be a role model or inspire others. That helping other women shine helps us all to shine. We now know for sure that many women are backing each other up in tricky workplace situations, and routinely cheering their own and others' achievements. And cheering each other up because women can be very funny, even when the chips are down.

And we know that the networks women run have been effectively addressing barriers and providing connections, collaboration and referrals that are helping women enjoy better working lives. Women have been doing this behind the scenes for decades, and with more recognition of the power of collaboration they are poised to grow stronger and more overt in their efforts.

We have seen that women are happy to lead, and are good at it — and most don't turn into Queen Bees. And the ones who do have faced much harder paths and been judged far more harshly than their male peers. And there's a particularly strong group of women in leadership helping the women coming behind them. Women have confidence in themselves and their ability to contribute when they are in safe environments, where sharing is celebrated and part of pressure for the greater good.

As women's place at the helm is revealed more clearly, the very nature of leadership and what it means is being renegotiated — and employers who understand and make the most of this will reap significant rewards. But they need to listen and tap into the wisdom of women, too. Men — particularly in leadership — are recognising that it's no longer the responsibility of women to prove sexism, discrimination and harassment exist. It's up to workplaces to address these issues, and this will only happen when women's interests and rights are central to the mainstream agenda.

Many influential people have seen the power of women supporting women and have been able to articulate why it matters. It's about 'collective courage', as director Holly Ransom (profile #90) says. Young women need to know 'your life is yours to define', as BHP executive Jacqui McGill (profile #66) explains. That bonds with other women matter, and to pass on courage. That friendship between women is life affirming, even life changing, not silly or trivial. And at the very top, those bonds are no less important.

As journalist Leigh Sales (profile #129) observed, when concluding an onstage conversation between Julia Gillard and Hillary Clinton in Sydney:

> There is something between you two that goes
> beyond politics. There is a warmth in this room,
> and it's because you have both broken ground in
> incredibly difficult circumstances and we've all
> watched the cost.

We have watched that too, but learned that many, like us, believe the momentum that saw #CelebratingWomen explode is unstoppable. As Angus Armour of the Australian Institute of Company Directors points out:

> At every level we are seeing that it is absolutely
> clear to anyone that equality is where our society
> is going, and it is essential to make the most of the
> social and economic potential of Australia.

This has been made all the clearer by the #CelebratingWomen campaign, which has helped to inspire women to find the tools, connections and confidence to take the reins in a way that was unimaginable a decade ago.

By supporting and standing together, women are finally grabbing their chance to change the story of their lives as they step up to shape and define a fairer world for themselves and women everywhere.

And that is worth celebrating.

ACKNOWLEDGEMENTS

Writing this book has been an exercise in the kindness of women. So many women, from all corners of the globe, have helped us produce this book and for that we are both incredibly grateful.

First and foremost, we wish to thank the 757 women who voluntarily participated in #CelebratingWomen, never realising that a simple Twitter thread and Facebook post would end up leading to this book. What may have seemed like a small decision to be involved in 2017 has had a lasting impact and we are very grateful for your willingness to be role models to others. While it was not possible to share every woman's story in this book, as much as we may have wanted to since every story is inspiring, we have named every woman from the campaign in the order in which they were profiled. You can find this list of inspiring women in the pages following and we also encourage you to visit the Twitter handle @CelebratingWom or the Facebook page of Kirstin Ferguson where you can scroll down and read the 757 women's profiles yourself.

We are also very thankful to the 65 women who agreed to provide us with feedback on your experience of being part of #CelebratingWomen. Your insights and experiences have helped enormously in articulating why the campaign resonated with so many women and we were thrilled to include your thoughts in our book. Thank you for your support and engagement.

To our publishers and editor, thank you. This book would not have been possible without the imagination, inspiration and intelligence of our publisher, Jane Morrow at Murdoch

Books and our editor, Katri Hilden. You have been wonderful colleagues in this process. And thank you also to all the team at Murdoch Books including Julie Mazur Tribe and Carol Warwick who have tirelessly worked to ensure this book is read by as many people as possible. A big thank you also to Fiona Inglis at Curtis Brown for your generosity and support.

To the many men and women we have interviewed for this book as well as those who offered us their time and wisdom behind the scenes, thank you. This includes Andrea Perry-Petersen, Andrew Stevens, Angela Priestley, Angus Armour, Annabelle Brayley, Bijna K. Dasani, Brianna Casey, Dr Caroline Ford, Catherine Cahill, Cheryl Hickey, Claudia Theis, Conrad Liveris, Associate Professor Darren Saunders, Dr David Cooke, David Perks, Denyse Whelan, Diane Smith-Gander, Emma Isaacs, Evelyn Ralph, Fay Calderone, Fiona Boyd, Fi Shewring, Gail Kelly, Gavin Fox-Smith, Georgie Dent, Georgie Somerset, Gillian Fennell, Dr Graeme Russell, Helene Young, Holly Kramer, Holly Ransom, Jacqui McGill, Jane Caro, Jane O'Connell, Dr Jillian Kenny, Julie Reilly, Jo Prigmore, Dr Julia Baird, Kate Barker, Kate Jenkins, Kathryn Fagg, Dr Kim Morgan-Short, Kimberley Cole, Kylie Walker, Leigh Sales, Leith Mitchell, Dr Leonora Risse, Libby Lyons, Professor Marian Baird, Marina Go, Megan Welch, Melissa Pouliot, Dr Mellissa Naidoo, Mary Ward, Ming Long, Dr Monique Beedles, Dr Muneera Bano, Nicola Hazell, Patricia Karvelas, Peter Warne, Hon. Philip Dalidakis, Dame Quentin Bryce, Rachel Scanlon, Professor Rae Cooper, Rebecca Gelding, Sabina Shugg, Sally-Ann Williams, Sharryn Naylor, Simon Mordant, Suzanne Young, Suzy Nicoletti, Tarla Lambert, Dr Tien Huynh, Tina Sipicki and Tracey Clark.

Finally, none of this would be possible without the love, support and kindness of our friends and family.

Kirstin would like to send much love and gratitude to her husband Glen and daughters Emily and Zoe, since she is quite convinced nothing in her life would be as fun, rewarding or meaningful without them in it. Kirstin's parents Irene, David as well as Lori and Brian, have all provided invaluable support and encouragement along the way — thank you and much love to you all. To the Camping Crew who are Kirstin's family in every possibly way other than genetics — you have provided more wonderful memories than anyone should be entitled to, and Michelle and Sue, you epitomise the title of this book; your friendship over decades means everything. And Ali, thank you for the adventures we have shared and for always being there. Other thanks from Kirstin must be made to the many role models, friends and colleagues who have provided constant encouragement, reassurance, practical advice and much-needed laughs and wine along the way. You know who you are. Thank you.

Catherine would also like to thank her posse: David, Simone, Evie and Antonia; Geraldine Roger and Brendan Fox; Margot Saville, Judith Hoare, Michele Jackson, Adele Miles, Helen Trinca, Beverley Uther, Rosemary Johnston, Aviva Lowy, Jane Caro, Julie Reilly, Narelle Hooper, Ming Long, Marina Go, the AFR chicks, Jane Counsel, Libby Lyons, Kate Jenkins, and role models par excellence Quentin Bryce and Wendy McCarthy.

#CELEBRATINGWOMEN
ROLL CALL

1	Irene Rogers	40	Claire Bibby
2	Alanna Ball	41	Kate Doak
3	Gene Moyle	42	Aprill Allen
4	Cassandra Heilbronn	43	Amanda Jones
5	Stacey Copas	44	Alex Atkins
6	Fay Calderone	45	Janne Ryan
7	Trish Kerin	46	Alicia Curtis
8	Diann Rodgers-Healey	47	Majella Beagley
9	Marina Go	48	Lea Slade
10	Audette Exel	49	Leith Mitchell
11	Erica Gavel	50	Monique Beedles
12	Christine Moody	51	Lisa Lamarre
13	Penny Reidy	52	Vanessa Waters
14	Naomi Kemp	53	Jane Caro
15	Pip Stocks	54	Emma Beckett
16	Diane Smith-Gander	55	Louise Ferris
17	Kylie Sprott	56	Paulina Skerman
18	Juliet Bourke	57	Jane Needham
19	Mary-Ellen Field	58	Leanne Beagley
20	Tanya Monro	59	Michelle Redfern
21	Shivani Harland	60	Kath Mazzella
22	Jacquie Fegent-McGeachie	61	Elisha Wright
23	Briony Scott	62	Fay Feeney
24	Carol Duncan	63	Kristie Fankhauser
25	Susannah Birch	64	Lauren Maxwell
26	Amali Perera	65	Kate Carruthers
27	Alice Korngold	66	Jacqui McGill
28	Jane Moran	67	Jayne Juvan
29	Sue Cato	68	Katherine Jorgensen
30	Ann Sherry	69	Sarah Fox
31	Penelope Twemlow	70	Karen Endicott
32	Rowie Webster	71	Lisa Fryar
33	Fi Shewring	72	Dina Medland
34	Arabella Douglas	73	Trish Jackson
35	Funke Abimbola	74	Benita Husband
36	Halla Tomasdottir	75	Kelly Lovely
37	Amy Leighton	76	Tasha Broomhall
38	Andi Csontos	77	Shannon Fentiman
39	Isobel Joyce	78	Lindsey Mask

79	Sandi Rhys Jones	126	Patricia Karvelas
80	Louise Adams	127	Zan Rowe
81	Bijna K. Dasani	128	Georgina Dent
82	Kelly Higgins-Devine	129	Leigh Sales
83	Heather Beach	130	Katie Bradford
84	Samantha Sharif	131	Tracey Spicer
85	Cynthia Nyamai	132	Shannon Byrne
86	Carolyn Tate	133	Pip Courtney
87	Viola Llewellyn	134	Leena Linnainmaa
88	Lesley Harris	135	Zantie O'Connell
89	Loren O'Keeffe	136	Sherry Lam
90	Holly Ransom	137	Kelly Bernish
91	Gabriela Burian	138	Lou de Beuzeville
92	Kristina Cain	139	Trish Crews
93	Rebekah Weston	140	Cordelia Nash
94	Sarah Daniels	141	Jessica Klarholm
95	Karen Stocks	142	Jen Geale
96	Mel Kettle	143	Sienna Scopel
97	Cecily Joseph	144	Georgia Lane
98	Janine Walker	145	Jennifer Wittwer
99	Victoria Hepburn	146	Anjee Davis
100	Shirley Chowdhary	147	Charlene Dipaola
101	Carolyn Ryder	148	Tokie Laotan Brown
102	Jessamy Gleeson	149	Stephanie Kurlow
103	Katherine Marquardt	150	Nicola Hazell
104	Sarah Oxenbridge	151	Stephanie Brown
105	Leanne Mulcahy	152	Lee Brentzell
106	Denise Shrivell	153	Jemilyn Bitun
107	Heidi Dening	154	Gabi Zedlmayer
108	Mary McMillan	155	Carole Labram
109	Adele Blair	156	Romae Calland
110	Sara Haslinger	157	Samantha Crisford-Eade
111	Shalom Lloyd	158	Jane Huxley
112	Jacqueline Onalo	159	Jaclyn Smith
113	Simone Moore	160	Nina Du Thaler
114	Fiona Landis	161	Angelle Kwemo
115	Laurice Temple	162	Carly Findlay
116	Donny Walford	163	Alison Hallworth
117	Faustina Anyanwu	164	Fiona Austin
118	Ana Sevo	165	Lisa LaMaitre
119	Kate Smith-Miles	166	Kate Seselja
120	Sharon Carvolth	167	Keren Rambow
121	Nicole Foster	168	Kylee Fitzpatrick
122	Jade Collins	169	Helen Goodman
123	Alexandra Thomas	170	Lisa Alexander
124	Tracey Holmes	171	Tina Šipicki
125	Nicole Sheffield	172	Laura Clise

173	Rae Cooper	219	Lacey Filipich
174	Verity Trott	220	Natalie Richards
175	Elyse Lithgow	221	Suzie Robertson
176	Louise Eyres	222	Theresa Apple Coss
177	Bianca Martin	223	Rebecca Smallwood
178	Claire Ledder	224	Jessa Rogers
179	Caryn Walsh	225	Kirsten Coventry
180	Eden Gillespie	226	Kimberly Humphrey
181	Debbie Hersman	227	Mathilde Desselle
182	Emily Webb	228	Chelsea Stutchbury
183	Sarah Gow	229	Simone McLaughlin
184	Lisa Dib	230	Meegan Jia-Good
185	Janine Thompson	231	Susan Dirgham
186	Pip Marlow	232	Kate Hobbs
187	Natalie Seegers	233	Amanda Webb
188	Endi Frydman	234	Neelima Fernandes
189	Ashley Love	235	Kylie White
190	Dominique Hes	236	Katie Spearritt
191	Linda Minassian	237	Mari Kikvadze
192	Juanita McGowen	238	Karen Becker
193	Cassandra Kelly	239	Demitra Sealy
194	Myf Clark	240	Kate Row
195	Alena Titterton	241	Sally Coldrick
196	Johanna Elms	242	Madonna King
197	Emma Hodgman	243	Diana Ryall
198	Nabila Farhat	244	Sabra Lane
199	Megan Kingham	245	Suzanne Young
200	Gemma Lloyd	246	Fatima G. Remtulla
201	Rosie Thomas	247	Selena Schimko
202	Margaret Jolly	248	Tamara Horton
203	Anne Graham	249	Fiona David
204	Julie Harris	250	Marie McMillan
205	Melissa Jardine	251	Carolyn Bendall
206	Peninah Achieng-Kindberg	252	Jo Mikleus
207	Jocelyn Hunter	253	Rachel Scanlon
208	Deirdre Anderson	254	Elizabeth Saunders
209	Emma Mugi-Turkington	255	Kerry Abbott
210	Jo Prigmore	256	Caroline Overington
211	Kerry Arch	257	Elise Margow
212	Libby Mitchell	258	Cathy Egan
213	Amanda Sartor	259	Michelle Tucker
214	Penny Paliadelis	260	Kay Danes
215	Dionne Drew	261	Vyla Rollins
216	Nikki Stamp	262	Louise Stanley
217	Fiona McLeod	263	Yemi Adenuga
218	Natalie Angel	264	Melissa Yeo

265	Shirley Randell	311	Molatelo Mainetje
266	Mary Konstantopoulos	312	Esline Turner
267	Rochelle Courtenay	313	Shwetal Shah
268	Rowan Brookes	314	Emelda Davis
269	Deborah Wilson	315	Vaishali Vijay
270	Ingrid Tomanovits	316	Mellissa Naidoo
271	Catherine Fox	317	Sarah Ross
272	Eliza Berlage	318	Laura Finn
273	Sarah Louise Brown	319	Georgia Banks
274	Rebecca Cross	320	Reeva Cutting
275	Julie Fleming	321	Sonia McDonald
276	Naomi Phillips	322	Claire Christian
277	Philippa Walker	323	Catherine Nelson-Williams
278	Maria Murphy	324	Nicki Page
279	Kate Kyriacou	325	Liz Helliwell
280	Melissa Wu	326	Fran White
281	Abigail Harrison	327	Gemma Mahadeo
282	Uma Patel	328	Ali Dale
283	Kate Leaver	329	Kez Wickham St George
284	Louise Milligan	330	Narelle Hooper
285	Claudia Theis	331	Vanessa Thiele
286	Danielle Logue	332	Nicki Williams
287	Emma Ryan	333	Helen Henry
288	Jane Alver	334	Amanda Ray
289	Susie Green	335	Louise Perram-Fisk
290	Jane O'Connell	336	Ginger Gorman
291	Rebecca Harcourt	337	Esline Moli Felix
292	Veronica Gravolin	338	Rebecca Colless
293	Kristen Holzapfel	339	Lexie Wilkins
294	Sarah Boyd	340	Christina Smerdon
295	Caitlin McGrane	341	Joanna Gaudoin
296	Heather Earl	342	Jenine Beekhuyzen
297	Shannon McDonald	343	Józefa Fawcett
298	Denyse Whelan	344	Rachel Hentsch
299	Tess Rouvray	345	Nina Joshi Ramsey
300	Menna Rawlings	346	Lauren Barns
301	Jowen Hillyer	347	Rachel Blackburn
302	Erin Cox	348	Julie Cavaney
303	Amber Cordingley-Erpf	349	Katy Barfield
304	Mellissa Lambert	350	Moninya Roughan
305	Anita Gurrieri	351	Emma Haller
306	Meg Burrage	352	Alice Vigors
307	Anita Erskine	353	Tia Brown
308	Neha Gupta	354	Catherine Cahill
309	Caroline Newman	355	Kath Sansom
310	Karen Loon	356	Mel Yeates

357	Liz Van Dort	403	Jude Towns
358	Jill Brennan	404	Dinah Davis
359	Michelle Blanchard	405	Susann Beier
360	Caitlin Scott	406	Teresa Dyson
361	Annie Parker	407	Tara Jacobsen-Neven
362	Heather Watson	408	Alicia Barry
363	Caroline Parkes	409	Sam Cornett
364	Samantha Bowen	410	Clare Anderson
365	Madeleine Pownall	411	Emily Campbell
366	Julie Wheway	412	Jill Hennessy
367	Leah Ong	413	Wilhelmina Huston
368	Julie Luxford	414	Margot Harley
369	Mara Antonoff	415	Anne Gleeson
370	Melissa Marquez	416	Julie Brown
371	Mary Darlington	417	Susan Redden Makatoa
372	Melanie Toomey	418	Jay Crisp Crow
373	Kayleigh Rhodes	419	Belinda Moore
374	Stephanie Reuss	420	Megan Welch
375	Erica Rees	421	Jeanette Purkis
376	Jennifer Crawford	422	Lynne Cazaly
377	Lynette Delane	423	Kellie Sloane
378	Peta Irving	424	Juanita Rayson
379	Paola Gutierrez	425	Jane Bell
380	Leanne Drew	426	Janine Larsen
381	Erin Watson-Lynn	427	Barb Cook
382	Emma Livingstone	428	Marianna Cherry
383	Jodie Fields	429	Phinnah Chichi Ikeji
384	Emily de la Pena	430	Morenike Ajayi
385	Ashleigh Morris	431	Kate Brow
386	Samantha Selmes	432	Sarah Bartholomeusz
387	Rachel Smith	433	Catriona Cowie
388	Kriti Colless	434	Michelle Choma
389	Sharon Smith	435	Alison Skrzypiec
390	Lou Pollard	436	Anna Dartnell
391	Annelies Cowin	437	Susan Seipel
392	Karen Johns	438	Fiona Jose
393	Scherazade Siganporia	439	Rose Ricketson
394	Rachel Neylan	440	Susan Burke
395	Kerry Ashbrook	441	Kate Allman
396	Camille Eddy	442	Amanda Glaze
397	Emily Bryan	443	Anne O'Donoghue
398	Sara Goldstein	444	Carol MacArthur
399	Bridie O'Donnell	445	Maria Allart
400	Karen Percy	446	Rebekah Outred
401	Carol Cooke	447	Gauri Maini
402	Ann-Marie Reid	448	Sandra Przibilla

449	Jenny Murphy	495	Holly Kramer
450	Tamika Smith	496	Julie Inman-Grant
451	Jane Wild	497	Princes Shelly-Ann
452	Mrinalini Venkatachalam		San Miguel
453	Oumakie Pieterson-Shayi	498	Julie Busch
454	Monica Dsouza	499	Catherine Osborne
455	Alanna Bastin-Byrne	500	Kristen Pressner
456	Lizzie Mettam	501	Belinda Brosnan
457	Amanda Connon-Unda	502	Sharon Brennan-Olsen
458	Grace Borsellino	503	Kay McGrath
459	Diane Curley	504	Shelley Watts
460	Jan Wild	505	Amy Coopes
461	Camilla Baker	506	Cheryl Kernot
462	Humsha Naidoo	507	Anastasia Cammaroto
463	Anna Wright	508	Kara Hinesley
464	Kathryn Harris	509	Suzy Nicoletti
465	Bronwen Sciortino	510	Julie Bishop
466	Kate Jenkins	511	Ruth McGowan
467	Gemma Godfrey	512	Upulie Divisekera
468	Ming Long	513	Alexandra Taylor
469	Van Badham	514	Anne Thériault
470	Drisana Levitzke-Gray	515	Kim Rayner
471	Linda Tirado	516	Michelle Ferguson
472	Dai Le	517	Ellen Fanning
473	Lauren Ingram	518	Von Slater
474	Xanthe Visram	519	Natasha Stott Despoja
475	Romilly Madew	520	Dhara Patel
476	Annabelle Brayley	521	Jane Saville
477	Helene Young	522	Kirsty Collins
478	Sandra Sully	523	Zora Artis
479	Murwarid Ziayee	524	Kirsten Galliott
480	Silvia Young	525	Catherine Ball
481	Kate Corkery	526	Kirsten Molloy
482	Josephine Sukkar	527	Melissa Hart
483	Sharon Schoenborn	528	Fiona Lang
484	Carol Hay	529	Edith Sztychmasjter
485	Danielle Price	530	Amber Hauff
486	Lisa Longman	531	Sharryn Naylor
487	Carla Harris	532	Ursula Hogben
488	Sarah Bennett	533	Chrys Stevenson
489	Kylie Green	534	Katie Dufficy
490	Lynette Gray	535	Andrea Sargent
491	Kristyn Haywood	536	Amy Miller
492	Nerida Cunneen	537	Leah Kivivali
493	Michelle Zaffino	538	Anna Beaumont
494	Maureen McVail	539	Tomoko Sugino

540	Joanne Gray	586	Kelly Tagalan
541	Pearl Goodwin-Burns	587	Roanne Blackler
542	Deborah Field	588	Belinda Kuehner
543	Tracey Clark	589	Nicole Mitchell
544	Nicole Ivens	590	Beverley Unitt
545	Kerryn Pennell	591	Vanessa Guthrie
546	Lama Tayeh	592	Janelle Weissman
547	Kathryn Germain	593	Sarah Styles
548	Gabrielle Dolan	594	Sara Safari
549	Nicole Brown	595	Gillian Fennell
550	Fi Slaven	596	Shalailah Medhora
551	Allison Macdonald	597	Vanessa Egli
552	Faustina Agolley	598	Paula Ward
553	Muneera Bano	599	Avani Dias
554	Serena Ryan	600	Melanie Brock
555	Linda Tapp	601	Elaine Stead
556	Rachelle Balez	602	Virginia Haussegger
557	Hannah Macdougall	603	Sally-Ann Williams
558	Kathy Caprino	604	Jo Hirst
559	Liza-Jayne Loch	605	Giovanna Fera
560	Joy Hopwood	606	Nicky Thomas
561	Jessica Lee	607	Rennae Stubbs
562	Natasha Wells	608	Elizabeth Boulton
563	Amanda Terranova	609	Heidi í Homrum
564	Leisa Bacon	610	Nazia Hussain
565	Liza Peapell	611	Sarah Macarthur-King
566	Katie Read	612	Kimberly Rowntree
567	Candice May	613	Angela Moonan
568	Melissa Ries	614	Andrea Josephs
569	Renae Ryan	615	Chelsea Ford
570	Jiayu Wang	616	Talitha Cummins
571	Jules Brooke	617	Sarah Zeljko
572	Paula Holden	618	Gail Creighton-Davies
573	Sareswari Selva	619	Diana Fraser
574	Abby Ferri	620	Mathuri Santhi-Morgan
575	Bianca Santi	621	Rebecca Gelding
576	Davida Forshaw	622	Heba Shaheed
577	Aliza Knox	623	Rebecca Davies
578	Anne-Marie Elias	624	Caroline Ford
579	Gayle Avery	625	Renee Eglinton
580	Liz Walder	626	Yvonne Kelly
581	Marijke Huisman	627	Holly Brennan
582	Mel Street	628	Bobbi-Lea Boucher
583	Nicole Bathurst	629	Niki Vincent
584	Simone Strachan	630	Cat Matson
585	Sara Cameron	631	Olga Shimoni

632	Nicola Jones-Crossley	678	Lucy Barnard
633	Sally Coldham	679	Jayne Powell
634	Deb Kirby	680	Emma Alberici
635	Beverly Simmons-Hurtado	681	Karyn Nimmo
636	Zeynep Sertel	682	Anna Dixon
637	Joanna McPherson	683	Naomi Caietti
638	Shelley Cox	684	Amelia Jones
639	Jo Smail	685	Julie Trell
640	Aradia Sayner	686	Edwina Bartholomew
641	Jess Caire	687	Kate Foy
642	Marijana Kagis	688	Patricia Jonas
643	Emily Mills	689	Natalie Chapman
644	Jillian Hishaw	690	Joy Taylor
645	Kirstin Harcourt	691	Dayle Stevens
646	Shirley Harring	692	Catherine McGregor
647	Susan Polson	693	Janett Egber
648	Sara Tasker	694	Deb Morandin
649	Danni Pirc	695	Deborah Dalziel
650	Chantal Vanderhaeghen	696	Tracey McGuinness
651	Lea Sharp	697	Kirsten Connan
652	Marion Edwin	698	Marianne Rose
653	Anthea Webb	699	Vanessa Romer
654	Annmarie Liddle	700	Ellen Maynes
655	Pip Cleaves	701	Kari Esplin
656	Jamie Klingler	702	Nicolle Bradford
657	Shirley Osborne	703	Georgie Somerset
658	Tanya Hill	704	Alice Zaslavsky
659	Sue Keay	705	Stephanie Peatling
660	Jane Morrow	706	Kumi Taguchi
661	Elyce Phillips	707	Andra Keay
662	Amanda Rose	708	Julia Baird
663	Kirsty Bradley	709	Cheryl Hunter
664	Maren Mossman	710	Layne Beachley
665	Kate Ross	711	Abigail McGregor
666	Hege Kjelbye	712	Kerryn Fewster
667	Katie Fitzgerald	713	Brianna Casey
668	Emma-Lee Whyte	714	Virginia Trioli
669	Katharine Jordan	715	Tanya Plibersek
670	Sonia Canton	716	Martine Westerlund
671	Leslie Cannold	717	Tabitha Laser
672	Zsuzsanna Gyenes	718	Janice Tong
673	Linda Burn	719	Victoria Jameson
674	Melissa Pouliot	720	Miranda Brawn
675	Jenny Woodward	721	Fiona Craig
676	Natasha Keir	722	Daniela Ion
677	Kate Callaghan	723	Jennifer Mackay-Ortiz

724	Andrea Perry-Petersen	741	Alicia Reti
725	Lina Duque	742	Saffron Hodgson
726	Jenny Brown	743	Emma-Louise Moss
727	Zoe Ferguson	744	Vanessa Vanderhoek
728	Hilda Smith	745	Paige Burton
729	Deborah Kent	746	Jill Nes
730	Saalihah Seedat	747	Vanessa Losada
731	Evelyn Ralph	748	Vicki Forbes
732	Amy Ho	749	Tamie McNiece
733	Shanna Hocking	750	Claudia Barriga-Larriviere
734	Sarah MacDiarmid	751	Salma Rizwi
735	Alessandra Golisano	752	Katie Grogan
736	Jenny Pearse	753	Kate McLoughlin
737	Susie Alexander	754	Marija Jovanovich
738	Wendy Wilson	755	Maxine Mawhinney
739	Paula Woodward	756	Sam Mostyn
740	Ivy Halstead	757	Emily Ferguson

STAYING
CONNECTED

This book has highlighted the power of connections and networks, especially via social media.

To stay in touch with us, you can do so via a range of ways, and we look forward to continuing to build networks with women and men around the world.

Dr Kirstin Ferguson

Email	contact@kirstinferguson.com
Website	www.kirstinferguson.com
Twitter	@kirstinferguson
LinkedIn	Dr Kirstin Ferguson
Facebook	Kirstin Ferguson
Instagram	Kirstin Ferguson

Catherine Fox

Email	catherine.fox17@gmail.com
Twitter	@corporatefox
LinkedIn	Catherine Fox

NOTES

INTRODUCTION

1   Matt Liddy and Catherine Hanrahan, 'Fewer women run top Australian companies than men named John — or Peter, or David', ABC News online, 8 March 2017, www.abc.net.au/news/2017-03-08/fewer-women-ceos-than-men-named-john/8327938

2   Workplace Gender Equality Agency, *Australia's Gender Pay Gap Statistics*, Australian Government, February 2018, www.wgea.gov.au/sites/default/files/gender-pay-gap-statistics.pdf

3   Antoinette Lattouf, 'Superannuation: Women on track to retire with half as much as men, study finds', ABC News online, 20 July 2017, www.abc.net.au/news/2017-07-20/women-on-track-to-retire-with-half-as-much-super-as-men/8727112

4   Our Watch, 'Understanding Violence: Facts and Figures', undated, www.ourwatch.org.au/understanding-violence/facts-and-figures

5   Oprah Winfrey acceptance speech at the 75th Golden Globes Awards in Los Angeles, 8 January 2018

1 AN ACCIDENTAL ACTIVIST: KIRSTIN'S STORY

6   Peter Beinart, 'Fear of a female president', *The Atlantic*, October 2016, www.theatlantic.com/magazine/archive/2016/10/fear-of-a-female-president/497564/

7   Karrin Vasby Anderson, 'Every woman is the wrong woman: The female presidentiality paradox', *Women's Studies in Communication*, vol. 40, no. 2, 2017, p. 132

8   ibid., pp. 134–5

9   Tyler G. Okimoto and Victoria L. Brescoll, 'The price of power: Power seeking and backlash against female politicians', *Personality and Social Psychology Bulletin*, vol. 36, no. 7, 2010, p. 923

10 ibid.

11 ibid.

12 Helen Clark, 'Breaking glass ceilings: Reflections on women's leadership', speech delivered at the Asian Development Bank in Manila, Philippines, 16 March 2018, https://helenclarknz.com/2018/03/18/breaking-glass-ceilings-reflections-on-womens-leadership-speech-by-helen-clark-at-asian-development-bank-in-manila-philippines-16-march-2018/

13 Michelle King, 'How powerful women experience extreme online sexual harassment and what you can do to stop it', *Forbes*, 14 November 2017, www.forbes.com/sites/michelleking/2017/11/14/how-powerful-women-experience-extreme-online-sexual-harassment-and-what-you-can-do-to-stop-it/#715738c67b73

14 Faye Raincock, Havas helia press release, 'Powerful women face daily, rampant sexism online says Havas UK social media study', undated, Havas Media UK

15 Women in Media, *Mates over Merit? The Women in Media Report — A Study of Gender Differences in Australian Media*, undated, www.womeninmedia.net/wp-content/uploads/2017/10/Mates-Over-Merit_full-report.pdf

16   Dr Kirstin Ferguson, 'Let's make 2017 the year of making noise #CelebratingWomen', *Women's Agenda* website, 15 January 2017, https://womensagenda.com.au/latest/the-year-of-making-noise-celebratingwomen/

17   Belle Derks, Colette Van Laar, Naomi Ellemers and Kim de Groot, 'Gender-bias primes elicit Queen Bee responses among senior policewomen', *Psychological Science*, vol. 22, no. 10, October 2011, pp. 1243–49

18   Quinn Lisbon, 'Mayors: Yes, we too', Route Fifty, 29 January 2018, www.routefifty.com/management/2018/01/mayors-yes-we-too/145571/

19   Mary Taylor, *Baked Beans in the Outback and Curry in Kashmir*, Steve Currie, Mountain Gate, Victoria, 1999

20   Helen Clarke, 'Galloping Granny', *Australian Traveller*, 24 July 2006, www.australiantraveller.com/australia/galloping-granny/

21   'Lego Lingo: The Cadets' Language', compiled by Bill Cowham, unpublished, 1987

22   David Fickling, 'Corporate Australia, stop blaming women', *The Sydney Morning Herald*, 18 May 2018, www.smh.com.au/business/workplace/corporate-australia-stop-blaming-women-20180518-p4zg1w.html

23   Emma Brockes, 'Me Too founder Tarana Burke: "You have to use your privilege to serve other people" ', *The Guardian*, 15 January 2018, www.theguardian.com/world/2018/jan/15/me-too-founder-tarana-burke-women-sexual-assault?CMP=share_btn_tw

24   ibid.

2   THE POWER OF SHARING STORIES

25   Emma Brockes, 'Me Too founder Tarana Burke: "You have to use your privilege to serve other people" ', *The Guardian*, 15 January 2018, www.theguardian.com/world/2018/jan/15/me-too-founder-tarana-burke-women-sexual-assault?CMP=share_btn_tw

26   Australian Government, Office of the eSafety Commissioner, www.esafety.gov.au/

27   Sean Coughlan, 'Theresa May attacks "vile" online threats against women', BBC News online, 8 June 2018, www.bbc.com/news/education-44402658

28   Elverson Positively Social blog, Why #CelebratingWomen matters, 13 June 2017, http://elverson.com.au/why-celebratingwomen-matters/

29   Anne Manne, 'Making women's unpaid work count', *The Monthly*, May 2018, www.themonthly.com.au/issue/2018/may/1525096800/anne-manne/making-women-s-unpaid-work-count

30   Marilyn Waring, *Counting for Nothing: What Men Value and What Women Are Worth*, Allen & Unwin, Wellington, New Zealand, 1988

31   Anne Manne, 'Making women's unpaid work count', *The Monthly*, May 2018, www.themonthly.com.au/issue/2018/may/1525096800/anne-manne/making-women-s-unpaid-work-count

32   ibid.

33   Deborah Cameron, *The Myth of Mars and Venus*, Oxford University Press, Oxford, 2007

34   Ellen Brait, 'Women and minorities penalized for promoting workplace diversity — study', *The Guardian*, 26 March 2016, www.theguardian.com/us-news/2016/mar/25/women-minoriites-penalized-workplace-diversity-study

35   Ruth Williams, 'Australia's 30-year-old sexual harassment laws have "real gaps" ', *The Sydney Morning Herald*, 11 March 2018, www.smh.com.au/business/companies/australia-s-30-year-old-sexual-harassment-laws-have-real-gaps-20180309-p4z3nc.html

36   David Swan, 'Tech titans not spared of "imposter syndrome" ', *The Weekend Australian*, 2 June 2018, www.theaustralian.com.au/business/technology/how-tech-titans-beat-impostor-syndrome/news-story/79ce80fcfda65252e75b51197ebb2c04

37   Mike Cannon-Brookes, 'Imposter Syndrome', TEDx Sydney, 16 June 2017, https://tedxsydney.com/talk/imposter-syndrome-mike-cannon-brookes/

38   L.V. Anderson, 'Feeling like an imposter is not a syndrome', *Slate*, 12 April 2016, www.slate.com/articles/business/the_ladder/2016/04/is_impostor_syndrome_real_and_does_it_affect_women_more_than_men.html

39   Marianne Cooper, 'For women leaders, likability and success hardly go hand-in-hand', *Harvard Business Review*, 30 April 2013, https://hbr.org/2013/04/for-women-leaders-likability-a

40   Julia Baird, 'My experience of the harassment that's been missing from the #metoo debate', *The Sydney Morning Herald*, 12 January 2018, www.smh.com.au/comment/my-experience-of-the-harassment-thats-been-missing-from-the-metoo-debate-20180111-h0h5kd.html

41   Dr Muneera Bano, 'Why are we #CelebratingWomen?', Illuminated Lady, 17 October 2017, https://illuminatedladyblog.wordpress.com/2017/10/17/why-are-we-celebratingwomen/

42   Shawn Achor, 'Do women's networking events move the needle on equality?', *Harvard Business Review*, 13 February 2018, https://hbr.org/2018/02/do-womens-networking-events-move-the-needle-on-equality

43   Alexandra Topping, '"Same old fudge": BBC women hit out at equal pay review', *The Guardian*, 31 January 2018, www.theguardian.com/media/2018/jan/30/bbc-women-hit-out-equal-pay-review-gender-bias

44   ibid.

45   Press Association, 'BBC suggests £320,000 pay cap for news presenters', *The Guardian*, 30 January 2018, www.theguardian.com/media/2018/jan/30/bbc-320000-pay-cap-news-presenters-proposal

46   Shawn Achor, 'Do women's networking events move the needle on equality?', *Harvard Business Review*, 13 February 2018, https://hbr.org/2018/02/do-womens-networking-events-move-the-needle-on-equality

47   Boris Groysberg, 'How star women build portable skills', *Harvard Business Review*, February 2008, https://hbr.org/2008/02/how-star-women-build-portable-skills

48   Issac Chotiner, 'Punishment is not enough', *Slate*, 11 December 2017, www.slate.com/articles/news_and_politics/interrogation/2017/12/the_limitations_of_punishment_in_the_metoo_moment.html

3   EVERY WOMAN IS A ROLE MODEL

49   Dr Kirstin Ferguson, 'Let's make 2017 the year of making noise #CelebratingWomen', *Women's Agenda* website, 15 January 2017, https://womensagenda.com.au/latest/the-year-of-making-noise-celebratingwomen/

50   Claire Ayoub, 'The lost female geniuses of history', Amy Poehler's Smart Girls, 26 April 2017, https://amysmartgirls.com/the-lost-female-geniuses-of-history-fb60b81742e8

51   Workplace Gender Equality Agency, *Submission — Senate Inquiry into Gender Segregation into the Workplace and its Impact on Women's Economic Equality*, Australian Government, March 2017, www.wgea.gov.au/sites/default/files/WGEA-Submission-Inquiry-into-Gender-Segregation-in-the-Workplace.pdf

52   RMIT ABC News Fact Check, 'Have women become better educated whilst the gender pay gap hasn't budged?', ABC News online, 2 August 2017, www.abc.net.au/news/2017-08-02/fact-check-women-education-gender-pay-gap/8760614

53   Roxane Gay, *Bad Feminist*, Corsair, London, 2014, p. xiii

54   ibid.

55   Australian Human Rights Commission, 'Leading for Change: A Blueprint for Cultural Diversity and Inclusive Leadership Revisited', April 2018, www.humanrights.gov.au/sites/default/files/document/publication/Leading%20for%20Change_Blueprint2018_FINAL_Web.pdf

56 ibid., p. 23

57 Jarni Blakkarly, 'My Australia: Ming Long', SBS News online, 16 January 2018, www.sbs.com.au/news/audiotrack/my-australia-ming-long

58 Minerals Council of Australia, *MCA Gender Diversity White Paper: Summary Document*, March 2014, www.minerals.org.au/file_upload/files/resources/education_ training/MCA_Gender_Diversity_White_Paper_Summary_FINAL.PDF

59 Workplace Gender Equality Agency, 'Gender equality spotlight: Mining', WGEA website, undated, www.wgea.gov.au/wgea-newsroom/gender-equality-spotlight-mining

60 Gosia Kaszubska, 'Boosting confidence doesn't help women at work: study', RMIT website, 5 March 2018, www.rmit.edu.au/news/all-news/2018/mar/confidence-women-work-study

61 The Mandarin, 'Confidence doesn't help women get ahead: survey call', *The Mandarin*, 6 March 2018, www.themandarin.com.au/89375-confidence-doesnt-help-women-get-ahead-new-survey/

4 TAKING THE STING OUT OF THE QUEEN BEE

62 Cordelia Fine, *Delusions of Gender*, Icon Books, London, 2010

63 ibid., p. 58

64 Belle Derks, Colette Van Laar, Naomi Ellemers, 'The queen bee phenomenon: Why women leaders distance themselves from junior women', *The Leadership Quarterly*, vol. 27, 2016, pp. 456–69, www.5050foundation.edu.au/assets/reports/documents/2016-The-Queen-Bee-Phenomenon-Why-Women-Leaders-Distance.pdf

65 Colin Kruger, 'High stakes at the Hyatt: AMP board to face investors at AGM', *The Sydney Morning Herald*, 18 April 2018, www.smh.com.au/business/companies/high-stakes-at-the-hyatt-amp-board-to-face-investors-at-agm-20180418-p4zaad.html

66 ibid.

67 Janet Albrechtsen and Andrew White, 'Chris Corrigan attacks business gender targets', *The Weekend Australian*, 19 May 2018, www.theaustralian.com.au/business/chris-corrigan-attacks-business-gender-targets/news-story/f2fcb8607a28ebb5abbc5bfcffbcdf39

68 David Fickling, 'Corporate Australia, stop blaming women', *The Sydney Morning Herald*, 18 May 2018, www.smh.com.au/business/workplace/corporate-australia-stop-blaming-women-20180518-p4zg1w.html

69 ibid.

70 Andrew Cornell, 'Diversity, boards & the specious theories of threatened series', Bluenotes, 30 May 2018, https://bluenotes.anz.com/posts/2018/05/women--boards---the-specious-theories-of-threatened-species

71 Workplace Gender Equality Agency, 'Gender workplace statistics at a glance', Australian Government, February 2018, www.wgea.gov.au/sites/default/files/Stats_at_a_Glance.pdf

72 Amy Langfield, '"Queen Bee" stereotype in the workplace is a rarity', *Today*, 9 March 2013, www.today.com/money/queen-bee-stereotype-workplace-rarity-1C8768020

73 Alana Piper, 'The myth that women secretly hate other women has a long history', *The Conversation*, 24 September 2015, https://theconversation.com/the-myth-that-women-secretly-hate-other-women-has-a-long-history-47919

74 ibid.

75 Kasey Edwards, 'Why employers don't hire smart women', *The Sydney Morning Herald*, 22 April 2018, www.smh.com.au/lifestyle/life-and-relationships/why-employers-don-t-hire-smart-women-20180422-p4zb2p.html

76 Olga Khazan, 'Why do women bully each other at work?', *The Atlantic*, September 2017, www.theatlantic.com/magazine/archive/2017/09/the-queen-bee-in-the-corner-office/534213/

77   ibid.
78   Belle Derks, Colette van Laar, Naomi Ellemers, Gauwrie Raghoe, 'Extending the Queen Bee Effect: How Hindustani Workers Cope with Disadvantage by Distancing the Self from the Group', *Journal of Social Issues*, vol. 71, issue 3, September 2015, https://spssi.onlinelibrary.wiley.com/doi/abs/10.1111/josi.12124
79   Abby Wambach, 'Remarks as delivered' for the Barnard College Commencement Address, 2018, https://barnard.edu/commencement/archives/2018/abby-wambach-remarks
80   Olga Khazan, 'Why do women bully each other at work?', *The Atlantic*, September 2017, www.theatlantic.com/magazine/archive/2017/09/the-queen-bee-in-the-corner-office/534213/
81   Sue Duke, 'The key to closing the gender gap? Putting more women in charge', *World Economic Forum*, 2 November 2017, www.weforum.org/agenda/2017/11/women-leaders-key-to-workplace-equality/
82   Sheryl Sandberg and Adam Grant, 'Sheryl Sandberg on the myth of the catty woman', *The New York Times*, 23 June 2016, www.nytimes.com/2016/06/23/opinion/sunday/sheryl-sandberg-on-the-myth-of-the-catty-woman.html
83   Allison Yarrow, 'Tonya Harding is having her moment of redemption. Now Nancy Kerrigan deserves hers', *The Lily*, 20 January 2018, https://thelily.com/tonya-harding-is-having-her-moment-of-redemption-now-nancy-kerrigan-deserves-hers-8925d617c5a0
84   Will Swanton, 'Serena v Sharapova: Latest chapter in a 14 year catfight', *The Australian*, 4 June 2018, www.theaustralian.com.au/sport/tennis/serena-v-sharapova-latest-chapter-in-a-14year-catfight/news-story/a506012787daae8f5f19830ad796f302
85   Tarla Lambert, 'Williams and Sharapova aren't catfighting, let's stop buying into this sexist trope', *Women's Agenda*, undated, https://womensagenda.com.au/life/williams-and-sharapova-arent-catfighting-lets-stop-buying-into-this-sexist-trope/
86   Katie Roiphe, 'Why do we hate successful women?', *Slate*, 6 March 2013, http://amp.slate.com/articles/double_x/roiphe/2013/03/backlash_against_sheryl_sandberg_and_marissa_mayer_why_do_we_hate_powerful.html
87   Sharon Mavin, 'Venus envy: Problematizing solidarity behaviour and queen bees', *Women in Management Review*, vol. 21, no. 4, 2006, pp. 264–76, www.emeraldinsight.com/doi/abs/10.1108/09649420610666579
88   Stefanie K. Johnson and David R. Hekman, 'Women and minorities are penalized for promoting diversity', *Harvard Business Review*, 23 March 2016, https://hbr.org/2016/03/women-and-minorities-are-penalized-for-promoting-diversity
89   Sharon Mavin, 'Queen Bees, wannabees and afraid to bees: No more "best enemies" for women in management?', *British Journal of Management*, vol. 19, no. 1, pp. S75–84, 19 February 2008, https://onlinelibrary.wiley.com/doiabs/10.1111/j.1467-8551.2008.00573.x
90   Stephanie Neal, Jazmine Boatman and Linda Miller, 'Women as mentors: Does she or doesn't she? A global study of businesswomen and mentoring', DDI, undated, http://www.ddiworld.com/ddi/media/trend-research/womenasmentors_rr_ddi.pdf?ext=.pdf
91   Sarah Dinolfo, Christine Silva and Nancy M. Carter, *The Promise of Future Leadership: Highly Talented Employees in the Pipeline*, Catalyst, June 2012, www.catalyst.org/knowledge/high-potentials-pipeline-leaders-pay-it-forward
92   Marianne Cooper, 'Why women (sometimes) don't help other women', *The Atlantic*, 23 June 2016, www.theatlantic.com/business/archive/2016/06/queen-bee/488144/
93   ibid.
94   Sheryl Sandberg and Adam Grant, 'Sheryl Sandberg on the myth of the catty woman', *The New York Times*, 23 June 2016, www.nytimes.com/2016/06/23/opinion/sunday/sheryl-sandberg-on-the-myth-of-the-catty-woman.html

95   Cristian L. Deso, David Gaddis Ross and Jose Uribe, 'Is there an implicit quota on women in top management? A large-sample statistical analysis', *Stategic Management Journal*, volume 37, no. 1, 15 November 2015, https://onlinelibrary.wiley.com/doi/abs/10.1002/smj.2461

96   Olga Khazan, 'Why do women bully each other at work?', *The Atlantic*, September 2017, www.theatlantic.com/magazine/archive/2017/09/the-queen-bee-in-the-corner-office/534213/

97   Tweet from Roxane Gay (@rgay), 28 February 2018

5 A BRIEF HISTORY OF WOMEN'S NETWORKS

98   Ann Friedman, 'The Social Sex: A history of female friendship', *The New York Times*, 18 September 2018, https://mobile.nytimes.com/2015/09/20/books/review/the-social-sex-a-history-of-female-friendship.html

99   Anonymous staff writer, 'Women Laud Women's Work; At Manless Dinner, They Speak of the Achievements of Their Sex', *The New York Times*, vol. 71, issue 3, 16 January 1916, p. 17, www.nytimes.com/1916/01/16/archives/women-laud-womens-work-at-manless-dinner-they-speak-of-the.html

100 Sophie Williams, 'BBC apologises to China Editor Carrie Gracie for paying her less than male counterparts', *Evening Standard*, 1 July 2018, www.standard.co.uk/news/uk/bbc-apologises-to-china-editor-carrie-gracie-for-paying-her-less-than-male-counterparts-a3875451.html

101 Fawcett Society, 'Carrie Gracie donates BBC backdated pay to Fawcett Society to support women fighting for Equal Pay', Fawcett Society website, 29 June 2018, www.fawcettsociety.org.uk/News/carrie-gracie-donates-bbc-back-pay-fawcett-society-women-fighting-equal-pay

102 Gloria Steinem, *My Life on the Road*, Nero, Victoria, Australia, 2017, p. 38

103 Nicole Busby and Rebecca Zahn, 'A Dangerous Combination?', *Dangerous Women Project*, 20 June 2016, http://dangerouswomenproject.org/2016/06/20/womens-trade-unionism/

104 ibid.

105 ibid.

106 Annika Blau and Leigh Tonkin, ' "History is written by women like us": The little moments that shape a woman's life', ABC News online, 8 March 2018, www.abc.net.au/news/2018-03-08/international-womens-day-moments-that-shape-lives/9523986

107 Fi Shewring, 'My Trade Story with Fi Shewring', The Builder's Wife website, 27 January 2017, http://thebuilderswife.com.au/trade-story-fi-shewring/

108 Anonymous author, 'Over 100 years of women in trades and counting', SALT website, undated, https://saltaustralia.org.au/over-100-years-of-women-in-trades-and-counting/

109 Workplace Gender Equality Agency, 'Gender Segregation in Australia's workforce', Australian Government, August 2016, www.wgea.gov.au/sites/default/files/20160801_Industry_occupational_segregation_factsheet.pdf

110 Anonymous author, 'Over 100 years of women in trades and counting', SALT website, undated, https://saltaustralia.org.au/over-100-years-of-women-in-trades-and-counting/

111 Louise Chappell and Natalie Galea, 'Construction work is the last frontier for women at work', *The Sydney Morning Herald*, 6 December 2016 www.smh.com.au/opinion/construction-is-the-last-frontier-for-women-at-work-20161206-gt4par.html

112 Country Women's Association of Australia website, www.cwaa.org.au

113 Eva Wiseman, 'Meet the new suffragettes', *British Vogue*, 8 March 2018, www.vogue.co.uk/article/the-new-suffragettes

114 ibid.

115 ibid.

116   Nick Miller, '"The suffragettes live on in #MeToo": Pankhurst's great-granddaughter', *The Sydney Morning Herald*, 6 February 2018, www.smh.com.au/world/the-suffragettes-live-on-in-metoo-pankhurst-s-great-granddaughter-20180205-p4yzeo.html

117   Ann Friedman, 'The Social Sex: A history of female friendship', *The New York Times*, 18 September 2018, https://mobile.nytimes.com/2015/09/20/books/review/the-social-sex-a-history-of-female-friendship.html

118   StartUp Muster, *StartUp Muster 2017 Annual Report*, available at www.startupmuster.com/reports

119   Ben Paynter, 'Women are fueling the growth of collective philanthropy giving circles', *Fast Company*, 20 November 2017, www.fastcompany.com/40497674/women-are-fueling-the-growth-of-collective-philanthropy-giving-circles

120   Women Donors Network Australia website, '2011 – Inaugural Research Findings', http://womendonors.org.au/inaugural_research.html

6   THE AMPLIFICATION EFFECT

121   Ann Friedman, Shine Theory website, www.annfriedman.com/shine-theory/

122   Abby Wambach, 'Remarks as delivered' for the Barnard College Commencement Address, 2018, https://barnard.edu/commencement/archives/2018/abby-wambach-remarks

123   Juliet Eilperin, 'White House women want to be in the room where it happens', *The Washington Post*, 13 September 2016, www.washingtonpost.com/news/powerpost/wp/2016/09/13/white-house-women-are-now-in-the-room-where-it-happens/?noredirect=on&utm_term=.8b3dff1fd898

124   Emily Crockett, 'The amazing tool that women in the White House used to fight gender bias', *Vox*, 14 September 2016, www.vox.com/2016/9/14/12914370/white-house-obama-women-gender-bias-amplification

125   Anonymous author, Tweet sent by @Now This (@nowthisnews) on 27 May 2018, with a video of an interview with Jennifer Palmieri, https://twitter.com/nowthisnews/status/1000459807638290433?s=12

126   Reed Alexander, 'Women who speak up at work get ignored while men get promotions', *New York Post*, 8 November 2017, https://nypost.com/2017/11/08/women-who-speak-up-at-work-get-ignored-while-men-get-promotions/

127   ibid.

128   Summer Meza, 'What is a whisper network? How women are taking down bad men in the #MeToo age', *Newsweek*, 22 November 2017, www.newsweek.com/what-whisper-network-sexual-misconduct-allegations-719009

129   ibid.

130   Georgina Dent, 'Why women and men need to negotiate pay rises differently', *The Sydney Morning Herald*, 23 March 2017, www.smh.com.au/money/planning-and-budgeting/why-women-and-men-need-to-negotiate-pay-rises-differently-20170322-gv3vs7.html

131   Marie Tessier, 'Speaking while female, and at a disadvantage', *The New York Times*, 27 October 2016, www.nytimes.com/2016/10/27/upshot/speaking-while-female-and-at-a-disadvantage.html

132   Christopher F. Karpowitz and Tali Mendelberg, *The Silent Sex: Gender, Deliberation, and Institutions*, Princeton University Press, New Jersey, 2014, https://press.princeton.edu/titles/10402.html

133   ibid.

134   Lianna Brinded, 'Women are going to have to start bragging if they want to close the pay gap', *Quartz at Work*, 8 March 2018, https://work.qz.com/1222670/closing-the-pay-gap-means-women-are-going-to-have-to-start-bragging/

135   ibid.

136   ibid.

137   Marian Baird, Rae Cooper, Elizabeth Hill, Elspeth Probyn and Ariadne Vromen, *Women and the Future of Work*, The University of Sydney Business School, Sydney, 2018, http://sydney.edu.au/business/__data/assets/pdf_file/0005/348053/Women-and-the-Future-of-Work-Report_Final_050318.pdf

7   LESSONS FOR LEADERS

138   Emma Brockes, 'Facebook's Sheryl Sandberg: Who are you calling bossy?', *The Guardian*, 5 April 2014, www.theguardian.com/lifeandstyle/2014/apr/05/sheryl-sandberg-facebook-bossy-interview
139   Heather Murphy, 'Picture a leader. Is she a woman?', *The New York Times*, 16 March 2018, www.nytimes.com/2018/03/16/health/women-leadership-workplace.html
140   Mary Beard, *Women & Power: A Manifesto*, Profile Books, London, 2017
141   ibid., p. 86
142   ibid., p. 87
143   ibid., p. 87
144   ibid., p. 86
145   Alyse Nelson, 'How women lead differently, and why it matters', *Fast Company*, 9 August 2012, www.fastcompany.com/3000249/how-women-lead-differently-and-why-it-matters
146   ibid.
147   Helen Clark, 'Breaking glass ceilings: Reflections on women's leadership', speech delivered at the Asian Development Bank in Manila, Philippines, 16 March 2018, https://helenclarknz.com/2018/03/18/breaking-glass-ceilings-reflections-on-womens-leadership-speech-by-helen-clark-at-asian-development-bank-in-manila-philippines-16-march-2018/
148   Miki Perkins, 'Clinton and Gillard discuss the tough path for women in politics', *The Sydney Morning Herald*, 10 May 2018, www.smh.com.au/national/clinton-and-gillard-discuss-the-tough-path-for-women-in-politics-20180510-p4zel7.html
149   Avivah Wittenberg-Cox, 'Turning #PayGaps into potential', *Forbes*, 6 May 2018, www.forbes.com/sites/avivahwittenbergcox/2018/05/06/turning-paygaps-into-potential/#2d27d8ec532b
150   David Perks, 'Gender bias in the language of performance review and feedback', Pay Compliment website, 28 November 2017, www.paycompliment.com/blog/post/2017/11/28/gender-bias-in-the-language-of-performance-review-and-feedback
151   Matt Liddy and Catherine Hanrahan, 'Fewer women run top Australian companies than men named John — or Peter, or David', ABC News online, 8 March 2017, www.abc.net.au/news/2017-03-08/fewer-women-ceos-than-men-named-john/8327938
152   Claire Cain Miller, 'How to raise a feminist son', *The New York Times*, 2 June 2017, www.nytimes.com/2017/06/02/upshot/how-to-raise-a-feminist-son.html
153   ibid.
154   Andrea Tokaji, 'Why #IDidThat is better than #MeToo', *The Sydney Morning Herald*, 27 February 2018, www.smh.com.au/national/why-ididthat-is-better-than-metoo-20180227-p4z1zo.html
155   Michael Flood, Graeme Russell, Jane O'Leary and Cathy Brown, 'Men Make a Difference: How to Engage Men on Gender Equality', Synopsis Report, Diversity Council Australia, 2017, www.dca.org.au/sites/default/files/dca_engaging_men_synopsis_online_final.pdf
156   Jenny Anderson, 'Are millennials more likely than their parents to think women's place is in the home?', *Quartz*, 31 March 2017, updated April 3 2017, https://qz.com/946816/millennials-are-more-likely-than-their-parents-to-think-womens-place-is-in-the-home/

157 ABC News online, 'University sexual assault report: Half of students harassed at least once in 2016', updated 1 August 2017, www.abc.net.au/news/2017-08-01/uni-sexual-assault-hrc-report-released/8762638

158 Georgina Dent, 'Liz Broderick hands down report into college culture at Sydney University', Women's Agenda website, 28 November 2017, https://womensagenda.com.au/latest/liz-broderick-hands-report-college-culture-sydney-university/

159 Sheryl Sandberg and Adam Grant, 'How men can succeed in the boardroom and the bedroom', *The New York Times*, 5 March 2015, www.nytimes.com/2015/03/08/opinion/sunday/sheryl-sandberg-adam-grant-how-men-can-succeed-in-the-boardroom-and-the-bedroom.html

160 Michael Flood, Graeme Russell, Jane O'Leary and Cathy Brown, 'Men Make a Difference: How to Engage Men on Gender Equality', Synopsis Report, Diversity Council Australia, 2017, www.dca.org.au/sites/default/files/dca_engaging_men_synopsis_online_final.pdf

161 Kim Azzarelli and Deanna Bass, 'The most common excuse for not having enough women leaders are myths', *Quartz at Work*, 24 January 2018, https://work.qz.com/1186120/the-most-common-excuses-for-not-having-enough-women-leaders-are-myths/

162 Michael S. Kimmel, 'Getting men to speak up', *Harvard Business Review*, 31 January 2018, https://hbr.org/2018/01/getting-men-to-speak-up

163 Michael Flood, Graeme Russell, Jane O'Leary and Cathy Brown, 'Men Make a Difference: How to Engage Men on Gender Equality', Synopsis Report, Diversity Council Australia, 2017, www.dca.org.au/sites/default/files/dca_engaging_men_synopsis_online_final.pdf

164 Gary Barker, 'Gender equality won't be achieved with small-scale work: The state of the field of engaging men', *Promundo*, 8 December 2016, https://promundoglobal.org/2016/12/08/gender-equality-wont-achieved-small-scale-work/

8   OPPORTUNITIES FOR ORGANISATIONS

165 Schumpeter, 'Diversity Fatigue', *The Economist*, 11 February 2016, www.economist.com/news/business/21692865-making-most-workplace-diversity-requires-hard-work-well-good-intentions-diversity

166 Fay Hansen, 'Diversity's business case doesn't add up', *Workforce*, 2 April 2003, www.workforce.com/2003/04/02/diversitys-business-case-doesnt-add-up/

167 Frank Dobbin and Alexandra Kalev, 'Why diversity programs fail', *Harvard Business Review*, July–August 2016, https://hbr.org/2016/07/why-diversity-programs-fail

168 ibid.

169 Shelley Correll, 'Reducing gender biases in modern workplaces: A small wins approach to organisational change', *Gender & Society*, vol. 31, no. 6, 1 December 2017, pp. 725–50; www.gsb.stanford.edu/faculty-research/publications/reducing-gender-biases-modern-workplaces-small-wins-approach

170 ibid., pp. 727, 735

171 ibid., p. 738

172 Livia Yap, 'How a business school exercise helped boost women's grades', *Bloomberg Businessweek*, 16 November 2017, www.bloomberg.com/news/articles/2017-11-15/test-gives-89-boost-to-women-mbas-now-a-bank-will-give-it-too

173 ibid.

174 ibid.

175 Catherine Fox, 'Taking care of business', *Virgin Australia Voyeur* magazine, March 2018, pp. 123–9, https://media.tfehotels.com/media/filer_public/c7/de/c7defeb5-a29f-444e-9552-fe7dc6ef6e6f/rachel_argaman_in_virgin_voyeur_mar18.pdf

176   Katie Hope, 'All-male job shortlists banned by accountancy giant PwC', BBC News online, 4 June 2018, www.bbc.com/news/business-44353536

177   Anonymous author, '5 Aussie companies actually doing something about gender diversity in the workplace', *Women's Weekly* online, 1 June 2018, www.nowtolove.com.au/women-of-the-future/the-weekly/australian-businesses-gender-equality-48620

178   Elysse Morgan, 'Energy Australia closes gender pay gap overnight, literally', ABC News online, 7 March 2018, www.abc.net.au/news/2018-03-07/energy-australia-closes-gender-pay-gap-overnight/9524770

179   Marian Baird, Rae Cooper, Elizabeth Hill, Elspeth Probyn and Ariadne Vromen, *Women and the Future of Work*, The University of Sydney Business School, Sydney, 2018, http://sydney.edu.au/business/__data/assets/pdf_file/0005/348053/Women-and-the-Future-of-Work-Report_Final_050318.pdf

180   Bernard Coleman III, 'Forget the "Business Case" for diversity and inclusion', *Forbes*, 23 January 2018, www.forbes.com/sites/forbescoachescouncil/2018/01/23/forget-the-business-case-for-diversity-and-inclusion/#6918f2a4a903

CONCLUSION

181   Acceptance speech given by Gail Kelly after she received the National Award for Excellence in Women's Leadership, conferred by Women and Leadership Australia, on 2 May 2018 in Brisbane, Australia

182   Tweet sent by Sally-Ann Williams (@sallyannw) on 5 June 2018

INDEX

statistics on women's representation
  as world leaders 20
  in engineering roles 261
  in science roles 175
  in senior corporate roles 11, 225
  in start-ups 176
  in trade employment 162
Steinem, Gloria 159, 171
STEMMinist Book Club 155, 170
stereotypes about women *see
  also* 'Queen Bee' myth
  women as conspiratorial 84
  women as 'talkative' 83–85
Stevens, Andrew 227
#StilleForOpptak movement 163
superannuation and women 11, 133
Superstars of STEM 170, 174, 175,
  176, 239
Supporting and Linking
  Tradeswomen (SALT) 162

T

Tavris, Carol 134
Taylor, Mary (Millie) 33–35
technology, women in 176–178
Telstra 261
Tessier, Marie 201
TFE Hotels 254
Thomson Reuters 247
#TimesUp campaign 12, 16, 69,
  163
trade unionism 160–161
trades, women in 161–163
transgender women in
  #CelebratingWomen
  movement 62
trolling *see* online abuse of women
Trump, Donald 11, 19, 20
Twitter *see also* Dorsey, Jack (Twitter
  founder); *see also* specific
  hashtags; *see also* Nicoletti, Suzy
  (Managing Director, Twitter
  Australia); *see also* social media;
  see also online abuse of women
  analysis of abusive tweets 23–24
  benefits for women 169

policies 72
Twitter Blue Room 73

U

Uber 263
university colleges, abuse by men
  at 236
unmarried women, stereotypes
  associated with 107
UN Women 155

V

victim-blaming 84–85

W

Walker, Kylie 175
Walker, Sophie 165–166
Wambach, Abby 141–142, 188–189
Waring, Marilyn 77–78
Warne, Peter 230
Weinstein, Harvey 11
Welch, Megan 197
Western Australia Cricket Association
  (WACA) 216
Westpac 260
Whelan, Denyse 117
whisper network 193–194
White, Laurie Dalton 95
Williams, Sally-Ann 266
Williams, Serena 143
Winfrey, Oprah 12
Wiseman, Eva 165
Wittenberg-Cox, Avivah 219
Women and Work Research
  Centre 198–199
Women Corporate Directors
  (network) 56, 156
Women in Construction (network)
  162
Women in Economics Network
  85, 124
Women in Media (network) 154
Women in Mining and Resources WA
  (network) 93, 119, 258–259
Women in Social Enterprise
  (network) 156

301